The Forgotten Queens of Islam

The Forgotten Queens of Islam

Fatima Mernissi

Translated by Mary Jo Lakeland

University of Minnesota Press
Minneapolis

English Translation © Polity Press 1993
First Published in France as
Sultanes oubliées
© Éditions Albin Michel S.A., 1990
This translation first published 1993 by
Polity Press in association with Blackwell Publishers

Published by the University of Minnesota Press
111 Third Avenue South, Suite 290
Minneapolis, MN 55401-2520
http://www.upress.umn.edu

Second paperback printing, 1997

A CIP record is available from the
Library of Congress.
ISBN 0-8166-2439-9 (pb)

Printed in the United States of America on acid-free paper

The University of Minnesota is an
equal-opportunity educator and employer.

Contents

Introduction
Was Benazir Bhutto the First?

—◦◦◦◉◉◉◉◉◉◉●◦•◦—

When Benazir Bhutto became Prime Minister of Pakistan after winning the elections of 16 November 1988, all who monopolized the right to speak in the name of Islam, and especially Nawaz Sharif, the leader of the then Opposition, the IDA (Islamic Democratic Alliance),[1] raised the cry of blasphemy: 'Never – horrors! – has a Muslim state been governed by a woman!' Invoking Islamic tradition, they decried this event as 'against nature'. Political decision-making among our ancestors, they said, was always a men's affair. Throughout 15 centuries of Islam, from year 1 of the Hejira (AD 622) to today, the conduct of public affairs in Muslim countries has been a uniquely male privilege and monopoly.[2] No woman ever acceded to a throne in Islam; no woman ever directed the affairs of state, we are told by those who claim to speak for Islam and who make its defence their battle cry against other Muslims. And, so they say, since no woman had ever governed a Muslim state between 622 and 1988, Benazir Bhutto could not aspire to do so either.

All the press, in the West as well as in the East, echoed this argument, overlooking an intriguing point: the Pakistani politicians resorted to Muslim tradition only after their failure in the election.[3] Paradoxically the leaders of the parties which claim to represent Islam ostensibly accepted elections as part of the rules of the game – that is, they accepted parliamentary democracy, which derives from the principles of the Declaration of Universal Human Rights, where the vote is the sovereign base of political power. After the triumph of a democratically elected candidate, how could they appeal to the past, to tradition, which is so alien to the new political order. It would hardly be possible for a French, German, English, or American candidate who lost an election to have recourse to the past to discredit a rival and thus annul the election result. This would not only be absurd; it would be completely unacceptable. So how is one to explain how a Muslim political man who fought an election against a woman could brandish the past and trot out tradition as a weapon to disqualify his rival? Exactly what political territory are we on?

Saying that Benazir Bhutto cannot govern Pakistan despite her triumph in the election is to leave the political arena of parliamentary democracy to slide into another arena where the vote is not the foundation of legitimacy. It is this passage from one political arena to another, as soon as a Muslim woman appears on the horizon, that is fascinating. Nawaz Sharif and his supporters could not have waged a similar campaign against the candidate who won the election if he had been named Hasan or Muhammad. The resultant ambiguity (always a bearer of violence in matters of rights) only comes into play when it is a question of a woman.

In this book I do not claim to resolve the enigma, to expatiate on the ambiguity which hangs over the political rights of Muslim women, nor do I try to establish what is obvious to fair-minded people – the mysterious link between the viability of the 'Rights of Man' and the non-violation of those of women. As a good obedient Muslim woman, I shall leave those serious matters to men. I know my place; I can only take up that which is my concern – trifles. And what could be more trifling than to investigate the women who maybe never existed – the women who directed Muslim affairs of state between 622 and 1989? Playing the detective – especially the private detective – is not a very serious activity. We turn to a private detective when we think that the public authorities will not take up our case. And this is apparently the situation with these queens. No one in the vast Muslim world has worried about their fate. No public authority seems concerned about them. Moreover, do we have the least proof of their existence?

The alternatives are simple. Either women heads of state never existed, and in this case the politicians who assert that Benazir Bhutto was the first one are right. Or in the past there have been women who led Muslim states, but they have been rubbed out of official history. In pursuit of the second hypothesis, you, the reader, and I, your very private detective, will be the first to bring to light one of the most fascinating purges in world history: the liquidation of a series of heads of state, passed over in silence.

Where to begin? Should we expect to stumble on the corpses of queens? What monuments should we excavate? What palaces should we turn to? Should we fly off to Asia, disappear into Africa, or pass through the Strait of Gibraltar to venture into Europe to breathe the mystery of the gardens of Andalusia? Should we explore Cordoba or favour Delhi? Should we excavate San'a and its surroundings or take ship to the islands of Indonesia? Should we fly over Basra and Baghdad, make a tour of Isfahan and Samarkand before sweeping into the steppes of Mongolia? Islam is huge; immense and dense, it spreads out in time and space. Where, in what direction should we try to reach the unreal places of the Muslim queens, if in fact they did exist?

If we are going to conduct a detective investigation, what should be the method? How does one begin an investigation of this kind? The problem is that I have very little experience in this domain. I am no proper reader of detective novels: as soon as the hero is killed, I jump to the last pages to catch the criminal. But I believe that even the greatest of the famous detectives would simply advise me to go to a library. And, believe it or not, I had not far to look. Just as in a fairy-tale, queens, malikas, and khatuns emerged little by little from the soft crackle of yellowed pages in old books. One by one they paraded through the silent rooms of the libraries in an interminable procession of intrigues and mysteries. Sometimes they appeared in twos or threes, passing the throne from mother to daughter in the faraway isles of Asiatic Islam. They were called Malika 'Arwa, 'Alam al-Hurra, Sultana Radiyya, Shajarat al-Durr, Turkan Khatun, or, more modestly, Taj al-'Alam (Crown of the universe) and Nur al-'Alam (Light of the universe). Some received the reins of power by inheritance; others had to kill the heirs in order to take power. Many themselves led battles, inflicted defeats, concluded armistices. Some had confidence in competent viziers, while others counted only on themselves. Each had her own way of treating the people, of rendering justice, and of administering taxes. Some managed to stay a long time on the throne, while others scarcely had time to settle down. Many died in the manner of the caliphs (either orthodox, Umayyad, or Abbasid) – that is, poisoned or stabbed. Rare were those who died peacefully in their beds.

The more queens I found, the greater grew my anxiety. Although I was involved in research on women heads of state, the queens that I found who exercised power were not all necessarily heads of state. How was I to distinguish those who had governed from the others? What can be the unquestionable criterion of a head of state, the symbol or symbols of sovereignty in an Islam where the crown has no place and where humility is the sole sign of greatness?

Before listing these queens, before making a study of their lives and classifying them, perhaps we should begin by answering a question that is both more prosaic and more fundamental: How did these women contrive to take power in states which, as a matter of principle, defined politics as an exclusively male pursuit?

There is no feminine form of the words *imam* or *caliph*, the two words that embody the concept of power in the Arabic language, the language in which the Koran was revealed. The *Lisan al-'Arab* dictionary informs us without qualification that *'al-khalifatu la yakunu illa li al-dhakr'* (caliph is used only in the masculine). In such a context, where the principle is exclusion, any infiltration into the realm of political decision-making by women, even under the cloak of and in the corridors of the harem, even behind dozens of curtains, veils, and latticed windows, is an utterly laudable and heroic adventure. How did the women of former times, supposed to have fewer advantages than we do, manage such an achievement in a domain where we moderns fail so lamentably? In many Muslim countries there is a sort of acceptance of democracy, of assemblies that represent the people, of institutions that are set up by universal vote, and of millions of Muslim women going to the voting booth each time elections are announced. Nevertheless, rare are the institutions in which women figure. In most cases, the Muslim parliaments, the People's Councils or Revolution Councils resemble harems – they house one sex only. One sex deliberates and strives to regulate the problem of the other sex – and in its absence. This is obviously not the best way to resolve the problems of either the sex that deliberates or the one that is absent, and still less the intersex problems that require dialogue.

At a time when those among us women who have advanced degrees are counted by the millions, thanks to an education paid for by the state, even if it still only benefits the rich and the middle class, at a time when we are supposed to be shrewder, better informed, and more sophisticated, we find ourselves firmly excluded from politics. The essential problem is in fact one of space. Women are disturbing as soon as they appear where they are not expected. And no one expects to see us where decisions are made. If the Pakistani reactionaries had been used to seeing more women in power circles, they would have reacted with a little more discretion upon seeing Benazir Bhutto appear on the horizon. So there is an urgent need for us to decode our grandmothers' secrets. Who were these mysterious queens? How did they succeed in achieving power without frightening the men? What strategies did they use to tame them? How did they manipulate them? Did they use seduction, beauty, intelligence, or wealth? I know many women from Arab countries who are politically ambitious, extremely pretty, and endowed with myriad charms, but who do not know how to succeed on the political scene. It seems that, as things go, seduction does not work or rather it is stalled at a very low level. Personally I know not a single woman who, thanks to seduction, has crossed the threshold that makes an insecure courtesan into a political partner.

What then is the secret of the queens of former days? How did they find a place in a political arena in which every woman who makes a move is subject to punishment human and divine? What were their names and their titles? Did they dare call themselves caliph or imam, or were they satisfied with more obscure and less prestigious titles?

In order to avoid any misunderstanding or confusion, let me say that in this book every time I speak of Islam without any other qualification, I am referring to political Islam, to Islam as the practice of power, to the acts of people animated by passions and motivated by interest, which is different from *Islam Risala*, the divine message, the ideal recorded in the Koran, the holy book. When I speak of the latter, I will identify it as *Islam Risala* or spiritual Islam.

PART I

Queens and Courtesans

1
How Does One Say 'Queen' in Islam?

Faced with the plethora of queens who in the yellowed pages of history books constantly contend with caliphs for power and with sultans for thrones, we must first of all ask the most obvious question: how does one say *queen* in Islam? Remember, the Koran refers to the queen of Sheba, without ever mentioning her name! Moreover do you call queens by their given name or by that of their father or husband or son? Do they have the right to titles, and to which ones if not to the two most specific titles of power in Islam: caliph and imam? Once again words are going to reveal what over the past 15 centuries has modulated Islamic mental attitudes, conscious and unconscious, at the most profound level.

I hasten to say that, according to the little I know, no woman has ever borne the title of caliph or imam in the current meaning of the word, that is, someone who leads the prayers in the mosque for everyone, men and women. One of the reasons for my caution is that I cannot help feeling guilty in simply asking the question: Has there ever been a woman caliph? I feel that asking the question in itself constitutes a blasphemy. The simple idea of daring, as a woman, to question history is experienced by me, programmed as I am by a traditional Muslim education, as a troubling blasphemy. On this sunny morning of 6 February 1989, just a few steps from the Jami' al-Sunna, one of the great mosques of Rabat, I feel guilty being here with my computer about to expatiate on women and the caliphate. This strange association of words creates a new and diffuse anxiety which I must try to respond to before the hour of prayer. I want to have everything in order before noon, when the muezzin will announce that the sun has reached its zenith. And order dictates that women must be in their place and the caliph in his.

No woman who has held power has borne the title of caliph or imam. For that reason are we to say that there have never been women heads of state in Islam? Is the title alone a sufficient criterion of exclusion? If one regards having the title of caliph as the criterion for governing, one is going to eliminate the majority of heads of state, because few bore that title. Caliph is an extremely precious title reserved to a tiny minority, because of its religious and messianic dimension. Even today, just as in the past, many Muslim heads of state would like to bear this title, but only the exceptional few have the right to it. The king of Morocco is one of those; he is *amir al-mu'minin* (Commander of the faithful) and caliph, the representative of God on earth, his dynasty being traceable back to the Prophet.

In order to understand what a caliph is, it is necessary to understand the contrary – a sultan or king. And what better master could we find than Ibn Khaldun, that gifted intellectual of the fourteenth century (732/1332–808/1406), who filled political offices in various parts of the Muslim world from Andalusia to Egypt and retired from public life at the age of 40 in Oranie, a few miles from Tiaret in Algeria, to reflect on violence and the reasons for despotism? He knew whereof he spoke: he came close to death on several occasions during his political career in the service of princes. According to him, all the woes of the Muslim world and the political violence that held sway in it came from the fact that the caliphate, the divine mission specific to Islam, had been perverted into *mulk*, archaic despotism, which knew no limits and was answerable to no law, only to the passions of the prince:

> *Mulk* . . . implies domination and coercion, which come from a spirit of rapine and animality. Most of the time the orders given by the leader are unjust and injurious to the material interests of those under his rule, because he imposes burdens on them that they cannot bear, in order to gratify his aims and desires.[1]

The caliphate is the opposite of *mulk* in that it represents an authority that obeys divine law, the *shari'a*, which is imposed on the leader himself and makes his own passions illegitimate. And therein, Ibn Khaldun explains to us, lies the greatness of Islam as a political system. The caliph is tied by divine law, his desires and passions checked, while the king recognizes no superior law. As a result, the caliphate has another advantage that *mulk* lacks. *Mulk* deals solely with the management of earthly interests, while the caliphate, given its spiritual nature, is also in charge of the Beyond:

> *Mulk* pursues only the interests of this world. . . . But the aim of the inspired jurist [*al-shari'*, he who applies *al-shari'a*], as it concerns people, is to assure their well-being also in the next world. Therefore it is an obligation under divinely inspired laws to influence the community to obey the prescriptions of these laws in matters that concern its interests in this world and the next. This power belongs to the guardians of divine law, namely *al-anbiya* [prophets] and those who fill their place, that is, the caliphs.[2]

The caliph, who deputizes for the Prophet, the Messenger of God on earth, therefore has lost the freedom of the despot, the king. He is tied by the *shari'a*, which is, of course, enforced on the persons under his jurisdiction, but which also binds him. And, according to Ibn Khaldun, that is what is new and specific about Islam as a political system. Not only is the caliph tied by divine law, but he may also not change it, because the prerogative of legislating is not his. In fact, the lawgiver is Allah himself. As powerful as the caliph may be, he does not have the right to make the law. It is God who is the lawgiver. The caliph's mission is to apply it.[3] Then what is the problem, we may ask with Ibn Khaldun (who suffered from despotism), since the caliphate is so different from *mulk*? The problem is that the caliphate necessarily includes *mulk* as one of its components, since it has to be concerned with the interests of the community on earth. This detail is important for understanding not only contemporary Islam but also the past, and especially why the queens could only claim earthly power. *Mulk*, the power of the leader to coerce people by the use of violence, exists, but Islam as a political system is protected from it by subjecting it to the *shari'a*, religious law. Muslims are protected from *mulk*, which is despotic by nature, if, and only if, the *shari'a* is followed to the letter by the spiritual leader, the caliph. It is through the caliph's submission to the *shari'a* that the miracle of ideal government is achieved: 'Everything in *mulk* that is done through coercion and domination is nothing more than iniquity and aggressiveness, acts which are reprehensible in the eyes of the Lawgiver . . . for they are decisions taken without the help of the light of Allah.'[4] And, according to Ibn Khaldun, this is what makes the caliphate an institution specific to Islam, for it binds the will of the leader by the *shari'a*, divine law, while *mulk* exists elsewhere, wherever people have gathered together in a community.

The caliph is by definition someone who deputizes for someone else. He replaces the Prophet in his mission, which is to make it possible for the group to live according to religious laws that guarantee a harmonious life on earth and a happy one in Paradise. Not just anyone can claim to be a caliph; access to this privilege is subject to strict criteria. By contrast, titles like *sultan*, the linguistic origin of which is *salata* (dominate), and *malik* (king), which has the same connotation of raw power not tempered by religion, are available to anybody.[5] And that is why women can carry them; they do not imply or signify any divine mission. But women could never lay claim to the title of caliph. The secret of the exclusion of women lies in the criteria of eligibility to be a caliph.

According to Ibn Khaldun, the Arabs decided with the coming of the Prophet to resolve the problem of conflict between a leader, who rules by force, and a subject, forced to obey, by adopting one law, the *shari'a*, which links the leader and the subject. The leader, in this case called the caliph, the one who replaces the Prophet, and the subject both have the status of believer. What links the two and subordinates the will of both parties is their belief in the *shari'a*, the law of divine nature. Remember that the two key words in Islam, *shari'a* and *sunna*, mean 'way, mapped-out route, path'. All one has to do is follow. Having a caliph is an innovation in the history of the Arabs, a privilege granted to them by God through the intermediary of an Arab prophet, which allowed them to bypass the inevitably violent relationship between leader and community. This is the reason why few non-Arab heads of state could claim the privilege of bearing the title of caliph, while any military man who succeeded in subjugating a country could claim the title of sultan or malik.[6]

Women are not the only ones who cannot aspire to the title of caliph. Rare are the men among those succeeding in taking power in the Muslim world who could carry this title and be convincing and credible. If one understands the mission of the caliph, one will have grasped the whole Muslim political system and the whole philosophy that underlies it, and especially why the emergence of women in politics is necessarily a challenge. The appearance of women on the Muslim political scene, which for centuries was subjected at least nominally to the supervision of a mythically pious caliph, signals the eruption of earthly oriented, necessarily unscrupulous, power-hungry agents. The emergence of women in the arena of power indicates a breakdown in the system: lower-ranking, normally excluded elements are in charge. And it is difficult to imagine anyone more excluded from political competition than women.

The caliphate turned out to be a dream difficult to realize after the Prophet's death. It was a mythical vision of a happy community ideally directed by a caliph who was made wise by divine law – a law that reduced him to a humble captive of God's project, which was to make the Muslims happy and powerful among nations. This mythical caliph has no personal narcissistic concern with power. He is the servant of the community's needs first. Strange as it may seem, the caliph – one cannot say it too often – has no legislative power and as a result can make no legal reforms, because it is God himself who is *al-Musharri'* (the Lawgiver), the creator of the *shari'a*.[7] The law was revealed once and for all. That is why women's calls today for reform of family law, which derives entirely from the *shari'a*, for the forbidding of polygyny and the repudiation of wives, and for equal rights of inheritance have provoked an outcry.

While according to the *Lisan al-'Arab*, the word *caliph* exists only in the masculine form and cannot be used in the feminine, *sultan* and *malik* on the contrary exist in both forms. The distribution of political power between the sexes seems to be evident in Arabic grammar. In any case, although no woman ever became a caliph (as far as I know), there have been many who managed to be *sultana* and *malika* (queen).[8]

One of the most famous was Sultana Radiyya, who took power in Delhi in the year 634 of the Hejira (AD 1236).[9] This is not far from Punjab, which is the fief of Nawaz Sharif, later prime minister of Pakistan, who was one of Benazir Bhutto's major adversaries during the 1988 election, when he unsuccessfully tried to defeat her by mobilizing fundamentalist votes. Radiyya took power in somewhat the same conditions as did Benazir Bhutto, by demanding justice before the people for a crime committed by the reigning sultan, her brother Rukn al-Din. In Ibn Battuta, the Moroccan traveller, we have a distinguished historian who can inform us about Sultana Radiyya's ascent to power. He travelled in her country in the fourteenth century, just a hundred years after her reign, which apparently made such an impression on the minds of the Muslims that they recounted it to their visitors. Ibn Battuta departed from Tangier on a tour of the world. He left Mecca in September 1332 to see *Bilad al-Sind*, which is none other than the native land of our Benazir. His description of the country and its rulers is part of our basic knowledge, since Ibn Battuta's works have been 'best-sellers' up to today – obviously not in the Western sense of the word, but in the Arab sense, that is, a not very attractive book with faded pages and an ordinary cover, moderately priced, which continues to be sold century after century in the shadow of the mosques.[10]

Another queen bearing the title of sultana was Shajarat al-Durr, a ruler of Egypt, who gained power in Cairo in 648/1250 like any other military leader, through her command of strategy. She brought the Muslims a victory which the French remember well, because she routed their army during the Crusades and captured their king, Louis IX.[11]

However, the Arab queens rarely bore the title of sultana; the historian more often gave them the title of malika. For the moment let me point out that both Radiyya and Shajarat al-Durr were Turks; they held power as members of the Mamluk dynasty which reigned in India and Egypt. In Yemen several Arab queens bore the title of malika; among them were Asma and 'Arwa, who exercised power in San'a at the end of the eleventh century. Asma reigned only briefly and jointly with her husband 'Ali, the founder of the Sulayhi dynasty. Queen 'Arwa on the contrary, held power for almost half a century; she directed the affairs of state and planned the war strategies until her death in 484/1090.

We might say that malika is a convenient title easily given to any woman who obtained a bit of power anywhere in the Muslim world from Delhi to North Africa. Many Berber queens had the right to this title. The most famous was Zainab al-Nafzawiyya, who shared power with her husband, Yusuf Ibn Tashfin, ruler of a huge empire extending from North Africa to Spain between 453/1061 and 500/1107.[12] Historians describe Zainab as *al-qa'ima bi mulkihi*, literally, the one in charge of her husband's *mulk*, that is, the main actor running the show. Arab historians seem to have no problem bestowing the title of malika on a woman. A woman holding earthly power did not appear as traumatic to them as it does to our present-day rather mediocre politicians.

Another title often given to women who exercised power was *al-hurra*. Etymologically *al-hurra* means 'free woman', as opposed to a slave. In a harem *al-hurra* described the legal wife, often of aristocratic descent, as opposed to the *jarya*, who was bought by the master on the slave market. In Arabic words such as *hurr* (free) and *hurriyya* (freedom) have nothing to do with the modern human rights connotation. Freedom in our tradition is not rooted in a history of struggle for individual autonomy and independence. Freedom is the opposite of slavery. This is a very significant distinction in understanding Muslim dynamics today. When French children say *liberté*, memories come to their mind of the people's demonstrations and struggles in the streets of Paris in 1789 drummed into them by their teachers. When Arab children say this word, the images that come to their minds are of the pomp of the Golden Age of the Abbasid aristocracy, which always sets our teachers dreaming of the *jawari*, those beautiful slaves who thronged the streets of Baghdad as never again in Arab history. The admiration of my teacher for Abbasid pomp was the essential message that I got as a child. It was only in secondary school that I heard about the extent of slavery during that period. The concept of *hurr* is associated in our minds with the paired words aristocracy/slavery. *Sayyida*, the feminine form of *sayyid* (master, lord) is opposed to *'abd* (slave). Nowadays in modern Arabic, whether classical or spoken, we use *al-sayyid* to say Mr and *al-sayyida* to say Mrs. The linguistic root of *hurr*, which means 'free', is associated with aristocratic sovereignty and not with the struggle against despotism, as is the case with the word *liberté* in the famous French motto of *'liberté, égalité, fraternité'. Hurr* in Arabic has no democratic or popular connotation; on the contrary, *hurr* is what distinguishes a person from being a slave, from being inferior. If freedom in modern French is linked with the struggle of the people for their rights against despotism, *hurriyya* is rooted in the opposite idea, that of the sovereignty of aristocrats. Ibn Manzur tells us that a synonym of *hurr* is *ashraf*, the privilege of aristocrats to trace their ancestors far back. In all things the *sharaf* is the superior part (*'uluw*), the part that dominates; and the *ashraf* among human beings are the superior ones.[13] *Al-hurr* is also the noble deed; the *hurr* in any category is the best. In this way a *hurr* land is a fertile land, a *hurr* cloud is a rain-filled cloud, and the *hurr* part of the house is the best and most comfortable part.[14] *Hurr*, then, is a concept intrinsically linked to *sharaf*, the aristocracy, the elite, the superior group. One of the names for eagle is *al-hurr*.[15]

Paradoxically, while Islam was born of a democratic design that limited the power of the aristocracies, the word *ashraf* was never devalued; in fact the contrary is true. The Quraysh nobles were the *ashraf* in pre-Islamic Arabia. But after the triumph of Islam, *ashraf* always designated the elite, the notables of a city or country, and especially and most particularly the descendants of the Prophet. *Al-ashraf*, the sharifs, are the privileged ones who can trace their

ancestry to Fatima, his daughter, and to 'Ali, his son-in-law and
cousin. *Hurr* also has to do with the idea of resistance, since one
says of a bride that she has spent the night *hurra* if she was not
deflowered on her wedding night, since her husband could not
penetrate her.[16] This idea of resisting, of concentrated energy contained in *hurr*, is evident in the word *harrara*, which means 'to
write'. When you decide to write a text, what you are in fact doing
is 'liberating words' (*tahrir al-kitaba*). You are arranging alphabet
letters in a specific order that makes sense and liberates meanings.[17]
Al-muharrir (the liberator) is one of the many words for a writer.
One of the duties of the *hurr*, the aristocrat, is to think globally, to
plan for others, to think for the group. A duty and a privilege, it
is the mark of honour of the elite. But what is surprising is that we
never find the title of *hurr* used for men. We never encounter it
given to a temporal or spiritual head of state, like the words *sultan*
or *malik*. We often find it used for women as a synonym for *malika*
or *sultana*, and in regions of the Muslim empire as different as
Spain, North Africa, and Yemen. *Al-hurra* is the title of two Yemeni
queens of the eleventh and twelfth centuries, Asma and 'Arwa,
whom we will meet further on. Later, in the fifteenth and sixteenth
centuries, several Andalusian queens, who played important roles
on both sides of the Mediterranean (Spain and North Africa) bore
this title. Women seem to emerge on the political scene at the
time of great catastrophes. The fall of Granada in 1492, when
the Christians ejected the Muslims from Spain, was one of those
occasions.

The most famous of these women was 'A'isha al-Hurra, known
to the Spaniards by the name Sultana Madre de Boabdil, Boabdil
being the distorted name of her son, the last Arab ruler of Spain
Muhammad Abu 'Abdallah. She won the admiration of her enemies
at the time of the Muslim debacle.[18] According to 'Abdallah Inan,
an expert on the fall of Granada, despite the silence of Arab
sources, which barely mention her name, 'A'isha al-Hurra played a
prominent role in Muslim history.[19] Only Inan's analysis of the
Spanish documents revealed that she was a remarkable leader who
took heroic action at a tragic moment; he calls her one of the 'most
noble and fascinating [personages] of our history'.[20] Her life, which
Inan calls 'a page of heroism', is little known, if not entirely
unknown, and is barely studied even by experts. Inan tries to retrace
several episodes of it. According to him, it was 'A'isha al-Hurra
who decided to transfer power from her ageing husband, 'Ali Abu
al-Hasan, who had taken power in 866/1461, to her son by him,

Muhammad Abu 'Abdallah, the last king of Granada. The son took power by following the instructions of his mother in 887/1482 and held it until the fateful date of 896/1492, that is, one year after the fall of Granada. He was the last king of the Banu Nasr (or Banu al-Ahmar) dynasty of Granada (629/1232 to 896/1492), and remains forever linked in Arab memory with one of the most unforgettable defeats of our history. It was his flight before the advancing armies of Ferdinand and Isabella, the Catholic monarchs, that sounded the death knell of the Muslim empire in Spain, which had lasted more than eight centuries. So we can understand why Arab history throws a veil over the role played by 'A'isha al-Hurra, witness of and actor in one of the most traumatizing periods in the history of Islam.

The emergence of 'A'isha al-Hurra on the political scene began with marital unhappiness. She resided in the sumptuous Palace of the Alhambra, after giving her husband two sons, Muhammad (Abu 'Abdallah) and Yusuf, and after living, not without some danger, through the series of military catastrophes that preceded the fall. She became involved in political action when her husband, much older than she, succumbed to the charms of Isabella, a Spanish prisoner of war who succeeded in becoming his favourite. Isabella had been captured by the Arabs when she was just a child during a military expedition. As an accomplished favourite who had mastered the art of seduction, she decided to convert to Islam, a gesture that could not but flatter the Arab sovereign, and took the name of Soraya. The sultan fell madly in love with her, freed her first, and married her soon after, according to Islamic tradition. Soraya bore him children, which strengthened her position, and in the existing explosive political situation started to use her ascendancy over the caliph to achieve the triumph of her own people. The elite of Granada, sensing the danger represented by the rise of the Spanish wife, responded to the call of the Arab wife, who had clear aims: depose the father, who was a traitor to the Arab cause, replace him with his son Abu 'Abdallah. 'A'isha played on the nationalist fervour of the Andalusians, who were anxious about their future.[21] The Palace of the Alhambra became a battlefield, divided between two women who represented two enemy cultures, one of which was fated to disappear. The Arab queen, al-Hurra, who occupied the wing of the palace which contained the famous Court of Lions, decided to take action. Fleeing the palace, she organized attacks from the outside until the overthrow of her husband and the accession of her son Abu 'Abdallah to the throne at the age of 25.[22]

The fall of Granada propelled other women on to the political scene, women of the elite who would otherwise have led a somnolent life in the harem and whom the debacle pitched into the political melee, obliging them to assume responsibility and participate in the momentous events shaking the community and with it the western Mediterranean. Freed from the iron grip of tradition that immobilized them in domestic space and despite their inexperience, women showed themselves to be clever strategists, at least as resourceful as men.

Such a woman as Sayyida al-Hurra, a Moroccan of Andalusian origin, found no better way to ease the humiliation of defeat than to launch into piracy. She displayed such talent at it that she soon became *Hakima Tatwan* (governor of Tetouán). The Muslim historians treat this second al-Hurra, like the first, with the same disdainful silence: 'One finds practically no information in the Arab sources about this queen, who exercised power for more than thirty years [916/1510, the date of the accession to power of her husband al-Mandri, to 949/1542, when she was deposed].' According to Spanish and Portuguese sources, al-Hurra was their partner in the diplomatic game.[23] She played a key role for many years as governor of Tetouán and as the undisputed leader of the pirates in the western Mediterranean. One of her allies was none other than the famous Turkish corsair Barbarossa, who operated out of Algiers.[24] But corsairs were not her only allies. After the death of her husband she married the king of Morocco, Ahmad al-Wattasi, the third king of that dynasty (932/1524 to 966/1549). In order to show him that she had no intention of giving up her political role in the north, she requested that the king leave his capital of Fez and come to Tetouán for the marriage ceremony. This was the only time in the history of Morocco that a king got married away from his capital.[25]

Her family, the Banu Rashid, was a family of Andalusian notables, who like many others decided to return to North Africa after the fall of Granada. The life of Sayyida al-Hurra began amid the anxieties of exile and the uncertainties experienced by all the Andalusian refugees who fled the Inquisition. Her family settled in Chaouen, and there she married al-Mandri, who belonged to another great Andalusian family living in the neighbouring town of Tetouán. Many émigré communities let themselves be deluded by the idea of a return to Andalusia. Conducting expeditions against the Spaniards became the obsession of the bravest among them, and piracy was the ideal solution. It allowed the expelled to obtain quick revenues (booty and ransom for captives), and at the same time to continue to fight the Christian enemy. The history of the rebirth of Tetouán is linked to, and reflects that of, the family of al-Mandri, al-Hurra's husband, who became head of the community of Andalusian exiles:

> Tetouán was restored about ninety years after its destruction, around 1490 or a little later, by Captain Abu al-Hasan al-Mandri, originally from Granada . . .. The refugees sent a delegation to Morocco's Sultan Muhammad al-Wattasi in Fez. He welcomed them and, upon their request, gave them authorization to settle in the ruins of the destroyed town and to fortify it against attack . . .. Upon receiving the authorization of the sultan, the Andalusians rebuilt the ramparts of Tetouán, constructed their dwellings, and erected the Great Mosque. Then, under the leadership of al-Mandri, they launched a holy war against the Portuguese, who were installed at Ceuta.[26]

The historical sources do not agree on the identity of al-Hurra's husband. Was it 'Ali, the founder of the new town of Tetouán and the leader of the community, or was it his son, al-Mandri II?[27] In the first case she would have had a husband decidedly older than herself, and the fact that he lost his sight at the end of his life would explain the precocious involvement of his wife in political affairs.[28] Others say that she was married to the son, and that he, seeing her ability in political matters, often called upon her to replace him at the head of the city when he went on a trip. The community grew accustomed to seeing her exercise authority, and later accepted her as governor without demur.[29]

As the governor of Tetouán, however, she did not have the right to the title of al-Hurra, that is, a woman exercising sovereign power, gaining the title only in 1515, upon the death of her husband. Confirmed first as prefect of Tetouán, she managed affairs so well that she got herself named governor of that city-state. She then made contact with the Ottoman pirate Barbarossa, assembled a fleet, and launched into privateering in the Mediterranean. The Spaniards and Portuguese maintained close relations with her, as the responsible naval power in the region, and negotiated with her for the liberation of their prisoners. And Sayyida al-Hurra is the only title given her in the documents of the Spanish and Portuguese, who even wondered if that was not her name.[30]

Another word for queen, used only by the Arabs, is *sitt*, literally 'lady'. One of the queens of the Fatimid dynasty of Egypt was Sitt al-Mulk (born in 359/980). She took power in 411/1021 after organizing the 'disappearance' of her brother, al-Hakim, the sixth caliph of the dynasty. She had her reasons. The outrageous behaviour of the caliph, towards women whom he had forbidden to leave their homes, and dogs which he had decided to exterminate, had gone too far. He awoke one morning and announced that he was God and that the population of Cairo, with Sitt al-Mulk in the lead, had to worship him.[31]

'*Sitt*' seems to have been a title borne by women of exceptional talent. *A'lam* by Zarkali (the 'Who's Who' of famous Arab men and women) cites several of them who were known as experts in theology.[32] Sitt al-Qudat (chief of qadis!), a *musnida* (expert in Hadith or traditions relating to the Prophet) who lived in the fourteenth century, taught in Damascus and wrote treatises on *fiqh*, religious knowledge. (A qadi is a religious authority and judge.) Sitt al-'Arab and Sitt al-'Ajam were also famous experts in *fiqh* in the fourteenth century.

We cannot close the list of titles given to women who have exercised political power in Muslim history without mentioning the cases – rare, it is true – of those who took power either as military leaders or as religious leaders. One of the fairly unusual titles in an Islam that carefully distinguishes between spiritual and secular (or more precisely military) power was that given to a Yemeni queen who was a religious leader, the daughter of Imam al-Zayd al-Nasir li Din Allah, and who took San'a by force of arms in her capacity as the Zaydi chieftain in the middle of the fifteenth century. The title she bore was Sharifa Fatima.[33] And there was Ghaliyya al-Wahhabiyya, a Hanbali from Tarba near Ta'if, who led a military resistance movement in Saudi Arabia to defend Mecca against foreign takeover at the beginning of the eighteenth century. She was given the title of *amira*, *amir* being the title of the leader of armies. The *amir* in chief (generalissimo) of the army is called *amir al-umara*. 'This dignity was originally confined to the military command.'[34] Her boldness and strategic ability led her enemies on the battlefield to credit her with the magic gift of making the Wahhabi forces invisible. Historians noted her appearance at the head of the bedouin army as a memorable event: 'Never had the resistance of the Arab tribes from the vicinity of Mecca been so strong as was that of the Arabs of Tarba . . ... They had at their head a woman who bore the name of Ghaliyya.'[35]

However, in the majority of cases the women who entered the political arena, like most of the men, were neither military chieftains nor peerless religious leaders. Even if they sometimes had to lead military operations, that was not their preferred field of action. As for religion, as good politicians, women tried like men to manipulate it rather than assert claim to the spiritual and its symbols.

If *malika, sultana, al-hurra,* and *sitt* seem to be titles used for women who ruled in the Arab part of the Muslim world, the title of *khatun* is the one most often found in Asian Islam, especially in the Turkish and Mongol dynasties. According to the *Encyclopedia of Islam,* khatun 'is a title of Soghdian origin borne by the wives and female relatives of the T'u-chüeh and subsequent Turkish rulers. It was employed by Saldjuks and Khwaraz-shahs.' Many women who took an active part in directing the affairs of state, whether with their spouse or alone, bore this title. One of the problems that confronted the Mongol princes, who came to Islam as conquerors and in a few decades were conquered by it, was how to reconcile the very public status of women in their culture with the very private status that the new religion imposed. After taking power in 694/1295, Ghazan, the seventh ruler of the Ilkhan dynasty, faced this problem when he converted to Sunni Islam.

Dokuz Khatun, the favourite wife of Hulagu, the grandson of Genghis Khan, who conquered a large part of the Muslim empire and occupied its capital Baghdad in 1258, played an important role in forming the attitude of the new conquerors toward the Christians. Belonging herself to the Nestorian sect, she favoured Christians and placed them in posts of responsibility.[36] Al-Sarim Uzbek, from the Arab court of Hims, was extremely surprised when he was received by Hulagu to 'talk politics' to see the latter's wife constantly present.[37] Islam had to comply with the customs of the Asian steppes as far as the role of women and their prominence in public life went. One of the things that struck Ibn Battuta as an Arab traveller, when he crossed the Mongol empire and visited the Turkish sovereigns, was the constant involvement of women in politics: 'Among the Turks and the Tatars their wives enjoy a very high position; indeed when they issue an order, they say in it, "By command of the Sultan and the Khatuns".'[38] Khatun was also the title of the queens of the Kutlugh-Khan dynasty of Kirman. This was the case, for example, with Kutlugh Turkan Khatun and Padishah Khatun, respectively the fourth and sixth sovereigns of the dynasty in 1257 and 1293.

However, whether they were a khatun, a malika, a sultana, or a simple courtesan plotting behind the scenes in the shadowy world of the harem, not one has ever borne the title of caliph. Can we conclude as a result that women were excluded forever from the

supreme role of head of state? One of the great debates that has
agitated the Muslim world since the death of the Prophet concerns
the ethnic origin of the caliph: must he be an Arab or can he come
from any other ethnic group, that is, can he be an *'ajami*? *'Ajami*
refers to foreigners, literally those who cannot speak Arabic cor-
rectly, who either speak it badly or have not mastered its subtleties.

Among the many non-Arab heads of state who have taken power
throughout the centuries, Persians, Mongols, Berbers, Kurds, Sudanese, Indians, or others, rare have been those who claimed any
other title than sultan or malik, or some variation of these. The
assumption of the title of caliph by the Ottomans in the sixteenth
century came as a violent shock. A caliph has to prove a link to
the Prophet, and for a Turk that becomes a rather awkward matter.
It is necessary to resort to fiction, and the Ottomans were obliged
to do just that.

Every Muslim head of state who claims the title of caliph has to
solve the problem of his descent from the Prophet, to certify a
family tree that links him to the Prophet's descendants, that is, to
the children of his daughter Fatima and her husband 'Ali. One of
the standard forms of challenge used by rebels against the Arab
caliphs, first the Umayyads and then the Abbasids, was precisely
to claim filiation going back to the Prophet. Obviously those who
ventured along this road put their life in danger and ended by being
physically done away with, for there could be only one caliph. And
the Umayyad caliphs, as well as the Abbasids, were going to pre-
serve order on earth and in Heaven by cutting off the heads of all
pretenders to their title. The Abbasids, who were Sunnis, began
their decline the day they failed to liquidate a Shi'ite pretender who
proclaimed himself caliph in 297/909. He was al-Mahdi al-Fatimi,
who founded a second dynasty of caliphs, the Fatimids (named for
Fatima, the Prophet's daughter). Having two caliphs at the same
time, one Sunni and the other Shi'ite, was absolutely incongruous
with the Muslim ideal, which is directed toward unity as the way to
ensure strength. In order to succeed, the Fatimids had to operate
far from Baghdad. They started in North Africa, and it was only in
358/969 that they transferred their capital to Cairo and laid hold of
Egypt and Syria. All this goes to show that declaring oneself caliph
is not something lightly undertaken by just any powerful man. The
idea that this is a privilege reserved for exceptional beings is deeply
rooted. For a woman to claim it would be an act of delirium, and
to my knowledge no woman has ever been so lacking in good sense
as to consider it.

Two of the criteria of eligibility for the caliphate are being a male and being an Arab. While the latter criterion has been violently challenged and thousands of Muslims have died to defend the idea that any Muslim can become caliph, no one has ever questioned the criterion of maleness. In any case, no one has ever endangered life and limb to contend that the criterion of maleness for occupying the position of caliph violates the principle of equality which is the base of Islam. How could Islam reconcile these two points: the principle of equality among all believers and the very restrictive criteria of eligibility for the caliphate? Here is one of the enigmas of political history that it is incumbent on the people of today to clarify. The aim of my voyage into the past in search of the sultanas and their titles is one small step in that direction. A foray into the past brings with it one absolute certitude: to return there is impossible, because what has changed in the world, including Muslim societies, is not just the demands of women and of men *vis-à-vis* the powers that be, but the very environment in which they live, the air they breathe, the Heaven they look to, the earth on which they walk. The Heaven of the Abbasid caliphs is no longer our Heaven, their earth is no longer ours. The earth revolves around the sun, but in their time for many people it was the sun that revolved around the earth. However, the struggle for democracy in the sense of equality did not begin with the importation of the Universal Declaration of Human Rights, which is Western, as everyone knows; it began in the first centuries of Islam with the Kharijite sect.

At the very beginning this sect, one of the many which challenged Islam as a political practice, questioned the requirement that the caliph must be from the Quraysh tribe, asserting that anyone, regardless of ethnic origin, had the right to be caliph, to lead Muslims. The Kharijites ('those who quit') refused to play the political game by the rules any longer, making dialogue with them impossible within the heart of Islam.[39] When the Kharijites declared their disagreement with the criteria of eligibility of the leader, it came as a shock. At that time there was consensus: only an Arab had the right to lead. In order to understand the atmosphere and mentality that reigned in the first centuries of Islam, it might be a good idea to consider the attitude of a refined intellectual like Ibn Hazm the Andalusian, a good Muslim who tried to conform to the Muslim egalitarian ideal, but who remained fiercely aristocratic in his soul.

Ibn Hazm cites the names of three men who were not of the

Quraysh tribe, but who were each, for a very short period, given the title of caliph. The first was Ibn al-Muhallab, an opponent of the ninth Umayyad caliph, Yazid Ibn 'Abd al-Malik (ninth century), who challenged his power, but in vain. The second was a ruler of the Moroccan city of Sijilmasa, Muhammad Ibn al-Fath, who was briefly given the title in the middle of the tenth century. The last was 'Abd al-Rahman Ibn Abi Amir, an Andalusian ruler who held the title 'for a single day . . . . He was so overcome with joy to hear himself called caliph that he tore off his clothes, but he recovered and renounced the title . . . and this is the most foolish story I have ever heard.' Ibn Hazm's scorn expresses the thinking of the majority of Muslims of his time. It was pure folly for someone not a member of the Meccan aristocracy to want to claim the title. He gives another list of three powerful rulers who approached the religious authorities about how to appropriate this title, but who renounced the idea when objections were raised.[40]

The sole exception was the ninth Ottoman caliph, Salim I, who managed to kidnap the title by magically transferring its symbols to Turkey. He arranged for the last Abbasid caliph, then living in Egypt, who moved there after the sack of Baghdad by Genghis Khan, to hand over to him the title and symbols of the caliphate, that is the Prophet's cloak, one of his teeth, and a lock of his hair, which were brought to the Topkapi Palace.[41] As one might imagine, this was a sensational moment in the Muslim world, for until the Ottomans, no one outside the Quraysh, the Prophet's tribe, had succeeded in claiming the title of caliph, nor tried to take on its privilege and magic, which transcended earthly power and its hazards. The hordes of Genghis Khan had managed to destroy Baghdad in 1258, and Hulagu, charged with subduing the Islamic lands, had massacred close to 80,000 people, including the last Baghdad caliph, al-Musta'sim. But what he could never have suspected is that twenty-four years later, in 1282, his own son and third ruler of the dynasty, Manku Timur, would succumb to the charm of the religion they denounced and take the name of Ahmad upon declaring his new faith. This act threw the Mongol warriors into confusion and brought about the fall of Ahmad (formerly Manku Rimur) two years later. But the conqueror did not seem to grasp the fascinating appeal of the newly conquered religion. Thirteen years later Ghazan, another grandson of Genghis Khan and seventh ruler of the dynasty, became a Muslim, and this time Islam became the religion of the court. However, at the peak of their power, the Mongols, having taken everything away from the Abbasids, their empire and its riches, their authority, and their grandeur, were never able to seize the title of caliph, which mysteriously transcended the power of armies and all their earthly triumphs.[42]

Thus we see the unique status the caliph has in the Muslim hierarchy: although he is a head of state, all heads of state are not caliphs. The claim of non-Arabs to this title remains problematical, and it becomes even more so if one considers the highly fanciful hypothesis of women heads of state. But is there really a fundamental incompatibility between the caliphate as the ideal model of authority and a woman ruler?

2
The Caliph and the Queen

A feeling of vertigo comes over me at the association of the words *woman* and *caliph*, and it affects anyone who, like me, has received a good, solid Muslim education. It is mitigated, without completely fading away, on reading the historical sources. A good Muslim education teaches you to be careful in what you say, to put everything and every person in its place, to respect hierarchies and limits. Associating the word *caliph*, the essence of Muslim monotheism, and the word *woman* seems blasphemous. History teaches that the caliph always thought a woman unworthy of exercising even any inferior kind of power, such as *mulk*, basely secular earthly power. As the representative of God on earth and in principle the supreme source of all delegation of divine authority, the caliph systematically opposed women becoming head of state, even though they never laid claim to anything but being a sultana and to managing earthly affairs. But even that was forbidden to them. The rare women who were able to rise high enough to want to direct affairs of state found themselves denied spiritual validation by the caliph each time they asked it of him. In order to exercise even secular power, without any claim to administer spiritual matters, a sultan needed the caliph's stamp of approval, his spiritual benediction. One cannot lead a Muslim community without some sort of link with the divine, however *pro forma* it may be. And being in charge of this link became one of the functions of the caliphs at the moment when they ceased to be powerful.

Paradoxically it was by losing his earthly power at the time of the conquest of Baghdad by the Mongols that the caliph discovered his spiritual power. It was with his decline as a military leader and the breakup of his empire and its partition among his former vassals and slaves that the Arab caliph understood that the ascendancy he exercised over them was the locus of divine authority. And it was precisely this decentralization and quasi-democratization of power, the formation of local autonomous governments, and the coming to power of the *'ajam* (non-Arabs) that opened the royal road of politics to women. But once they succeeded in establishing their authority locally, queens, just like kings, had to seek the blessing of the caliph. He became the dispenser of the certificates of legitimacy. Queens, however, unlike their fathers, husbands, or brothers, encountered scathing rejection, usually without any possibility of challenging the decision. And rejection often played into the hands of other pretenders to the throne and precipitated the queens' more or less rapid defeat and sometimes their tragic death.

A militarily powerless caliph, who distributed honorific titles to generals who had seized power in the four corners of the empire – titles, such as *Rukn al-din* (Pillar of the faith), *Sayf al-dawla* (Sword of the state), *'Amid al-mulk* (Pillar of power), or *Nasir al-din wa al-dawla* (Victor of the faith and the state) – served the interests of both parties when the Muslim empire began to disintegrate. On the one hand, the new local chieftains, gaining power by force of arms, needed a facade of legitimacy, a kind of religious blessing. The caliph, militarily weakened and economically impoverished, was on the other hand only too happy to still have in his power something needed by the conquerors. The honorary titles were a sort of investiture, and the conferring of the title was done according to a solemn ritual. 'Recognition by the caliph, involving an investiture charter . . . plus the other insignia of power such as honorifics, a richly caparisoned charger and banners, might give a contender for power in a disputed succession the edge over his opponent.'[1] The ceremony of conferring a title took place in Baghdad as well as in the local capital in a lavish celebration with exchange of gifts. In the fourth century titles constituted the most important source of income for the caliph. In 423/1031 when the amir of Baghdad received the title of *Malik al-dawla* (King of the state) he gave the caliph '2,000 dinars, 30,000 dirhams, 10 pieces of silk cloth, 100 pieces of silk brocade of superior quality, and 100 others of lesser quality.'[2]

One of the first women who aspired to the sultanate for herself was Turkan Khatun,[3] the wife of Malikshah, the Seljuk sultan who made Baghdad and its caliph tremble and who reigned between

465/1072 and 485/1092. Of Turkish origin, Malikshah demanded from his caliph grandiose titles in exchange for protection, for the caliph was incapable of defending even his capital. After the death of Malikshah, Turkan Khatun tried to take power, since her son Mahmud, the crown prince, was only four years old. As a matter of principle, Islam forbids power being given to a child, so the stakes were enormous: 'The Friday *khutba*, which was recited in the mosques in the name of Malikshah, was heard throughout an empire that extended from the borders of China in the east as far as Syria in the west and from the Muslim countries of the north to Yemen in the south.'[4] Malikshah was the steel in the sword of Islam defending the Sunnism incarnated by Baghdad and its caliph from the attacks of the Shi'ites, who had become a formidable force.

In order to assure the succession as she understood it and to defend herself against the other pretenders to the throne, Turkan Khatun needed the complicity of the Abbasid caliph of the period, al-Muqtadi, the twenty-seventh of the line, who ruled between 467/1070 and 487/1094. She kept the death of her husband secret and tried to reach an agreement with Baghdad. The caliph began by saying that Mahmud was a child. Turkan managed to get a *fatwa* (decree) saying that Mahmud could reign despite the 'detail' of his age. But the caliph was not ready to let a woman install herself on a throne, however powerful she might be. What was important to him was that the *khutba*, the privilege that went with sovereignty, not be said in the name of a woman. The *khutba* (literally 'sermon') was officially preached at Friday prayers and was of both religious and political significance, affirming the caliph's right to rule. Al-Muqtadi insisted that the *khutba* be issued in the name of her son. But that was not enough; he imposed a vizier of his choice on Turkan. At first she balked, considering the caliph's conditions too humiliating.[5] Finally, she accepted all his conditions, for without the blessing of Baghdad she had no chance against her rivals.

Another Abbasid caliph, al-Musta'sim, also violently opposed the accession of a woman to the throne of Egypt. This was Sultana Shajarat al-Durr, the wife of Malik al-Salih Najm al-Din Ayyub, the eighth sovereign of the Ayyubid dynasty of Egypt, who decided to succeed her husband after his death in 648/1250.[6] At that time Egypt was within the control of the caliphate of Baghdad, and Shajarat al-Durr had just won a great military victory against the Crusaders. She certainly deserved at least one of the many titles of her husband, who held, among others, the most grandiloquent title that a general could dream of claiming: 'Sultan of the Arabs and the non-Arabs, King of the Lands and the Seas, King of India and China, of Yemen, of Zabid, San'a, and Aden, Master of the Kings of the Arabs and the non-Arabs, and Sultan of the Countries of the Rising and the Setting of the Sun'.[7] Shajarat al-Durr probably did not demand such a grand title, but asked for a simple recognition by al-Musta'sim of her power as Egyptian head of state. The caliph then sent to the Egyptian amirs the famous message, so humiliating to her, in which he proclaimed that he was ready to provide them with some capable men, if no more existed in Egypt, since they were reduced to choosing a woman.[8] Shajarat al-Durr tried to operate without his authorization, believing that she had the essential thing: the support of the army, an army that under her leadership had just beaten the Crusaders at Damietta. She gave herself a title that was less long than that of her husband, but which was a gesture of defiance to the caliph because it challenged his prerogatives. The title was *Malikat al-Muslimin*, Queen of the Muslims. But she did not last long, because the caliph's rejection proved fatal to her and brought on her tragic end, despite all the talent she displayed to hold on to her position and despite her desperate struggle to overturn the rules of the power game. She seemed to have perfectly mastered its most violent and ruthless dimension, since in a very short time she had succeeded in wiping out all her rivals.[9] The paradox is that al-Musta'sim, who took it upon himself to ridicule Shajarat al-Durr and her claim to rule, was militarily powerless. Furthermore, through his irresponsible behaviour toward the Mongols he brought on the sack of Baghdad in 1258 and the extermination of thousands of Muslims by Hulagu, the grandson of Genghis Khan. He was the symbol of a bankrupt, centuries-old Arab dynasty, in contrast to Shajarat al-Durr, who was the leading star of her own rising dynasty, that of the Mamluks, Turkish slaves, who were the only ones with the power to face the Mongol armies. Thanks to the combative Mamluks, the Mongols were never able to occupy Egypt. Al-Musta'sim's rejection of Shajarat was hardly justified in terms of the defence of the Muslims' interests, and he was certainly in a poor position to judge and evaluate her abilities. But, as he was the caliph, it was he who won. As soon as the attitude of the caliph became known, dissensions appeared; the administrators of Syria, which was a dependency of Cairo, refused to recognize Shajarat al-Durr; Cairo's army was soon divided; and finally the decision to depose her was taken.

A constant of Muslim history is that the upholders of orthodoxy saw every occasion that a woman claimed power as an aggressive violation of the rules of the game. The meaning of this orthodoxy obviously varies in different epochs and places, depending on the culture and the interests of those who have the power of the sword and can extort taxes. But this one constant endured throughout the empire and its states: as soon as a woman came close to the throne, a group whose interests she threatened appeared on the scene and challenged her in the name of the spiritual, the name of the *shari'a*. This was true even when she operated in an obviously unstable revolutionary context, as did Shajarat, who emerged when former slave Mamluks decided to take over.

One exception, perhaps, was Radiyya, another Turk, who took power in Delhi a decade before Shajarat al-Durr and who owed her rise to her father, Sultan Iltutmish, originally a slave who came to power through his own merits. It was he who established Muslim sovereignty over India and who decided to name his daughter as his heiress, despite having three sons. The religious authorities, whom he liked to surround himself with and who were very influential in the country, tried to dissuade him.[10] That did not keep Radiyya from acceding to power. But opposition in the name of the spiritual was latent and was brandished by her rivals during her reign.

Nor did Indonesian queens escape this obstacle, despite their geographical and cultural distance from Baghdad. Four of them, however, managed to hand down power to each other in the Atjeh empire in the northernmost part of Sumatra at the end of the seventeenth century. Not surprisingly, they faced religious opposition, which contested their right to rule, on the basis of a *fatwa* brought all the way from distant Mecca.[11] Nevertheless these Indonesian queens monopolized power until the beginning of the eighteenth century. They bestowed on themselves lavish titles that would have scandalized the Abbasid al-Musta'sim. The first (1641–75) called herself very humbly *Taj al-'alam safiyyat al-din shah* (Crown of the world, purity of the faith); the second (1675–8) chose the name *Nur al-'alam nakiyyat al-din shah* (Light of the world, purity of the faith); the third (1678–88) chose an exotic half-Persian title, *'Inayat shah zakiyyat al-din shah*; the fourth (1688–99), *Kamalat Shah*, ruled tranquilly until the dawn of the eighteenth century.[12]

Women, then, have reigned over the lands of Islam and directed their governments, but always in violation of the spiritual principles that underpin and legitimize political authority. Why? We know that gender and politics are so closely tied that it is absolutely impossible to separate them, especially in cultures where man/-woman subordination incarnates and symbolizes authority. Societies that have defined the identity of a man by his virile ability to control and veil women do not seem ready to relinquish such a definition of self, nor are they ready to enjoy democracy. Any infiltration of women into the Muslim political arena is seen as disruptive; the credibility of all the protagonists, especially the most pompous, seems to suffer grievously. And this unfolds on time's double stage: that of the present and that of the past, with memory playing the role of an artfully distorting mirror, creating a present which cannot be supported by any other logic. In this regard, the general outcry against Benazir Bhutto and her strangely brief career is more than eloquent.

What is the origin of this conflict between politics and women? The simplest way to probe the philosophical bases of the conflict is to go back again to the key concept of the caliph. This title has always been, and is still today, very rarely claimed, despite the many nation-states and the sovereign autonomy of each ruler. The coldness of the mullahs of Teheran, who claim to be the spiritual leaders of the universe, toward the king of Morocco is due, among other things, to the fact that he is one of the rare heads of a modern Muslim state to bear the title of caliph. And to make it worse for them, the kings of Morocco have inherited this title for centuries. Moreover, at a very early stage Morocco was one of the first regions of the Muslim empire to set up autonomous institutions and assert its claim to be an independent Muslim territory which did not accept just any claimant to spiritual authority. The sovereigns of the Almoravid dynasty (488/1056 to 541/1147) adopted the title of *Amir al-Muslimin* (Commander of the Muslims) to make known their desire for autonomy without going as far as repudiating the authority of the Abbasid caliph, who alone had the title of *Amir al-mu'minin* (Commander of the faithful). The example of the rivalry between Teheran and Rabat allows us to understand the permanence, the continuity, and the gravity of the symbolism of titles and their importance on the Islamic political scene and the ever-powerful import (today essentially spiritual) of the word *caliph*.

Although the caliph is always an imam, an imam is not necessarily caliph. One can very well dispense with the word *imam* when in the presence of the caliph, for he is both. An imam is he who positions people in space, while the caliph positions them in time. The grammatical origin of the word *imam* is *'amma*, to be the first, to be at the head, to lead and conduct people on the *sirat al-mustaqim* (the right path), the most common meaning of which is the leading of prayers. The imam of a mosque is the one who leads the prayers. The origin of the word *caliph* is very different; it derives from *khalafa*, which means to come afterward, to succeed someone in time. The first to bear the title of caliph was Abu Bakr; he was called caliph because he replaced the Prophet after his death. The caliph necessarily inherited both the spiritual and the material leadership of the Muslims, since the Prophet ensured well-being on earth and in Heaven through the *shari'a*, the divine law. The very nature of power is religious: the political leader's function is to enforce the law of God on earth. This is the only way to guarantee order and justice. The caliph's duty is to use religion to harmonize the political administration of the universe, politics and religion being inextricably linked. This cosmic entangling of Heaven and earth, and the caliph as the executor of divine will on earth, necessarily imply the exclusion of women, the divine being both One and male. We are taught at school that the caliph is the representative of God on earth, and repeating this formula mechanically makes women's exclusion an inevitable cosmic law.

However, at the beginning the first caliph, Abu Bakr (from 11/632 to 13/634), known for his great modesty, was a little frightened by the title and advised the Companions not to call him 'caliph of God on earth'. He told them: 'Call me the caliph of the Prophet – may the prayer of Allah and his peace be upon him – because one can only take the place of someone who is absent. One cannot take the place of him who is present.'[13] At any rate, it is because of this entangling of the spiritual and the earthly, explains Ibn Khaldun, that 'we call the caliphate the greater imamate [*al-imama al-kubra*] by contrast with the lesser imamate [*al-imama al-sughra*], which consists of leading the prayers. The responsibility of the greater imamate, or the caliphate, includes the leading of the prayers [*al-salat*], legal consultation [*al-futya*], adjudication [*al-qada'*, the function of qadi], holy war [*al-jihad*], and municipal administration [*al-hisba*].'[14] So the leading of the prayers (the lesser imamate) is only one of the functions of the caliph, who is both head of state and head of government and fills all the important cabinet posts, if we want to use modern terminology. He is at one and the same time minister of justice, finance, and defence. Since for many religious authorities the lesser imamate, the simple act of leading the prayers, already excluded women, one understands that for the greater imamate the question seems superfluous.

According to Ibn Rushd:

Opinion is very divided on the ability of women to be imam for a congregation of men [that is, to lead the prayers]; some even question her ability to lead the prayers for a congregation of women . . ... Shafi'i authorizes her to lead the prayers of women; Malik forbids it; as for Abu Tawr and Tabari, they allow her to be imam in both cases. Nevertheless, the consensus of the majority [of religious authorities] is to forbid women to be imam for a congregation of men.[15]

Since the ability of women to manage something 'lesser' is disputed, it goes without saying that their candidature to manage something 'greater' will not even be considered. However, *a priori* nothing excludes them if we consider the four conditions of eligibility for being caliph. According to Ibn Khaldun in the *Muqaddima*, everybody agrees upon these. The first is knowledge (*al-'ilm*), the second is equity (*al-'adala*), the third is competence, and the last is physical fitness. Knowledge is 'obvious, because the caliph must apply divine law, which he can only do if he knows it'. As for *al-'adala*, it is a matter of both integrity and probity, of a life without excess or licentiousness of any sort, because it is a religious function that is at issue. It is the idea of equilibrium that is the essence of this concept: as far as possible a caliph must be a man who does not violate ethical interdictions, who is not guilty of *bid'a*, innovation. Any innovation amounts to derailment, straying from the straight and narrow path of the *shari'a*, which has already been completely laid out. Competence is required 'because he must be able to impose respect for boundaries and to undertake wars'.[16] The last condition requires that the caliph be in good health and that he be 'neither mad nor blind nor deaf nor mute'.[17]

At the end of his chapter on 'the caliphate and its conditions', in order to explain why this does not apply to women, Ibn Khaldun reminds us that

Allah does not give orders directly to a person unless he knows the person is capable of carrying them out . . . . Most religious laws apply to women just as they apply to men. Nevertheless, the message is not directly addressed to them; one resorts to analogy in their case, because they have no power and are under the control of men.[18]

Islam is crystal-clear about principles. So if one acknowledges *a priori* that women effectively have no power, then one cannot directly transmit any divine mission to them. And Islam's essential institution, the caliphate, leaves no doubt about this exclusion of women from politics. If Benazir Bhutto's enemies had taken their stand on the level of principles and had specified that they were only speaking about the function of caliph, inaccessible to a woman, they would have been unassailable. But the problem is that Zia al-Haq was not caliph either, despite his religious pretensions and his brandishing of the *shari'a* to hide the arbitrariness of his military regime. What the fundamentalists in fact blamed Benazir Bhutto for was winning the election. Normally good Muslims who want to hold to the letter of Islamic tradition should not participate in popular elections with universal suffrage because elections are completely foreign to the spirit and tradition of the choice of the leader by *bay'a*:

> *Bay'a* is the solemn commitment that one makes to obey. He who makes this promise pledges to his prince that he gives up the right to decide his personal affairs and those of the Muslims, that he will raise no challenge thereto, that he will obey everything that he is commanded to do, whether he likes it or not.[19]

Bay'a has nothing to do with elections with universal suffrage because it contradicts them on two basic levels. The first is that *bay'a* is final, while the vote with universal suffrage is temporary and renewable at regular intervals. The second is that *bay'a* is the privilege of the notables, of those who already have a part in decision-making, *ahl al-hal wa al-'aqd* (literally, those who have the ability to tie and untie). Another word for the elite is *ahl al-ikhtiyar* (those who choose). Never at any moment in Muslim history was there an attempt to involve everybody, to include the *'amma*, the people.

The word *'amma*, the common people, must not be confused with *umma*, whose origin is *umm* (mother) and which means the community of the faithful. Both words refer to the body of the faithful, but while *umma* is a very positive concept, *'amma* is an extremely pejorative concept. The *'amma* is the uncultivated mass, ignorant and undisciplined by nature; being incapable of reflection or reason, it must be excluded from power. *Al-'aql*, the ability to reason and discriminate, is essential for all Muslims, and especially for the one who is to lead; thus the exclusion of the masses is necessary since they lack *al-'aql*. Only the elite, the *ahl al-hal wa al-'aqd*, who can tie and untie, that is make decisions, are in a position to guide them. The *'amma*, the popular mass, is always described in the historical literature as a monster which unreflectingly follows rebels and so must be muzzled, constantly watched, and, if need be, repressed. The role of the elite is to help the caliphate in repressing the *'amma*. The *'amma* and women are necessarily excluded from the stage. We will see that women are not the only ones to wear a *hijab* (veil); the *'amma* is also separated from the caliph by a *hijab*. Elections with universal suffrage constitute a rending of the veils that organize the caliphate's stage by identifying the actors and fixing the place of the spectators.

Nothing better symbolizes the relationship of authority to the constantly rebellious *'amma* than the sermon of al-Hajjaj Ibn Yusuf, sadly the most famous scourge in the history of despotism in Islam. The fourth Umayyad caliph, 'Abd al-Malik Ibn Marwan (65/685 to 86/705), dispatched him as governor to subdue a rebellion in Iraq. The speech that he made on that occasion is so important and significant in our culture that in my day it was one of the texts used in primary school. As we knew nothing of the purport of the words, only their poetic rhythm, we used to chant them in the schoolyard while rope-skipping. Here is what al-Hajjaj proclaimed from the pulpit, after blessing God and praying for his Prophet:

> Inhabitants of Iraq, Satan resides in you; he is in your flesh and blood and bones, in your limbs and organs. He circulates in you with your blood; he has penetrated your sides and the marrow of your bones; he has infused revolt, rebellion, and perfidy therein. He is established within you; he has built his nest, laid his eggs, and hatched them . . .. People of Iraq, what can I expect of you? What can I await from you? Why do I let you live? . . . Inhabitants of Iraq, if a crow croaks, if an impostor raises his voice, if a troublemaker incites you to disorder, you become his auxiliaries and his votaries. Is experience of no use to you? Can suggestions not protect you? Have events not taught you anything?[20]

After that, al-Hajjaj let loose his troops in the city with orders to teach the inhabitants of Iraq respect for authority. All from near or far who had an air of challenge about them were liquidated and their fortunes were confiscated. When we later studied this proclamation in class, we fell silent, horrified by the masscre of the Iraqis. Our teacher, wishing to defend the reputation of authority (the caliph's and indeed his own), felt obliged to add that the caliph was very upset once he learned of the excesses of al-Hajjaj. He read us the letter of the caliph to al-Hajjaj, which reassured us about the innocence of the spiritual authority:

> The Commander of the Faithful has learned that you have spilled rivers of blood and wasted treasure. These are two acts that the Commander of the Faithful cannot tolerate in anyone. Consequently, he has decreed against you the payment of blood money for every involuntary death, and for premeditated murder the law of retaliation.

The tyrant's power over the people in this instance had exceeded the limits, and the duty of the caliph was to protect the faithful. *Realpolitik*, alas, proved that the Commander of the Faithful had need of al-Hajjaj and, despite his atrocities, he was kept on as one of the strong men of the regime.

The tragedy of the caliphate has always been due to the gap that separates the caliph and the '*amma*, a gap filled by the elite and the military. The vote with universal suffrage, which introduces the '*amma* to the political stage as principal actor, opens up a whole new political horizon for Muslim politics. It is a strange horizon in relation to practice, but not in relation to the ideal of just government. Parliamentary democracy unveils a scene where those of yesteryear who had no responsibility, the '*amma*, with women in their wake, become principal partners in the game. The world is turned upside down. It is enough to give you vertigo, and sometimes this kind of vertigo is a good thing, but we should find a remedy for it, not try to revert to the past. In this sense, the Pakistani experience of a woman as head of government thanks to the vote of the '*amma* is an unparalleled opportunity to learn how to live in a century filled with challenge. A century in which those excluded in the past, including women, no longer need to be veiled in order to play a leading role, as did the *jawari* of yesteryear.

3
The jawari or Revolution in the Harem

Every history has its landmarks and its reference points, its periods of order and disorder, its golden ages and its eras of decadence, and, among them all, the events that 'count'. One of the traumatic events studied by historians, which they always view from the point of view of the palace, is the revolt of the *zanj*, black slaves, which took place under the Abbasids in 255/869. However, it could be argued that the first slave revolt was that of women slaves, the *jawari*, who well before that date launched an assault on the caliphs. The only difficulty is dating the event, which might be done by identifying the first caliph who became hostage to the charm of his slave singer. Was it Yazid II, Ibn 'Abd al-Malik, the ninth Umayyad caliph, who took power in 101/720, according to Tabari, only to surrender it to Hababa, his *jarya*?[1] It was she, the slave, who had to remind the besotted caliph of his mission on earth and the necessity not to depart too far from it.[2] Or was it al-Mahdi, the third Abbasid caliph, who took power in 158/775, and whose wife Khayzuran was not content like Hababa just to captivate her husband, but made him share power with her? After her death her influence continued in the reigns of her two sons, al-Hadi and then Harun al-Rashid.

The power of the women slaves over the caliphs effected some transformations not foreseen by the *shari'a* – transformations at the very centre of the system – –in the relations of women with 'the representative of God on earth'. Unlike the *zanj*, who tried to seize power from the periphery of the system, the *jawari* operated within the caliph's palace itself, in the bed and heart of the man whom the law set up as absolute master of souls and possessions. However, in order to make a comparison, we must begin by looking at the slave revolt that the Muslim historians have officially recorded as the first one.

The *zanj* were black slaves from the Sudan who worked in very harsh conditions in the salt marshes near Basra. They took up arms, occupied the city, and set out on the road to Baghdad. For years this cut the great communication routes that linked Baghdad to the Persian Gulf. They were halted only 27 kilometres from the capital. Their revolt lasted about 14 years, covering several reigns and disturbing the life of more than one caliph. It began in a way that Islam, as a government linked to the sacred, has been familiar with right up to the present day: a group rebelling in the name of *al-'adl*, divine justice. The *zanj* rebelled against the working conditions imposed on them, which they declared unjust according to the *shari'a*, divine law. In the name of that law they refused to obey the caliph who, according to them, had violated Allah's covenant with them.[3] In the beginning, the revolt was led by a certain 'Ali Ibn Muhammad. According to Tabari, he was a troublemaker who claimed descent from 'Ali Ibn Abi Talib.[4] He told his companions that he could change their miserable conditions in the marshes, and make them masters, rich and respected, if they would take up arms. This they did. The slaves left their masters and rallied in large numbers around the religious leader. The first time the people of Basra heard about the revolt they could not believe their ears and went to the 'preacher' to get back their fleeing slaves. To their great surprise, the religious leader ordered each slave to give his master 500 blows before releasing him, to symbolize their purpose and demonstrate the nature of their programme.[5] As a consequence, the slaves organized themselves, named a commander, and launched an assault on the cities under the nose of the government forces. But, like many of the popular uprisings that continually shook the Abbasid era (which is stubbornly presented to us as a golden age), the revolt ended in a blood bath. It was finally crushed in 270/883 under the fifth Abbasid caliph, al-Mu'tamid. The revolt was such a shocking event that so meticulous a historian as Tabari never manages to call their leader by his name in the 17 pages of his *Tarikh al-umam wa al-muluk* (History of nations and kings) devoted to the event. He calls him either *sahib al-zanj* (the *zanj* fellow) or *'aduw Allah* (enemy of Allah) or even *al-khabith* (the wicked one).[6] Obviously all the great names among the official historians took the same line, with Ibn al-Athir in the lead. Centuries later, in his discussion of the year 255 and the revolt of the *zanj*, Ibn al-Athir repeated Tabari's account, including his insults.[7] Compared to the limited impact of the revolt of the *zanj*, because it was only of a military nature, the revolt of the *jawari* was deep and enduring, because it operated on the level of emotions and sex, of eroticism and sensuality. The women slaves never made war on their master. They made love! And we know how defenceless we are in that state. When we love, we let defences fall, blur boundaries, and eliminate barriers, and are no longer concerned about limits.

The historians have been very impressed by the image of Yazid II, a caliph so infatuated with his slave singer/poetess that he went into a trance and uttered meaningless phrases. Even Mas'udi, who usually liked anecdotes, lost his sense of humour when it came to the caliphate of Yazid II: 'One day while Hababa was singing, Yazid experienced such great pleasure that he burst out: "I want to fly away!" Hababa told him: "Commander of the Faithful, if you leave the *umma* and also us, who will take care of us?"'[8] When Hababa died accidentally during a picnic, after choking on a pomegranate seed between two songs, Yazid's grief was so great that he forgot the world and his duty, the faithful and the infidels. The Muslim capital was obliged to say prayers without the caliph. He refused to bury Hababa and wept over her body, from which he refused to be separated, forgetting prayer, the state, the mosques, and the Friday ritual. A few weeks later the believers followed his coffin to the grave; Yazid was the first and perhaps last caliph to die of an ailment until then considered to be minor: love of a *jarya*, a slave. Yazid II was stigmatized by all the historians and only recovered prestige and respect as a caliph through the pen of Abu al-Faraj al-Isbahani, the author of *Kitab al-aghani* (Book of songs), in which Hababa figures as one of the artists who contributed to the development of poetry and song. Contrary to the interpretation of Mas'udi and Tabari, who both adopted the establishment point of view, which describes Hababa as evil and the enemy of God and his religion, the author of *Kitab al-aghani* regards her as a poet and musician of talent and sees Yazid as a man whose aesthetic taste was developed enough to appreciate her.[9] It is true that *Kitab al-aghani* is not a classic work of history; its author devoted its 24 volumes to describing the caliphs and viziers in situations of relaxation and not on the battlefield. It is an attempt to analyse the development of music and song in Arab civilization, and as the best singers and poets gravitated to the palaces, the *jawari* occupied a central place among them because of their contribution to the development of these arts. Abu al-Faraj al-Isbahani was writing a history of art, not of power, and *jawari* like Hababa are presented to us in a very different light.

Good Muslims that they were, Mas'udi and Tabari could only see Hababa as a slave who led the caliph astray. It is interesting to note that the historians held Yazid II in such contempt for publicly loving a *jarya* that they never paid tribute to him for his innovative approach to practical politics, passing over in silence his attempts at dialogue with the opposition. While until the time of his predecessor harsh treatment, even death, was the traditional mode of treatment of political opponents, Yazid II, a peacemaker, encouraged dialogue and opened negotiations with those who challenged and opposed him – not a trifling achievement. Although similar initiatives won praise for his predecessor, 'Umar Ibn 'Abd al-'Aziz, the first Umayyad caliph to renounce killing the Shi'ite opponents and to inaugurate dialogue with them, there was no praise for Yazid, who nevertheless continued his policy. Yazid was consistently regarded as a degenerate and incompetent in political matters. Rereading Muslim history today with a modern outlook and the preoccupations of our time, namely democracy and human rights, makes one think about what our historians call 'a great head of state'.

Another sovereign, who was categorized as great and outstanding, carried his 'duty as a good Muslim sovereign' to the extent of killing the *jarya* he loved, claiming that his passion for her was in flagrant contradiction to his political mission. Let me add that he was not an Arab, for seeing the conflict between amorous passion and political performance in such extreme terms is certainly foreign to Arab Islam as it was preached and practised by the Prophet Muhammad.[10] The person in question was Adud al-Dawla (338/949 to 372/982), the second sovereign of the Shi'ite dynasty of the Buyids, who reigned over Baghdad in the fourth century of the Hejira. At that time the power of the Abbasid caliph was only nominal and symbolic. The Buyids, an Iranian dynasty, were aristocratic military men who took power locally, first in Persia, where they became established as the secular authority. Although they were Shi'ites, when they entered Baghdad as a military force, they respected the symbolic prerogatives of the Abbasid caliph, who was Sunni. He gave them titles; they accorded him the military protection he needed. The enthronement rituals of the secular leader by the caliph, the leading of Friday prayers, and other ceremonies allowed this rather bizarre marriage between religion and the military to endure and create harmony in daily relationships. Neverthe-less, Adud al-Dawla took two steps that were shocking in the eyes of every good Muslim, and that heralded the beginning of the decline of the caliphate as supreme authority. First, he was the first Muslim leader to claim the title of Shahanshah, a grievous insult to Islam because it was the title of the pre-Islamic kings of Persia, who had from the beginning warred against Islam and from whom Adud al-Dawla proudly claimed descent. Adud al-Dawla's second trans-gression was that he demanded that the Arab caliph have his name proclaimed after that of the secular leader during the Friday prayers in the mosques of Baghdad. This was the crowning humiliation for what I will call the caliphal system, given the symbolic importance of the Friday prayers. Adud al-Dawla is nevertheless described as a great sovereign. Historians as important as Miskawiya, who entitled his book *Kitab tajarib al-umama* (Book of the experiences of nations), and Hanbali, the author of *Shazarat al-dahab* (Golden splendour), expatiated at length on his abilities as an excellent leader and accomplished military chief.[11] The fact that he ordered the death of an innocent *jarya*, who had the misfortune of pleasing him too much, did not diminish his stature as a political man. We are entitled to know the details of the prince's decision-making process. What Adud al-Dawla found disturbing about love is that he could no longer concentrate. After his first 'isolation' with the *jarya*, which apparently lasted several nights, he noted that govern-ment business had accumulated and he felt miserable at having so neglected his duties. He decided not to see her again, but his will gave way before *al-shaghaf*, the consuming passion she inspired in him. He arranged a second meeting and the same phenomenon occurred. 'He imagined his situation as if it were in a picture, and thus he could detect what caused his imbalance . . .. He summoned Shukr and ordered him to take the *jarya* and drown her in the river.'[12] His reasoning was simple and straightforward; he explained it to Shukr, the executioner: 'He who gives way to pleasure will become a bad politician and will inevitably lose earthly power.' Luckily the Arab caliphs did not all have the bizarre idea of killing the women they loved, even though other *jawari*, unlike Hababa, did not merely seduce the caliph but developed such an appetite for political power that they quickly began acquiring a share of it.

The first *jarya* who sought a political career and enjoyed influence that was no longer that of a harem woman was Khayzuran. She exercised power for a very long time, during the reigns of several caliphs – her husband and her two sons. Through them she directed the affairs of the *umma* and the empire.[13] Another *jarya*, who appeared on the political scene during the Abbasid caliphate, Shaghab, the mother of the eighteenth caliph, al-Muqtadir (died in 321/933), succeeded in manoeuvring the religious and military bureaucratic elite into recognizing her son as caliph, despite the fact that he was only 13 years old. The qadi Ahmad Ibn Yaqub persisted in not recognizing al-Muqtadir, maintaining in his capacity as a religious authority that al-Muqtadir was still a child and therefore not qualified to become caliph. He was put to death with the whole group that shared his opinion.[14]

Once they gained power, women indulged in atrocities that men might envy, making use of the sole political argument that was effective before the discovery of the vote – brute force. Like men, women used political murder as much as necessary, with perhaps 'softer' methods such as suffocation and poisoning rather than the sword. The difference should be studied at this level of technical detail rather than otherwise. In any case, the execution of the qadi gave great political credibility to this queen, whom the historians do not cite by name, but rather designate by her biological function, Umm al-Muqtadir (mother of al-Muqtadir) or by her political func-tion, *al-sayyida*, the title, as we have seen, given to high-ranking free women, which very quickly came to be given to all those who exercised political power in a more or less official fashion.

This queen had a conception of politics that today one could call very 'feminist'. According to her, the affairs of the *umma*, especially justice, were better managed if a woman was in charge. To cries of scandal by the viziers and the qadis, she put Thumal, one of her assistants, in charge of *mazalim* (injustices), a post equivalent to what today we would call minister of justice. The religious authori-ties, especially the qadis, who had to work under the orders of Thumal, began to balk at this, condemning the appointment and finally repudiating it as repellent.[15] They trotted out their misogyn-istic litanies and refused to collaborate with the new official. But when they realized *al-sayyida* had no intention of yielding on the subject of Thumal, they bowed their heads and agreed to collaborate with their new supervisor. They still remembered the fate of qadi Yaqub.

We must acknowledge the objectivity of the great historians of the past, like Tabari, on the subject of women, an objectivity that is rarely found in contemporary historians. Tabari tells us that Thumal carried out her duties very well, and consequently, despite the initial aversion, *al-nas* (the people) loved her and appreciated her way of acting, and with good cause. The first order given by caliph al-Muqtadir, after the naming of Thumal, was to put an end to corruption and to lower court fees. Plaintiffs had only to pay a minimum fee to initiate a case; in addition they only had to pay the cost of paper and were not obliged to give anything at all to the minor officials who swarmed around the senior justice officials.[16] These important details about one of the most spectacular events in Muslim history, the naming of a woman to head the administration of justice and the joy of the little people in having an official who fought against corruption in the judiciary system, naturally disappeared from the biographies of Umm al-Muqtadir by modern historians. Writing only a century after Tabari, Ibn Hazm presents the naming of Thumal as chief administrator of justice as one of the bizarre acts in a series of 'scandals whose equal has not been seen to this day'.[17]

With the modern historians we are seeing something more subtle: the erasing of details. In his book on the women who played a part in the history of Islam, Dr 'Ali Ibrahim Hasan, professor of history at the University of Cairo, describes Umm al-Muqtadir as the perfect example of the decadence that overtook the dynasties 'which let women interfere in the affairs of state'.[18] His way of presenting the 33 biographies of women whom he selected as examples hardly makes you want to pursue a political career. The most accomplished women are either Companions of the Prophet (an honour impossible to achieve today) or learned women intellectuals (which scarcely guarantees access to power). And we know that the domain in which Muslim women of today have been able to get a foothold is the university. A woman intellectual does not upset the system. It is women politicians who shake the foundations. Balqis, the queen of Sheba, with whom Dr 'Ali Ibrahim Hasan begins his series of biographies, has her life broken into two sections, the first part before her encounter with King Solomon being uninteresting, and the second part afterwards being quite admirable. He tries to convince us that everything that has been said about her throne is exaggerated and that the historians fantasize too much about her power. He has to reduce the size of her throne and the value of its jewels.[19] Reducing the importance of the queen of Sheba is a risky undertaking, for she is one of the few Arab women whom it is difficult to hide or veil, since she is mentioned in the Koran as a powerful sovereign. The great event in the life of Balqis is supposed to have been meeting King Solomon, who held power, the real kind – with an impressive spiritual dimension. The greatness of Balqis, then, is to have understood this immediately and to have decided to please him rather than do battle with him. Dr Hasan's unconscious misogyny reveals itself in a more subtle and much more pernicious way when it comes to writing about the Islamic queens. He eliminates all the positive information regarding them, like the enthusiastic reception given to the measures adopted by Thumal. He writes instead about the rejection of Thumal by the *'ulama*. And he stops with that, leaving out the details that the early historians like Tabari noted – 'religiously' – one might say, because the mission of the historian was regarded by the ancients as a religious mission. This technique of eliminating pertinent details explains how today we find ourselves with a collective Muslim memory that is uniformly misogynistic. And this is why we must take a fine-tooth comb to the historical scenario that is presented to us as eternal truth and 'Muslim tradition', especially the mixing of women and politics as maleficent and the bearer of disaster.

Let us return to the *jawari* who preferred to rule the caliphs from within their harem rather than spending their time worrying about the obstacles that barred their access to power. Dr Hasan seems to have been shocked by one detail concerning Umm al-Muqtadir: her foreign origin. He puts great emphasis on the fact that she was *rumiyya*, that is, of Roman origin. First and foremost, the word *rum* designates the Byzantine empire, the traditional and closest enemy of the Muslim Empire, which extended beyond the whole Roman Empire.[20] One might legitimately ask how it could be that the mother of a Muslim caliph, the representative of God on earth, could be of foreign origin. Does the sublime sovereign caliph have the right to marry and have children with a foreign woman? And what happens when this foreigner holds such a strong place in the heart of the caliph that he entrusts the administration of the *umma*, the Muslim community, to her? Were there cases in which the caliphs let themselves be seduced by foreign *jawari*, particularly Christian ones? One of the most famous examples is Subh, the *jarya* of the caliph al-Hakam, one of the greatest Umayyad caliphs of the Muslim Empire in Spain.

Subh was consumed by ambition. She had two major faults to answer for to the Muslims: she was a foreigner and a Christian. Obviously such things could take place without unrest only in Muslim Spain, that particularly open and cosmopolitan civilization. Subh is usually called by the historians Sabiha Malika Qurtuba, queen of Cordova, Sabiha being one of the diminutives from the root word *sabah*, dawn. Her original name was Aurora, which had to be

Arabicized without misrepresenting it too much. But others said that the prince, entranced by the beauty of the foreigner, called her Subh because she had that amazing soft glow of the Mediterranean dawn. She was the wife of al-Hakam al-Mustansir, the ninth Umayyad caliph of the western branch which reigned in Spain with Cordova as its capital for almost three centuries (138/756 to 422/1031). Al-Hakam's reign lasted 16 years (350/961 to 366/976). All the historians agree in recognizing him as a great head of state. Ibn Hazm, one of the most eminent of the Muslim Andalusian historians, himself an Andalusian and known for not handing out bouquets in judging sovereigns, said that al-Hakam 'was of good conduct' and that he 'put his energy into the sciences, which he valued highly'.[21] According to Ibn Hazm, al-Hakam was one of those who helped Islam to become a great cultural and scientific centre through his systematic policy of book-buying throughout the world and because of his proverbial generosity toward men of science, whom he valued and honoured.[22] Al-Hakam, he writes, 'sent emissaries to every country to seek out books, with orders to buy them at any price and bring them back to him'.[23] According to al-Maqarri, another Andalusian historian, al-Hakam 'had libraries built that no one succeeded in equalling . . .. He gathered around him the most able experts in the art of copying manuscripts, of correcting them and binding them.'[24] For example, he sent a thousand dinars in pure gold to al-Isbahani for a copy of *Kitab al-aghani*. He was the first to read it, even before the rival caliph who ruled in Baghdad.[25]

Thus al-Hakam was the picture of an ideal caliph, his interest in learning equalling his deep faith. Ibn Hazm, who at one time in his life served as a judge (qadi), reports that al-Hakam 'ordered the destruction of all the stocks of wine in the country and was strict about it . . . and he consulted his agents in the provinces before ordering the uprooting of all the vineyards in Andalusia'.[26] The uprooting was not carried out, because the experts explained to him that even if the vines were destroyed, the people would continue to produce wine from other fruits which abounded in the mild Spanish climate. To complete this ideal portrait, let us add that al-Hakam was famed as a great *mujahid* (holy warrior) who 'never stopped battling against the *rum*'. And one might say that he had plenty on his hands in this regard, given that the *rum* in this case were first of all the Spanish, then the French, and finally the whole western Roman Empire. The Umayyads, fleeing from Abbasid repression, escaped to the West via Africa and then created a new

Muslim Empire in Spain, right in the heart of Christian Europe. As we have seen, a caliph worthy of the name had to divide his time between his spiritual mission (seeing to the application of religious law) and his earthly mission (comprising among other duties collecting taxes, administering justice, and defending the territory). *Jihad* (holy war) took up a lot of time in the lives of the great Umayyad caliphs in general, and in the life of al-Hakam in particular. He began his reign with a spectacular offensive against the Christians. 'The booty from his conquests was incalculable, whether it was in money or arms, in livestock or in prisoners of war.'[27] In fact, the Christians never gave the Umayyads any respite. The conquest of Andalusia having to be refought every day, the great sovereigns themselves went out at the head of their armies. It was in the course of one of these expeditions that Subh was captured and made a slave.

How did Subh, who was only a prisoner of war, succeed in taking the reins of power over the *umma*? We must stop here a moment to consider the secret of the ascent to power of a *jarya* in a Muslim harem where there were many beautiful prisoners of war and where competition was intense. How to make oneself stand out, how to retain the attention of the caliph? Contrary to what one might suppose, youth and physical beauty were not sufficient. Something else was needed, and that other thing for the Arabs was intelligence, intellect, and culture. Without exception all the *jawari* who succeeded in impressing the master to the extent that he shared power with them were women endowed with that analytical intelligence that even today guarantees success to whomever possesses it, whether man or woman. Refusing to give one's opinion lightly on a situation or event or person before analysing it calmly and deliberately reveals a form of intelligence particularly appreciated by Arab men; it has made a success of more than one man or woman, whether yesterday or today. In a woman such an intelligence, especially when accompanied by a certain modesty and a bit of humour, will lead you directly to the heart of your caliph. It goes without saying that it needs to be cultivated; all sorts of information must be gleaned and then sorted and classified to be used where and when needed. Poetic wordplay, Koranic quotations, and historical references were indispensable tools. And in order to indulge in verbal wit one must know words. Many *jawari* who succeeded in becoming favourites were women who were particularly well informed about what was going on in the empire, and they were well versed in key areas of knowledge like the history and power of words, being both poets and linguists. Subh was a perfect example of this.

Al-Hakam's excessive interest in knowledge and books was cited by many as one of the reasons that led him, as he grew older, to neglect the routine management of political affairs and leave it to his wife. She was an unrivalled assistant. But soon she herself felt the need for an assistant, and she was given a secretary who was going to shake up both her life and the life of the Muslim Empire. His name was Ibn 'Amir; he was 26 years old, of Arab stock, young, very handsome, superbly educated, with exquisite manners, versed in all manner of religious knowledge, and endowed with the ability to bend time and people to his will. As he later admitted, since earliest youth he had a single fixed idea – to rule Andalusia.[28] Subh, like the officials who had sent him to her at the palace, was dazzled by him. The queen and her secretary embarked on an intense relationship that did not escape the notice of the caliph himself. One day in conversation with his intimates on the subject of Ibn 'Amir, he said, 'That young man has an incredible sway over the minds in our harem.'[29] Were they lovers, or did the queen sacrifice her desires to her duty as wife of the caliph and as mother of a future caliph who as regent on the death of al-Hakam would be responsible for the *umma*? Did she limit her relationship with one of the most fascinating men in Muslim history – or any other history – to a strict collaboration in the political domain? The question was debated by the early historians and is still being debated by the modern historians. And it is one of the many incidents that gives us the opportunity to measure the misogyny of both camps.

The debate on the sexual life of Subh is extremely edifying in this regard. Al-Maqarri, the seventeenth-century author of *Nafh al-tib min ghusn al-Andalus al-ratib*, begins by saying that Ibn 'Amir always aroused jealousy and intrigues against himself. He very quickly became the effective sovereign of Andalusia, supplanting Subh, and he held her son, Caliph Hisham Ibn al-Hakam, hostage in his own palace. Al-Maqarri explains that there is always resentment when a person has an unparalleled opportunity in life along with prodigious talent, and in consequence has too great success in everything – which was the case with Ibn 'Amir.[30] He continues by saying that in this way one can understand the rumours about his being the lover of Subh. The rumours were soon put into rhyme in satiric poems which proclaimed that the Muslims were on the verge of an apocalypse 'for the caliph plays in his office while his mother is pregnant', etc.[31] Al-Maqarri then proceeds to exonerate Subh and defend her against such accusations, concluding that only Allah knows the truth of all things.

The modern writers systematically reduce Subh to a vulgar schemer and, to boot, a simpleton who lets herself be seduced by a secretary interested only in her power. This is the line taken by 'Abdallah Inan in his book *Tarajim Islamiyya* (Muslim biographies).[32] He reduces both Caliph al-Hakam and Subh to characters in a second-rate soap opera like those on Egyptian television, adding a racist and chauvinistic tone that totally denigrates the cosmopolitan essence of our culture:

> Our Muslim history presents us with a large number of foreign women, including slaves and prisoners of war, who have shone in the palaces of caliphs and sultans, and who have enjoyed power and influence. But it does not show us how ordinary citizens reacted to a foreigner, a Christian, who exercised a despotic, totalitarian power over them, under the protection of a powerful Muslim nation . . ..
> We can never find a more perfect example than Subh, Aurora, the beautiful Christian who ruled the caliphate of Cordova for 20 years, thanks to her charm and influence.[33]

Ahmad Amin, one of the great names among modern Muslim historians and the author of the prestigious trilogy *Fajr al-Islam*, *Duha al-Islam*, and *Zuhr al-Islam*, makes Subh into an octopus who devours men and power. Amin's trilogy, which comprises no fewer than nine volumes and has been a bestseller ever since its publication, has had a very harmful effect on Muslim women, because one cannot find fault with it on scholarly grounds.[34] His completely involuntary and unconscious misogyny is all the more pernicious as the quality of the work is without equal. His scholarly blending of events with short, striking commentaries, his incessant weaving together of past and present, his gift as a born narrator, and his encyclopedic knowledge have made his book bedside reading as well as a basic reference for generations since its first appearance. His misogyny is all the more insidious in that it is as though it is distilled into the watermark, lightly dispersed here and there, mixed in with proud accomplishments like the scientific contributions of our ancestors and their love of books and knowledge. In his work Subh becomes a cynical, repulsive schemer:

> And things got still worse when Hisham Ibn al-Hakam came to power while still a 10-year-old child. He was proclaimed caliph, and his

mother Subh became regent. She was a Christian from Navarre, who had a very strong personality. She succeeded in extending her power over her husband, al-Hakam, and in interfering in the affairs of the Muslim state despite its greatness and power. But while her son was still a child, her power became enormous . . .. Subh first took Ibn 'Amir as her secretary even before the death of her husband . . .. She became very fond of him and he of her. She named him *hajib* [chief of viziers] and gave him free access to power. And in this way he took over all the functions of the caliph.[35]

In the words of Ahmad Amin, Subh is neither *malika* (queen) nor *sayyida* (Madame); she has no title. She is Subh, the Christian.

Al-Murakushi, a thirteenth-century historian, gives a less simplistic explanation of the relationship between Subh and Ibn 'Amir; he portrays them as partners in the political game, one complementing the other and each benefiting from the collaboration:

The stature of Ibn 'Amir continued to grow until he made the acquaintance of Sayyida Subh, the mother of Hisham, the son of al-Hakam. He took charge of her business affairs and managed her lands. In this way he earned her appreciation. Things continued like this until the death of al-Hakam. Hisham was still young, and there was fear of trouble. Ibn 'Amir provided Subh with the security and calm necessary for her son to be able to reign. Ibn 'Amir was very competent and circumstances worked in his favour. Subh made available the necessary funds, and he was able to win over the army. There then followed a train of circumstances that allowed him to rise even higher, until he became practically the sole manager of the affairs of state.[36]

The relationship between Subh and Ibn 'Amir lasted for more than 30 years. They became acquainted ten years before the death of al-Hakam (Ibn 'Amir was named secretary in 356/966, and al-Hakam died in 366/976). Their collaboration continued for 20 years afterwards, until the first notorious quarrel between them, when the queen tried to escape from his domination by seeking support from other men in her entourage. This attempt failed lamentably because there was no one as brilliant and astute as Ibn 'Amir, who managed to reduce to powerlessness all the men she tried to set as rivals. In 388/997 the conflict between Subh and Ibn 'Amir took a turn in his favour. His star continued to shine, but for Subh it was the beginning of the end. It was not because Subh was stupid or a bad politician that Ibn 'Amir seized power, but simply because she played the game of politics and lost, just as in any political joust.

It seems that the early historians saw women's relation to politics in a different light than do the more modern historians. They called the queens by their title, tried to understand their motivations as they did with men, and noted that women slaves could marry caliphs and give birth to future caliphs.

The most illuminating way of understanding the phenomenon of the *jawari* and how, in an apparently very hierarchical Islam, women could not only dominate caliphs but share their power might be to spend some private moments with Khayzuran and the different caliphs who succeeded each other in her life. Her example will allow us to measure the limits of power of the *jawari*, which was often of a territorial nature. Operating from the harem, the territory of women, none of the *jawari* mentioned, neither the mother of al-Muqtadir, nor Subh, nor Khayzuran, can be considered women heads of state. They failed to cross the threshold that separated women's territory from that of men.

4
Khayzuran: Courtesan or Head of State?

The great obstacle to a political career for a woman like Khayzuran, who had a great appetite for politics and apparently exhibited exceptional talent for it, was not biological (the fact of being a woman) nor legal (the fact of being a slave), but territorial – the fact of belonging to the harem, inner space (the territory of peace) rather than to public space (the space of war). All the historians are fond of telling us over and over that she ruled, commanded, and governed the Muslim Empire under three caliphs: her husband al-Mahdi, the third Abbasid caliph (158/775 to 169/785); her elder son al-Hadi; and her younger son, whom she cherished and who returned her love, Harun al-Rashid. The fabulous, noble Harun al-Rashid, whom nature endowed with unparalleled gifts and whom memory treasures as a jewel, had the grace to live out his dreams without succumbing to their spell. Once he became caliph, he acknowledged the talents of his mother and showed the Muslim world that he was not ashamed to share power with a woman, as long as she had the good judgement of Khayzuran. But having done this, Harun al-Rashid would only prove once again the limits for action of a woman of the harem, be she courtesan or regent: she only held power with the consent of, and through, a man. Her political actions could only appear on the public stage masked by the presence of a man.

To the end Khayzuran's political career had the fatal stamp of harem life: her authority was cloaked in secrecy and was only the radiation of someone else's power. On the day of her death Baghdad understood the greatness of the mother in the grief of the son. A caliph is supposed to show great restraint and moderation at the death of a woman very dear to him, and above all to avoid showing his grief in public. Harun al-Rashid violated all the rites of the caliphate and of burial. And, great man that he was, filled with self-confidence, he saw his prestige only grow from it. Tabari reports the testimony of a man who was present at the burial of Khayzuran in the year 173: 'I saw al-Rashid that day . . .. Barefoot, he accompanied the casket through the mud to the cemetery of Quraysh. Upon arriving, he washed his feet . . . and intoned the funeral prayer. Then he went down into the tomb to pay final homage to his mother before leaving the cemetery.'[1] Right up to her death Khayzuran defied the empire and its traditions.

The name Khayzuran means 'bamboo', the plant that symbolizes both beauty and suppleness. Her life has fascinated both the members of the elite, who adopted her styles of coiffure and adornment, and the common people, who could only admire her in the tales from the *Arabian Nights*, that popular fiction that rightly depicts her life as the ultimate dream of a woman's life, in which seduction, fortune, and power are intimately linked and sensually entangled. She made political decisions that were so important that it can be said without exaggeration that she put her mark on one of the most momentous epochs of the Abbasid dynasty and the history of Islam. There is almost no information about her physical appearance, says Nabia Abbott, who devotes half of her book *Two Queens of Baghdad* to her.[2] Today bamboo, because of its slender suppleness and deceptive fragility, is still considered to suggest some of the inexpressible mystery of the female body. In the medinas of the traditional cities of Morocco, as young girls walk by, one of the murmured compliments one hears, still reflecting the charm of the past, is: '*Allah la qtib al-khayzuran*' (Allah! What a stem of bamboo!). But Khayzuran infused bamboo with a magical dimension it lacked before her. As in fairy-tales, she had a very difficult early life before she rose to dizzying heights.

She was born free in an area of Yemen called Jurash. All the historians except Ibn Hazm agree on this fact.[3] He is probably wrong, and this detail is important. Yemeni women are known for never agreeing to leave men in sole charge of politics. Was it because the memory of the queen of Sheba remained vivid despite Islamicization? According to the overwhelming majority of sources, Khayzuran arrived at the palace in Baghdad as a slave. As the *shari'a* specifies, no Muslim may ever be reduced to slavery by another Muslim, yet no classic historian ever took the trouble to raise the question of slavery only a century after the death of the Prophet, who specified in his laws and principles that only a *kafir* (infidel) taken as a prisoner of war could be made a slave.[4] The laws of war enabled a Muslim sovereign to conquer a country by war and reduce its inhabitants, both men and women, to slavery. Two conditions had to prevail for a person to be made a slave: first, to be an infidel; and then to be part of the booty captured in war. Yemen was one of the first countries to be Islamicized during the first decade of Islam. How are we to explain that a Yemeni, and therefore Muslim, woman like Khayzuran could be made a slave? In any case, she was brought to Mecca by a bedouin and sold there. From the slave market, she is next found in the palace of Caliph al-Mansur, the father of al-Mahdi.[5] She made herself noticed by al-Mansur from the first words she spoke when asked about her origin:

> 'Born at Mecca and brought up at Jurash (in the Yaman).'
> 'Have you any relatives?' continued the caliph.
> 'I have none but Allah; my mother bore none besides me.'
> Deeply moved by her words, the caliph ordered her to be given to his son al-Mahdi: 'Take her to Mahdi and tell him that she is good for childbearing.'[6]

Thus she found herself in the presence of the man who, once he became caliph, would put the empire at her feet. It must be noted that she lied to Caliph al-Mansur. She was not an only daughter, nor was she without family. She revealed the existence of her mother, her two sisters, and her two brothers only when her future was assured, after giving birth to her two sons. Once her family, who were living in Yemen in poverty, were brought to the palace in Baghdad, their fortunes greatly improved. Apparently the seduction of powerful men was a family speciality. Asma, one of her sisters, tried to steal al-Mahdi from her, but he returned repentant.[7] Her sister Salsal fixed her choice on another prince, Ja'far, the brother of Caliph al-Mahdi, and married him. And her brother Ghatrif was named governor of Yemen.

Although Khayzuran was al-Mahdi's favourite *jarya*, she was not the only woman in his life. The fact that she succeeded in marrying him in due form gives an idea of her influence. According to the law, a Muslim did not have to marry his slave. He could very well have sexual relations with and have children with her without the act of marriage, and this would have been completely legal. This situation allows us to refine a bit more the concept of polygyny and to understand why the harems were full of *jawari* at the time of the great Muslim conquests. Everybody knows that Islam permits a man to marry no more than four women. However, it must be added that that limit refers only to free women, because the *shari'a* gives to the happy husband, in addition to the four free women married with a marriage contract, the right to have sexual relations and children with as many *jawari* (women slaves) as he possesses. The authorization for this comes from verse 3 of sura 4, 'Women', which is the unassailable foundation for polygyny as an institution;

> marry of the women, who seem good to you, two or three or four; and if ye fear that ye cannot do justice (to so many) then one (only) or (the captives) that your right hands possess.[8]

There is no limit to the number of concubines, Tabari tells us in his *Tafsir*, because the believer 'does not have towards them the same duties that he has towards free women', since they are *amlakuhu* (his property).[9] The master was not constrained by law in his treatment of a slave, and he could have any number of them. The great danger to Khayzuran as the reigning favourite came above all from the *jawari*, slaves like herself, whom the winds of destiny ceaselessly deposited on the steps of the palace.

Sometimes *jawari* were offered to the caliph as part of the booty of conquest; sometimes they were proferred by one of his governors; sometimes sent as gifts by those who hoped to better themselves with al-Mahdi; and obviously sometimes bought if they had exceptional talents. Developing their intellectual skills, such as learning the *fiqh* (religious knowledge) or poetry, or improving their musical talents for playing the lute or singing were the only avenues open to these women, sometimes Arabs but very often foreigners torn from their country of origin and having to survive in a strange environment.

One of the *jawari* of whom Khayzuran was very jealous was named Maknuna. She had 'a very beautiful face and was *raskha*' (that is, with slender hips and legs), and she was renowned in Medina, her home town, as a *mughanniyya*, a singer. Al-Mahdi had bought her when he was still the royal heir and had paid 100,000 dirhams for her. This was an exorbitant price and had to be kept secret, for his father, al-Mansur, would not have approved of such extravagance.[10] Al-Mahdi was so captivated by her charm that Khayzuran later admitted: 'I never had such fear of another woman as I had of her.'[11]

The price of a *jarya* increased according to her education and mastery of the arts. So education of *jawari* became a veritable institution which brought solid rewards to those who engaged in it. And it was during the reigns of al-Mahdi and his father that the education of *jawari* took on unprecedented importance. One of their contemporaries, Ibrahim al-Mawsili, a master of Arab music and song who frequented the court of the two caliphs, was 'the first to begin to instruct the beautiful *jawari*',[12] and to give them an elaborate education in poetry, music, and singing. He had, al-Isbahani tells us, 'a regular school with 80 resident students in training with him, in addition to his own'.[13] Ishaq, the son of Ibrahim al-Mawsili, continued his father's work under the sons of Khayzuran. Harun al-Rashid bought from him a number of his student *jawari*, and their price was so high that he had to bargain very hard with the great artists who organized his evening parties after battles.[14] Ibrahim al-Mawsili and his son were of Persian origin. They not only infused music and song with new rhythms and melodies from their own culture and from that of the foreign slaves, but they also larded poetry and song with Persian words and concepts. Sharya, a *jarya* bought by Ibrahim, another son of Caliph al-Mahdi, who declared himself an artist despite being a prince, cost 300 dinars when he bought her. He had her given lessons for a year, during which she was exempted from all domestic work. She devoted herself to study and practice. At the end of a year he called in the experts to evaluate her, and they told him that if he put her on the market she would be worth 8,000 dinars, that is 26 times her original price.[15] Some years later a would-be buyer heard of her and her incredible talent and offered 70,000 dinars for her, that is, 233 times her original price. Prince Ibrahim Ibn al-Mahdi obviously declined the offer. We can understand that for Khayzuran competition came from the *jawari* and not from al-Mahdi's aristocratic wife, whom she had stripped of all her prerogatives, including the right to have her sons named royal heirs.

Khayzuran's *coup d'état*, if I may call it that, was to induce al-Mahdi to have her children designated as heirs apparent and those of the other women excluded. Among those excluded were the children of al-Mahdi's aristocratic wife and cousin Rayta, a princess of royal descent, the daugher of Caliph al-Saffah, the founder of the dynasty, whom he had married in 144/762. A century earlier the first Umayyads 'did not permit sons of slaves to become caliph'.[16] The sovereign could only be the son of a free woman. Hisham Ibn 'Abd al-Malik, the tenth Umayyad caliph (105/724–125/743), is supposed to have said to Zayd Ibn 'Ali, a pretender to the throne:

'I have learned that you are entertaining the idea of becoming caliph. This office cannot be given to you because you are the son of a slave.'[17]

Ibn 'Abd Rabbih, who devoted one volume of his book *Al-'iqd al-farid* to women, tried to understand the phenomenon of the rise of the *jawari* and how they succeeded in upsetting an Arab society that, despite Islam, remained fiercely aristocratic and elitist. He recalled that the Prophet himself had two women slaves: one was Maria the Copt, mother of his son Ibrahim, who died young; the other was Safiyya, whom his co-wives insulted by calling the Jewess: 'When she complained to the Prophet, he advised her to counter-attack the next time, reminding those jealous women of aristocratic Arab stock: "My father is Isaac, my grandfather is Abraham, my uncle is Isma'il, and my brother is Joseph." '[18] Despite the attitude of the Prophet and of Islam against hierarchization and for equality between masters and slaves, 'the people of Medina', reports the author, 'detested women slaves.' There were precise terms for labelling children born of mixed marriages: 'The Arabs called an *'ajam* who became Muslim *al-muslimani* . . .. A child of an Arab father and an *'ajam* mother was called *hajin*; a child of an Arab mother and an *'ajam* father was called *al-mudarri'*. The author adds that the Arabs called *'ajam* any person who did not speak Arabic very well, even if he was a Muslim, and before Islam they excluded a *hajin* from inheriting.[19] It took a long time for the idea of equality, which was so strongly supported by the Prophet and the Koran, to overcome the resistance of the Arabs. The Prophet was not followed either in his ideas favouring emancipation of slaves or in his very positive attitude toward women in general and toward his (to whom he had given the possibility for self-development), in particular. It took a long time for equality between slaves and masters to begin to penetrate Arab customs, especially those of the elite and especially when it threatened their class interests.[20] When 'Abd al-Malik Ibn Marwan, the fifth Umayyad caliph (65/685–86/705) learned that 'Ali Ibn al-Husayn, the grandson of caliph 'Ali, had freed a *jarya* and married her, he sent him a letter reproaching him for binding himself to a woman of inferior rank. 'Ali reminded him that 'Islam came to raise the station of inferiors, and it is a religion which brings perfection to him who is incomplete and generosity to the stingy. It is not shameful for a Muslim to marry a slave woman.'[21] Not long after, adds Ibn 'Abd Rabbih, one witnessed the rise of the *jawari* and the appearance of poems and proverbs against free women.[22]

Khayzuran persuaded al-Mahdi to choose her two sons as royal heirs. First he officially designated the elder, Musa al-Hadi, as heir in 159/775. As part of its struggle against slavery, Islam forbade men to marry a woman slave before freeing her. Once she has been freed, the man might conclude a marriage contract with her in due form. Her status, before being freed, is that of *umm walad*, literally 'mother of a child', in contrast to the free woman, who was called *umm al-banin*, mother of sons. One of the innovations introduced by Islam was to declare that the son of an *umm walad*, a slave woman, and a free father was free. And afterwards the slave mother could be partially liberated by acquiring a status much more advantageous than that of *umm al-banin*; her husband could no longer sell her after the birth of a child and she became free after his death. The heirs of her master could no longer exclusively inherit her as they had done before Islam. The children of the *umm walad* had the same rights and privileges as those born of a free mother. They could inherit a share of the father's possessions equal to that of the other children and according to the prescriptions of the *shari'a*. The *jawari* were also going to make certain that their sons could inherit everything, even the throne.

In Muslim history the number of caliphs whose mothers were slaves is more than impressive. The phenomenon deserves an indepth study, for from it we can learn, beyond the love stories, about an extremely important aspect of the struggle between classes and cultures during the Muslim Golden Age – the sexual aspect. Ibn Hazm remarks that 'among the Abbasids only three caliphs were sons of a *hurra* [free woman], and among the Umayyads of Andalusia not a single son of a free woman succeeded in becoming caliph'.[23] Sallama, the mother of Caliph al-Mansur (the second of the Abbasid dynasty), who was the father of al-Mahdi, was a Berber slave. The mothers of caliphs al-Ma'mun (the seventh), al-Muntasir (the eleventh), al-Musta'in (the twelfth), and al-Muhtadi (the fourteenth) were Roman slaves; the mother of al-Mutawakkil (the tenth) was Turkish.[24] However, Khayzuran surpassed all of these by becoming the mother of two future caliphs. Not satisfied with the naming of her first son as the heir, she doubled her chances by insisting that al-Mahdi also name Harun, her second and favourite son, as a royal heir. In 166/782, seven years after naming Musa al-Hadi as heir, Caliph al-Mahdi designated Harun al-Rashid as second in line to succeed. Al-Mahdi adored Khayzuran's children, especially Banuqa, his daughter by her, whom he loved to such an extent that he did not want to be separated from her. He dressed her as a boy in order to take her with him when travelling: 'A witness recounts that he saw al-Mahdi advancing with his armies when he visited Basra, with the chief of police in front and between them Banuqa wearing a black cloak, dressed as a young boy with a sword by her side. And her breasts could be seen pointing beneath her clothes.' Another describes Banuqa as 'dark-haired, slender, and very pretty'. Banuqa died very young, and al-Mahdi was inconsolable. The whole court and all the high dignitaries were obliged to render their condolences to him according to strict protocol – to such a point that the religious authorities began to find that it was a bit too much for a woman. Her death, even if she was a princess, should have been treated with the greatest discretion, especially since she was the daughter of a *jarya*.[25]

At the time of Khayzuran, Islam was at its apogee as a religious and military empire. It continued to expand and conquer other nations. Harun al-Rashid was a great conqueror, like his father, whom he accompanied to battle from the age of 15. At the age of 17, in year 165, he won a great victory, crossing the snow-covered mountains of the Byzantine Empire and besieging Constantinople. The Byzantine queen-regent was forced to sign a three-year truce that was extremely advantageous for Baghdad. One of the conditions was that the queen had to give him 'guides' to lead him back over the mountains to Baghdad. He succeeded in persuading the 95,700 men of his army, inspired by his enthusiasm and courage, to dare the crossing 'along hazardous routes that frightened the Muslims'.[26]

His many conquests led to the enslavement of great portions of the conquered peoples, and the palaces swarmed with *jawari*, who brought with them their own culture and exoticism. There were Persians, Kurds, Romans, Armenians, Ethiopians, Sudanese, Hindus, and Berbers. Harun al-Rashid had a thousand *jawari*. Al-Mutawakkil (232/847–247/861) had four thousand.[27] The harems became places of the greatest luxury where the most beautiful women of the world played their cultural differences and mastery of diverse skills and knowledge like winning cards for seducing caliphs and viziers. In order to seduce these men, it was not enough just to bat one's eyelashes. One had to dazzle them in the fields that fascinated them – astrology, mathematics, *fiqh*, and history. On top of these came poetry and song. Pretty girls who got lost in serious conversations had no chance to be noticed, and even less chance to last; and the favourites, who knew this very well, surrounded themselves with competent teachers. In order to retain the favour of al-Mahdi, Khayzuran took courses in *fiqh* from one of the most famous qadis of the time. And finally, sexual techniques and sensual refinements were another area that the *jawari* developed, each one drawing on the secrets of her own culture. By comparison, aristocratic Arab women lost out, especially in the last area, inhibited as they were by the rigid moral code that the governing class applied to their women, and which was not at all imposed on the *jawari*. As the number of masters increased, the *jawari* deepened their knowledge of male pleasure and its whims.[28]

Soon each region of the world became known for the specific qualities of its women. The women of the West were the principal winners: 'He who wants a *jarya* for pleasure should choose a Berber; he who wants a reliable woman to look after his possessions should take a Roman. For the man who wants a *jarya* to bear him children, the best choice is a Persian. If he wants a *jarya* to suckle a child, he should choose a Frankish woman. And for singing, a woman of Mecca cannot be equalled.' These are the counsels of Ibn Batalan, an eleventh-century Christian doctor, famous in Baghdad for his expertise, who became even better known when he wrote a treatise on the purchase of slaves, *Risala fi shari al-raqiq*.[29] The tract is fascinating, because it gives tips for thwarting the tricks of the pedlars who put makeup on sick slaves to give them the bloom of health and provided cosmetics for changing hair and skin colour according to prevailing fashion:

> The *nakhkhasin* [slave traders] can change the colour of the skin. They can transform the dark-skinned woman by giving her skin a golden hue . . . . They can give a blush to pale cheeks . . . . The same for hair: they can make blond hair raven black . . . . They can put a curl in straight hair . . . . They can lengthen hair by adding on a false piece . . . . They can make tattoos disappear, as well as smallpox marks, freckles, or black spots.[30]

Some of these tricks can still be used.

Ibn Batalan had more advice. One should absolutely beware of those with wide eyes – they are lazy or voluptuous. Those with deep-set eyes are envious. Blue eyes denote stupidity, and the woman who blinks all the time is malice personified. But if you have business with a person in whose eyes the black part is larger than the white, you should pick up your feet and run – that person is mad. Too fine hair is a sign of foolishness, and thick, wiry hair denotes courage. According to Ibn Batalan, trying to communicate with a person with a large nose is lost effort, because that denotes a fool. A person with a high forehead is lazy but a low forehead is no better, because that person is ignorant. A large mouth denotes courage, and thick lips are the mark of a fool.[31] But where Ibn Batalan breaks all records is when he advises the slave buyer on the attributes of each race. After the Arabs, it is the Hindu *jawari* that he recommends for their faithfulness and tenderness; but, he says, 'their problem is that they die very young'. The Turks are recommended for their good qualities and beauty, but they are rather stocky, and one very rarely finds a slender one. The Romans make very good slaves and often possess good manual skills. The monsters to avoid are the Armenians, who are faithless and thieving; you have to use the rod to get something out of them.[32]

What is astonishing about a text like this is that the Muslim countries, whose Prophet and Koran directed them towards the elimination of slavery, are found instead to be its supporters and defenders, right up until the nineteenth century when the European nations renounced it. In the middle of the eighteenth century a Muslim published a book of tips for examining a slave in order to avoid being swindled. Lutfallah al-Ghazali, a citizen of Ottoman Egypt, gave his text the very edifying title of *The Best Way for Buyers to Inspect Slaves*.[33] As the size of the Muslim Empire began to stabilize during the time of Harun al-Rashid, and since for centuries Islam had not been a conqueror, but rather the object of conquest, one might well ask where its slaves came from. The answer is that they could only be Muslims. How is it that the religious authorities, so solicitous of Islam and the defence of its essential principles, including justice and equality, did not organize campaigns against slavery? This is a question which must sooner or later be investigated.

Upon the unexpected death of her husband Caliph al-Mahdi in 169 (785), Khayzuran took centre stage. The death of a caliph was always a period of unrest, and her two sons were far from Baghdad. She summoned the viziers for consultation and ordered them to unblock funds immediately to disburse to the army the equivalent of two years' pay, a substantial sum. It was necessary to calm the soldiers, who were beginning to be restless upon hearing the news. In the course of an expedition to Tabaristan with his son Harun, al-Mahdi had been taken ill with a malady which proved fatal. He died immediately, and after consultation Harun decided to bury him on the spot and return to Baghdad. There he rejoined Khayzuran, and the two of them took charge of the ritual of succession in the absence of the person most concerned. They arranged that al-Hadi should be designated the new caliph, and the dignitaries swore the oath of loyalty to him in the presence of his brother. It took al-Hadi 20 days to return to the capital. Meanwhile, the soldiers 'had set fire to the door of the vizier al-Rabi's house and had opened the gates of the prisons and freed the prisoners'.[34]

When Khayzuran summoned the two most important ministers, al-Rabi and the famous Yahya al-Barmaki, they immediately presented themselves at her door. Then came an incident of the utmost importance, because it indicates the limits of Khayzuran's power. When she told the two waiting ministers to enter, only one obeyed her order, the other refusing: 'Al-Rabi accepted her invitation to enter, but Yahya refused, aware of al-Hadi's jealousy.'[35] In fact, upon hearing the news, al-Hadi, less tolerant than his father of his mother's interference, sent a courier to al-Rabi threatening him with death. He had transgressed the threshold of the forbidden space – the harem. This insistence on the threshold that separates the world of men from that of women would come up again in another incident that took place several months later.

During the life of her husband, Khayzuran had given audiences. Many important people thronged her door. After the death of the caliph, she showed no desire to change: 'She continued to monopolize decision-making without consulting him [al-Hadi]. She behaved as she had before, during the reign of al-Mahdi . . .. People came and went through her door.'[36] Unsure of himself, al-Hadi felt threatened by the ambition of his mother and was morbidly jealous of his brother Harun al-Rashid, who was greatly loved by the people and the elite and admired for his military prowess. He made several attempts to strip his brother of the title of heir apparent in order to give it to his own son, Ja'far.[37] Harun adopted the tactic of avoidance and reduced the occasions for being in his brother's presence. But this was not Khayzuran's style. She continued to involve herself in what in her view concerned her – which above all was the management of the affairs of the empire. Al-Hadi thought just the opposite. He continually told her that 'it is not in the power of women to intervene . . . in matters of sovereignty. Look to your prayers and your prayer beads.'[38] She insisted. One day she went to him to force him to grant a favour. She was interceding for a certain 'Abdallah Ibn Malik. Al-Hadi refused to grant her request, but did it publicly in a very Arab manner by giving no answer. Khayzuran committed the blunder of insisting: 'You are obliged to answer me because I have already made a promise to 'Abdallah.' She had made the mistake of exposing her game too openly.[39] In his anger her son let loose a tirade which very neatly summarized his views on women and politics: as she made her way to the door, he told her:

> Wait a moment and listen well to my words . . .. Whoever from among my entourage – my generals, my servants – comes to you with a petition will have his head cut off and his property confiscated. What is the meaning of those retinues that throng around your door every day? Don't you have a spindle to keep you busy, a Koran for praying, a residence in which to hide from those besieging you? Watch yourself, and woe to you if you open your mouth in favour of anyone at all.[40]

She left her son 'without knowing where she placed her feet', the historians say. War was declared.

Al-Hadi died prematurely at the age of 24, after a brief reign of a year and two months. Many historians say that his death was the work of a politically frustrated Khayzuran.[41] Some say that she had to act hastily because she learned that he intended to kill Harun al-Rashid. Accounts of the method of the murder vary, the most cruel being that she ordered his pretty *jawari* to creep into the room where he was napping and smother him with cushions.[42] They are supposed to have playfully placed the cushions around the head of the sovereign and then sat on them. Tabari, who very rarely takes sides against anyone, felt obliged to tone down, as it were, the monstrosity of Khayzuran's act by saying that al-Hadi had tried at least once to kill his mother. He sent her a tasty dish, saying that it was so delicious that he wanted her to enjoy it. The tender, sentimental Khayzuran gave a first taste of it to her dog, and it fell instantly dead.[43]

Powerful as she was, Khayzuran nevertheless never considered changing the rules of the game, of taking power directly. She accepted the division of the world into two parts – the harem for women and public life for men. She tried to manipulate the public sphere from the private sphere, instead of breaking down the division and taking her place officially on the other side, where power is found, outside the house, in the public arena, where one can be recognized as head of state.

It was not so much her status as a woman or as a slave that blocked Khayzuran's political career. It was the fact that, as a woman, she belonged to the harem, the territory of obedience.

Theoretically, in Islam, public space is the arena for taking the initiative and making decisions in all matters, especially political affairs; but public space was forbidden to a woman. Again, involvement in political matters necessarily means taking charge of war-making; it assumes the act of killing. By contrast the household, women's territory, is the territory of life, of sex, and of reproduction. Women give birth, men make war and go hunting. The *harim* (known to Westerners as the harem) has its linguistic roots in sacred space, the sanctuary at Mecca, and shares in its privileges and laws. During the period of the pilgrimage, war (killing human beings) and hunting (killing animals) are forbidden in the *haram* area, the sanctuary at Mecca, and this was true before Islam as well as after. It is one of the pre-Islamic traditions that Islam kept, with only a few changes.[44] In the pre-Islamic pilgrimage ritual, the word *haram* applied to the clothing that the pilgrims had to remove during the procession that they, men and women, carried out in the nude. The clothing, symbol of the sins to be cast off, was not allowed to be touched.[45] The *haram*, then, was the sanctuary and at the same time a man's household where his women and children lived, a space forbidden to others.

Khayzuran's elder son, al-Hadi, wanted his mother to return to her place, to her territory, the house. In his eyes, the people of the empire who came for an audience with her transgressed the threshold of his harem. Al-Hadi's argument against his mother, when he finally decided to take action four months after the death of his father, was not at all based on any evidence of her incompetence. According to him, interfering in power is not one of the prerogatives of women. And this was because of a distribution of duties based on assignment to one territory or the other.

After reminding his mother of her place, that is, the harem, he summoned the persons who were seeking an audience with her and made them recognize that they were violating a territorial law, a law to do with honour. When al-Hadi became exasperated by the retinues of his generals who took turns at his mother's door, he called them together:

'Who is the better among us, you or me?' asked Caliph al-Hadi of his audience.

'Obviously you are the better, Commander of the Faithful,' the assembly replied.

'And whose mother is the better, mine or yours?' continued the caliph.

'Your mother is the better, Commander of the Faithful.'

'Who among you', continued al-Hadi, 'would like to have men spreading news about your mother?'

'No one likes to have his mother talked about,' responded those present.

'Then why do men go to my mother to speak to her?'[46]

It was because Khayzuran loved power and suffered from being relegated to the harem that she decided to resort to the only weapon which represented the essence of power – the decision to kill. She planned al-Hadi's murder from the harem, although it was the place of peace.[47] The harem is both the place and the women who live in it, and this confusion between place and beings is absolutely central to all Muslim architecture. The *harim* is protected space, and a man may kill in order to deny access to it. Murder happens outside, not within. The duty of the *'ulama* is to keep watch over thresholds, and to remind us that Islam is nothing but this: respect for *hudud*, non-violation of thresholds and boundaries. The *'ulama* are right to insist that sexual desegregation, women leaving the house to do the same work as men, is the beginning of the end. Those who say that Islam and Western democracy (and that is the only kind there is, as far as I can see) are compatible – that is, that the difference in privileges in the political domain between men and women is no problem for Islam – are in fact trying to avoid asking the fundamental questions, especially about the individual and the place of individualism in decision-making. Each person in his or her own territory is the principle of the traditional architecture. All individuals have the right to all territories is the message of modern democracy. This is a cosmic conflict in nature and scale.

This idea of territoriality can also explain another bizarre phenomenon here at the end of the twentieth century: the almost irrational fear of terrorism in the West. You only have to read or hear the news in Berlin or Paris to realize that the media vision of current events reflects a collective frenzy about the power of Islam, a deep, atavistic fear of Islam, despite the military and technological weakness of the Muslim states. This is because Islam is a cosmic phenomenon and, as a territorial concept, is threatening. It should not be forgotten that the Prophet said that the whole earth is a mosque.[48] If a worker in an automobile factory in France has access to water for performing the purification ritual and faces toward the east, the direction of Mecca, he can turn an aisle in the factory into a mosque, a space for prayer. Islam is a cosmic phenomenon, a precise relationship to space. And this cosmic dimension is what makes the difference between the sexes architectonic.

Women belong to interior space, the *harim*, forbidden space, and a head of state belongs to exterior space, public space. So we must discover the ritual, which must necessarily be spatial in character, by which women heads of state are going to assert their existence in men's space. How will it be done, with what signs and what symbols?

It was neither Khayzuran's intelligence nor her competence that were questioned by her son when he challenged her right to pursue the political career that she had engaged in under her husband: 'Khayzuran wanted to dominate her son as she had previously dominated his father, al-Mahdi.'[49] Her brilliance and charisma were never in doubt, and they explain how she was able to stand out from the group of favourites surrounding al-Mahdi and eclipse his cousin Rayta, the aristocratic wife. By contrast, the intelligence of her son, who bore the name of Musa before receiving the title of Caliph al-Hadi (he who guides), is far from being established. The historians never fail to give us physical descriptions of the caliphs, and that of Musa al-Hadi contains a detail that lets us guess that mental agility was not his strong point: 'He was tall, strong, handsome, with a lightly tanned white skin. He had a very short upper lip. He was called Musa Atbiq [literally Musa Close-it].'[50] And Ibn al-Athir, who was a stickler for details, explains that he was called that because his father, Caliph al-Mahdi, had charged a slave to tell Musa '*atbiq*' every time his son forgot to close his mouth, and so he was given the name Musa Atbiq.[51] Since competence was not grounds on which Caliph al-Hadi could measure himself against his mother, he used another weapon against her: her duty to return to her territory, the harem.

Another word comes from *haram*: *mahram*, the person with whom the law of incest forbids marriage, 'the person with whom there is a uterine [*rahm*] relationship, which makes that person forbidden'. Territory, a man's *haram*, is that which belongs to him, that which he defends against the covetousness of others. The *haram* of a well is the space that surrounds it and to which access is forbidden: 'A well which a man has taken the pains to dig is forbidden to others, and one may not challenge his monopoly of it, and it is called *muharram* because its use is forbidden to all except the one who dug it.'[52] We see that the word *harim* in fact expresses an idea of threshold, of boundary, of separation between two territories. It is rooted in the idea of space as a field linked to life (sexuality) and to death (war), the ability to defend oneself and to protect. It is a threshold which organizes the universe and distributes beings in space, according to their relationships to power, their power to kill and to defend thresholds.

Islam is one of the few religions to have erected the difference between the sexes into a social architecture. Before Khayzuran, 'A'isha, the Prophet's wife, the first Muslim woman to claim and assume a political career, was confronted by the same territorial logic. 'A'isha's intelligence was also obvious: "A'isha was, among all the people, the one who had the most knowledge of *fiqh*, the one who was the most educated.'[53] She led the first armed resistance against a caliph. She put herself at the head of an armed insurrection in 36/658 against the fourth orthodox caliph, 'Ali Ibn Abi Talib. She went to the mosques to harangue the mobs and call on them to take up arms against 'Ali, and she then led some thousands of men into battle. This battle is known as the Battle of the Camel, referring to the camel ridden by 'A'isha, the only woman on the battlefield. On that day 7,000 Muslims fell in the space of a few hours. It was the first civil war, which traumatizes Islam right up to today, and which marked the division of Islam into the Shi'ites (those who remained the supporters of Caliph 'Ali and his descendants) and the Sunnis (those who accepted as caliph the man who would stop the civil war and restore peace, even if he was not of the Prophet's family).

'A'isha was the first woman to transgress the *hudud* (limits), to violate the boundary between the territory of women and that of men, to incite to kill, even though the act of war is the privilege of men and belongs to territory outside the harem. A woman does not have the right to kill. Deciding on war is the function and *raison d'être* of men. 'A'isha, as the first woman who took a political decision by leading armed men, remains forever linked in Muslim memory with *fitna* (disorder and destruction).[54] When 'A'isha went on a campaign to recruit supporters, especially among the Companions of the Prophet who held decision-making posts as governors of provinces and thus could help her in raising an army, the argument of those who opposed her initiative and decided to remain loyal to Caliph 'Ali was never an argument based on her competence. It was always systematically an argument based on territory.[55] And that territoriality is symbolized by what Caliph 'Ali said to 'A'isha after her defeat as she sat slightly wounded on her camel, which was riddled with arrows: 'Humayra, is that what the Messenger of God ordered you to do? Didn't he order you to remain quietly in your house?'[56] *Humayra*, referring to her very white skin made radiant by a light sunburn, was the loving pet name that the Prophet gave 'A'isha. More than a century later, Khayzuran, like 'A'isha but in different circumstances, found herself confronted by an impassable threshold.

A woman head of state will be the one who will assert her right to exist beyond the threshold of her house. She will seek to make herself visible in the most eminently public territory: the *minbar*, the pulpit of the mosque, where divine power and earthly power are in intimate communion and manifest themselves one through the other, one in the other.

PART II

Sovereignty in Islam

5
The Criteria of
Sovereignty in Islam

There are two indisputable criteria of sovereignty in Islam: the name of the head of state is proclaimed in the *khutba* at the Friday service in the mosque and it is inscribed on the coins. Nevertheless, if one had to choose which one of these seems to be permanently and clearly indispensable since year 1 of the Hejira (622) when the Prophet built the first mosque in Medina with his own hands, it would be the *khutba*, the sermon at the Friday prayers. We have seen that the titles of heads of state in Islam vary according to the nature of the power they exercise. There is the caliphate with its intimately linked spiritual and earthly powers, and there is *mulk* in Ibn Kaldun's sense, that is, earthly power with no other claim. It is true that their authority varies according to how much military power they wield, but one thing remains certain: only the person whose name is proclaimed in the Friday *khutba* is recognized as the official sovereign.

The Friday *khutba* is both the mirror and the reflection of what is going on in the political scene. In the case of war, one learns what is happening at the front by listening: the name of the sovereign that is mentioned is the one who currently controls the territory by military means. And the name changes with events in periods of political trouble. The *khutba* is the accurate barometer of subtle negotiations between the spiritual (the caliph) and the secular (the military chieftains who declare themselves head of state). In 428/1038 when the militarily weakened Abbasid caliph agreed that the *khutba* should be delivered in the name of the Buyid sovereign, who had given himself the Persian title of Shahanshah (emperor of emperors), a near-riot ensued.[1] The title of Shahanshah, in Arabic *malik al-muluk* (king of kings), was deemed blasphemous by the pious, because only Allah is described as *malik al-muluk*, for instance in verse 26 of sura 3. In order to re-establish order, the caliph had to summon the *'ulama* and ask them for a *fatwa* on the subject. As always, the *'ulama* were divided according to their own interests, their courage, and the degree of their faith. Many of the qadis granted the Buyid sovereign what he wanted, declaring that it was not heretical for him to claim the title of *malik al-muluk*. But one of them, Abu al-Hasan al-Mawardi, stood out as the voice of conscience and preferred to tell the truth, even if he risked losing his head. He declared it heretical for a head of state to claim such a title, and his *fatwa* was all the more important because he occupied the position of *qadi al-qudat*, judge of judges, a prestigious office and ultimate reference in matters of *fiqh* (religious knowledge). 'After such a *fatwa*, he remains at home, fearful.'[2]

In cases of rebellion, which were and are almost always of a religious nature, the first act of a rebel is to deliver the *khutba* in his own name if he has claims to power, or in the name of the sovereign who backs him. The Sunni world was traumatized in 450/1052 by a *khutba* delivered by rebels in the name of a Shi'ite sovereign in Baghdad itself, the capital of the empire and of Sunnism, when the city was occupied by a Turkish general, al-Basasiri.[3] This *khutba* took place during a blood bath when *fitna* (disorder) was at its height.

So now we understand the importance of the *khutba* as a criterion for distinguishing between women who have officially exercised power and those who like Khayzuran are content to exercise it by virtue of their position as wife or mother. The idea of the *khutba* being delivered in the Iraqi mosques in the name of Khayzuran was absolutely blasphemous. Nevertheless the Iraqis did quietly listen to the *khutba* preached in the name of the queen of the Jallarid dynasty, Malika Tindu, who reigned over the country in the fifteenth century.[4]

If the Friday *khutba* is so symbolically charged, even overdetermined by its double spiritual and material significance incarnated by the physical presence of a group of the faithful, the *umma*, united for public prayer under the leadership of an imam, it is all the more so in the case of women, who are considered as outsiders in political space. The few women who had the *khutba* delivered in their name from the *minbar* (pulpit) of mosques are exceptional in the political history of Islam, because they thus succeeded in officially forcing acceptance of the violation of an interdict. If one understands the conflictual relationship between women and the religious and the ambiguity that hangs over the right of women 'to exist' in the mosque (an ambiguity that was differently applied in various locales, cultures, and historical epochs), one can better appreciate the incredible symbolic and political importance of those rare women who attained the summit of having the *khutba* delivered in their name.

The minting of coins, the other criterion of sovereignty, is one of the privileges of sovereign power. However, the difference between the two criteria of legitimacy is enormous, in that the *khutba* is the specific insignia of Muslim power, while the coining of money is a royal emblem that Islam shares with other cultures and religions. The Arabs began by making use of the money of their neighbours, which is surprising if we recall that Mecca was a great trading centre at the time of Islam's early years. They used Persian or Roman money, and for decades after the coming of Islam they continued to be dependent on foreign money. The historians date the decision of a Muslim sovereign to ban the use of foreign money to year 65 of the Hejira. They credit this decision to 'Abd al-Malik Ibn Marwan, the fifth Umayyad caliph, who enforced the use in Muslim territory of a new official coin inscribed in Arabic with the *shahada* (Muslim declaration of faith) on one side, and the year of the coining and the name of the sovereign on the other.[5] Such a gesture of independence did not at all please the Roman emperor, who threatened the caliph with flooding the market with a coin that would insult the Prophet. Furious at the idea of blasphemies inscribed on metal and distributed in infinite numbers, the caliph consulted his religious authorities, who advised him to ignore the Roman's threat and summon artisans to coin dinars (in gold) and dirhams (in silver) stamped in Arabic. Later caliphs took similar steps, notably Khalid Ibn al-Walid. But he merely coined dinars in collaboration with the Romans, engraving his name in Latin on the Roman money, which carried a cross and a crown, both symbols equally spurned by Islam.[6] Mu'awiya, the first Umayyad caliph, like Khalid Ibn al-Walid, had his name inscribed on a foreign coin, a Persian dinar.[7]

Islam had a difficult time imposing its own coinage as the symbol of sovereignty during the years of conquest. But right from the beginning of the Hejira, the *khutba*, the short sermon delivered by the *khatib* (the imam in charge of leading the religious service), was an unalterable element of Muslim ritual, celebrated in the mosque on very precise occasions: the Friday religious service, services for the great feasts, and finally special services for unexpected, troubling cosmic events such as drought or an eclipse. In principle prayer precedes the *khutba*, although on Friday the order is reversed. The *khutba*, a sermon, is verbal, while prayer is primarily gestural, with each gesture accompanied by ritual words which intensify the symbolic meaning of each movement. The *khutba* contains invocations of Allah and his prophets, a reading of Koranic verses, and finally *du'a' li-al-mu'minin* (prayers on behalf of the faithful). It is the latter which concludes with mention of the ruling sovereign and asking God's help for him in the performance of his duty. The naming of the reigning sovereign, which constitutes both a sort of publicity for the sovereign whose name is mentioned (especially in times of political troubles) and a renewal of recognition of him and loyalty to him (in times of peace), is accompanied by prayers and intercessions to Allah to assure the sovereign support and a long life. The prosperity and security of the faithful depend on the sovereign's good management of the affairs of state. Therefore, wishing him long life and praying for him during the Friday sermon strengthens the idea so dear to Islam of a complete harmony between Heaven and earth, the spiritual and the material, the leader and the led. The Friday *khutba*, the central religious ritual of the system, expresses its very essence – namely, the fact that religion is political, and politics is religion. It is always supposed to be spoken in Arabic, although there are exceptions to this rule in non-Arabic speaking Muslim countries. The ritual unfolds according to a precise convention:

> It is commendable (*sunna*) for the *khatib* to be on a pulpit or an elevated place; to salute the audience when directing himself towards them; to sit down until the *'adhan* is pronounced by the *mu'adhdhin*;[8] to lean on a bow, a sword or a staff; to direct himself straightaway to his audience; to pray (*du'a'*) on behalf of the Muslims; and to make his *khutba* short.[9]

The Friday religious ritual is so important that it is the subject of a special chapter (*kitab*) in all the works of *fiqh*.[10]

In order to understand its importance, its traditional roots in memory, and the aesthetic emotion that it engenders, we have to go back to the famous first sermons delivered by the Prophet himself in the world's first mosque in Medina – a mosque whose grandeur and beauty were simplicity and lack of adornment. It is a mosque that still fascinates us today, because the strength of the leader, the Prophet, was expressed precisely by his great humility and rejection of the vanities of power. He was regarded as the *hakam*, the arbiter, the simple catalyst of the will of the group, and not as a despot.

After he fled Mecca in the company of his supporters and set up the first Muslim community in Medina, the Prophet's first act was the construction of a mosque: 'Before that, the Prophet was accustomed to praying in the stables [*marabid al-ghanam*] or practically anywhere he might be at the time of prayer.'[11] But the first mosque was not only a place for prayer. Today, with the coming of parliaments and people's assemblies on the Western model, we tend to forget that the mosque was the first and sole political space in which Muslims debated their problems in a group. That was the Prophet's idea of the mosque, and he thought of his residence as an integral part of it, as Ibn Sa'd tells us:

> The Prophet decided to construct his mosque at the place where his camel stopped. He bought the land for ten dinars . . . gave instructions for removal of the palm trees that stood there . . .. There were also some tombs from the *jahiliyya* [pre-Islamic times] . . .. He gave instructions to open them and to bury the bones in deep graves . . ..
> And they [the Muslims] began to construct *al-masjid* [the mosque] . . .. Then the Prophet built alongside it three rooms with roofs of palm fronds. When he finished the construction, he married 'A'isha, and the wedding night was spent in the room that was directly connected to the mosque.[12]

The Prophet was in such haste to get settled in order to attend to essential matters, that is, the management of the affairs of the community, that he decided to leave the mosque without a ceiling. When the Companions asked him if he did not intend to build one in due form, he replied: 'There are other more urgent problems.'[13]

Thus, simply, did Islam begin, as the experiment of a group under the direction of a Prophet who never made any decision alone. He always took care to debate it with those concerned, and to do it within the mosque, which was the place of worship and of the regulation of day-to-day affairs. The mosque of the Prophet Muhammad was the assembly hall and court of justice, the headquarters and centre for decision-making; and the Friday *khutba* was the occasion when the community, including women, gathered for prayer, was informed of the latest news, and received instructions:

The call of the muezzin was used to gather the people for prayer and also to announce an event that had happened, such as the conquest of a new territory or some other matter that concerned them. The call of the muezzin for prayer was used to bring the people together even when it was not the hour of prayer.[14]

The *khutba* on feast days was also an occasion for announcing planned expeditions, strategic plans for the immediate future, as it were:

When Muhammad had concluded the *salat* on the days of festival by the *taslim*,[15] he remained on his feet and turned to the sitting audience; when he wanted to send a mission or when he desired some other arrangement, he gave his orders on it; he used also to say: give alms, give alms . . . then he went away.[16]

It is true that at the beginning the community consisted of under a hundred households: 'There were 45 Muhajirun [the Meccans who came to Medina with the Prophet] and 45 Ansar [his original supporters in Medina].'[17]

The idea that the mosque is a privileged place, the collective space where the leader debates with *all* the members of the community before making decisions, is the key idea of that Islam which today is presented to us as the bastion of despotism. Everything passed through the mosque, which became the school for teaching new converts how to do the prayer ritual, the principles of Islam, how to behave toward others in places of worship and elsewhere. Was it fitting to come armed or not? Could one do buying and selling there (the Prophet and his Meccan supporters were originally merchants)? Could one keep prisoners of war in the mosque courtyard (to keep better watch on them) or not?[18] These simple, everyday, even banal questions show us that the mosque was something other than a mere place of worship. It was a place where showing ignorance was permitted, where asking questions was encouraged, both activities that today are strongly prohibited. But, above all, it was a place where dialogue between the leader and the people could take place. The apparently simple decision to install a *minbar* (pulpit) in the mosque was treated by the Prophet as a matter that concerned all Muslims:

The Prophet used to say the Friday prayers standing, leaning against a palm trunk. One day he announced that standing made him tired. Tamim al-Dari answered: 'Why not build a pulpit like I have seen in Syria?' The Prophet asked their advice on the question, and they agreed to the suggestion.[19]

The Medina carpenter cut a tree and built a pulpit with a seat and two steps up to it. Other versions say that the Prophet was urged to take his place on the *minbar* at the time of prayer so that he could be seen by everybody, because in a few months the number of Muslims had grown considerably, and this seemed a more plausible reason than physical fatigue. The Prophet was only 54 years old at the time of the Hejira and was in the prime of life. As military commander, he himself led all the most important expeditions right up until the day of the triumphant conquest of Mecca, his native city, eight years later. According to Mas'udi, the expeditions commanded by the Prophet himself 'numbered 26'.[20]

In any case, direct contact between the Prophet, as the imam who led the prayers, and those who attended seems to have been an important element of the Friday *khutba*:

When he mounted to the *minbar*, the Prophet was accustomed first to pronounce the *salam* [Peace be upon you]. When he sat down, the muezzin proclaimed the prayers . . .. On Friday he preached the *khutba* leaning on a staff . . .. And the people were in front of him, their faces raised toward him; they listened as they watched him. He was accustomed to conduct Friday prayers at the moment when the sun began to set. That day he was wearing a *burd* [Yemeni cloak] . . . a shawl woven in Oman . . .. He only wore them for the Friday prayers and on feast days, and they were carefully folded afterwards.[21]

However, that mosque, a place of worship and a place for the conduct of matters of common concern, the place for direct contact between the Prophet, head of state and imam, and his community, was not long to endure.

Thirty years after the death of the Prophet, Mu'awiya (41/661–60/680), the first Umayyad caliph, who used force to come to power, thus shattering the orthodoxy that required that the caliph be selected, continued the Prophet's traditional way of using the mosque, but introduced a significant innovation: the presence of guards. Mas'udi tells us that Mu'awiya

used to come to the mosque, and after making his ablutions, would sit down on his chair, and, leaning on the *maqsura* and surrounded by his guards, he would let those who wished approach – the poor, bedouin, women and children, people who had no protector. One would complain of an injustice: he ordered it redressed; another, of an attack: he ordered some men to take care of it; a third came to complain of some injuries: he ordered an inquiry. When there were no more petitioners, he left, seated himself on his throne, and received the courtiers according to rank.[22]

A century later the direct contact between caliph and community at the Friday prayer ritual was finally sundered. Harun al-Rashid was the first to entrust someone else with the duty of conducting the Friday service in his place.[23] The *khutba* became the business of a specialist, the *khatib*, who preaches the Friday sermon in the name of the sovereign. From then on, the sovereign would only lead the prayers on important feast days such as *al-adha*, the feast of sacrifice.

As with any profound change in an institution, the renunciation by the sovereign of personal interchange with the faithful, which the regularity of the Friday *khutba* imposed, had to have several causes. One was the psychological tensions that such a confrontation inflicted on the sovereign. Caliph 'Abd al-Malik Ibn Marwan was asked why he had white hair when he was still young. He answered that 'sovereignty would have been a heavenly pleasure if it had not been for the difficulties of the *minbar*.'[24] It was an exhausting duty, which required a particular kind of eloquence – namely, conciseness, *ijaz*, as the essayist al-Jahiz, the master of eloquence, called it. The sovereign had to summarize very rapidly the most important facts in a harmonious way that informed the audience of everything while taking account of their differences and conflicts.

The Prophet's custom in delivering the *khutba* was to be particularly concise. His Friday *khutba* was very short. It should be noted that his personal charisma was unrivalled:

> The Prophet was endowed with wisdom and eloquence, that is, with pertinence, moderation, and concision of language that expressed numerous thoughts and diverse ideas full of meaning and usefulness. In fact, his language was both the most beautiful and the most concise, for he reduced a great number of thoughts into a few words.[25]

The long *khutba* of ministers and other officials, especially the interminable televised discourses that are the custom in many Muslim countries today, are certainly an abominable *bid'a* (heretical innovation) that has nothing to do with the tradition of the first Companions. They were, like the Prophet, hard-pressed men of action, up at dawn and busy reconciling a pious life with military discipline, and they thought that the faithful had no time to waste either. Abu Bakr, the first caliph (11/632–13/634), who took power after the death of the Prophet, was concerned that a Muslim leader should not drown the faithful in words. He advised one of the generals whom he sent to conquer Syria to be brief: 'In your relations with those under your jurisdiction, be sparing with words; one part of a long discourse makes one forget another part.'[26]

The Friday *khutba* thus obliged the sovereign to develop his ability to communicate directly with the group, to pass information along rapidly by sticking to the essential facts, and to assume political responsibility for what he said. The leader's heavy responsibility was linked as much to what he chose not to say as to what he said. One can easily understand why the Muslim sovereign very quickly tried to get out of such an obligation and thus avoid the anxiety of direct contact with the group. But he thereby deprived the mosque of its political function, its function as the assembly of the faithful, who are well informed and asked to give their opinion. The caliphs rapidly cut themselves off from the community and deserted the mosque-residence of Muhammad, where the leader lives and works next to the mosque. Between themselves and those they governed they raised the *hijab*, literally the veil. The institution of the *hijab*, that is, a curtain in the sense of a barrier that separates the sovereign from the people and impedes their access to him – which was considered by the Prophet and the first four caliphs as a grave failure in duty by the leader – was very quickly adopted in political practice.[27]

The name of the official responsible for controlling access to the sovereign was coined from the same linguistic root as *hijab*; he was called *al-hajib*, literally, the one who veils the caliph. The *hajib* was the one who acts as a buffer; he received the applicants for an audience in place of the caliph and decided who should be received and who sent away. The institution was strongly challenged at the beginning, especially by the *ashraf*, the elite, who were upset by the caliph's decision to put a *hajib*, a man-veil, between them and him, thus shattering the intimacy and solidarity that had united them before. The famous epistle of al-Jahiz on the *hijab* is an attempt to document the incidents that took place when the caliphs ceased to be visible and accessible.[28] Once the institution of the *hijab* was adopted, the caliph faced another problem no less thorny than had been direct contact: the choice of the ideal *hajib*. According to Caliph al-Mahdi, the husband of Khayzuran and the father of Harun al-Rashid, a *hajib* must be neither ignorant nor foolish, neither absent-minded nor a worrier, neither disdainful nor disdained. How many sovereigns found such a pearl? Only Allah knows.

The institution of the *hijab* can be considered a key event in pushing the caliphate into despotism, for it constituted a rupture with the Prophet's tradition of the Friday *khutba* being carried out by the sovereign in person. It is possible to imagine another political Islam, which little by little would have developed from the mosque, a mosque-based democracy, a real parliamentary practice of interchange and resolution of conflicting opinions and interests. One can imagine the transformation of the *masjid*, the mosque, into a popular assembly with the expansion of the *umma* and the growth in the number of Muslims. We might have seen the birth in the heart of Islam of a democratic practice founded on a neighbourhood mosque/local assembly, since mosques are found everywhere where there is a community of Muslims and someone to lead them. The Prophet left everything in place for moving in that direction. A parliament could have been created without arguing about it as a satanic Western importation. We would have given to the world, well before other nations, that ideal which inspired the Prophet and his whole strategy: a group led by a *hakam*, an arbiter, the title he loved the most and was most proud of. But history took a different turn. With the seizure of power by Mu'awiya, who founded the first Muslim dynasty in the year 41, Islam as a political practice started down the road to despotism. By introducing guards into the mosque, he had already transformed its nature.

Nothing better expresses the betrayal of the Prophet in this matter than the attitude toward the access of women to mosques. In the *Kitab al-jum'a* (Book of Friday) of Imam Bukhari,[29] who wrote two centuries after the death of the Prophet (he died in year 256 of the Hejira), we find the following famous Hadith: 'Do not forbid the mosques of Allah to the women of Allah.' A half-century later, Imam Nisa'i, who wrote his *Al-sunan* (Traditions) in the tenth century, 300 years after the death of the Prophet, never forgot to give directions for arrangements between men and women during prayers. In his chapter on '*al-masjid*', for example, he gives specifications for the rows of men and women: how crowded they may be and how far from each other. The problem, according to him, is to regulate the coexistence of the sexes in the mosque and not to forbid it, as happened later.

Imam Nisa'i begins by declaring that 'the Prophet said that saying one's prayers in the mosque is worth a thousand prayers said elsewhere, with the exception of the Ka'ba.'[30] Then he added that the best way to wash away sin is to go to the mosque. The Prophet said: 'When a man leaves his house to go to the mosque, the foot that advances exhibits a good act, and the other wipes out a bad act.'[31] And he concludes naturally by saying that a man has no right to forbid his wife to go to the mosque. The Prophet said: 'When a woman asks authorization from one of you to go to the mosque, let him grant it to her.'[32] He terminates the question of access to the mosque by asking 'Who is really forbidden access to the mosque?' And he replies that, according to the Prophet, only those who have eaten garlic or onion are excluded. The Prophet had a very keen sense of smell; he loved perfumes, emphasized cleanliness, and had a horror of dirt and slovenliness. According to him, coming to the mosque after letting yourself be tempted by garlic was unbearably gross:

> 'Umar Ibn al-Khattab said: 'I see you, O people, eating of those two plants that are so bad, garlic and onion. I saw the Prophet, peace be on him, require those who came smelling of garlic and onion to leave the mosque. May those among you who are tempted by these two things have them cooked in order to lessen the odour.'[33]

For Nisa'i, access to the mosque had nothing to do with one's sex, and the importance of attending the Friday service is for women the proof of that fact. Three centuries later the Hanbali imam, Ibn al-Jawzi (died in year 597 of the Hejira) wrote a book on the laws that govern women in Islam and devoted his chapter 24 to 'Women's Friday Service'. He had to acknowledge that they had a right to it since the Hadith on that subject were incontrovertible. However, he took four steps that created doubt. First, when he took up the question of rows, he said that 'the prayers of men who are seated behind women are worthless.'[34] It often happened that men came to the mosque late and were blocked by the rows of women who had taken the pains to arrive on time. It is very easy to imagine the fatal next step: ban women from the mosque, since the mere presence of women risked creating a problem. So Ibn al-Jawzi then asks a question which in itself constitutes a betrayal of the ancient texts: 'Is it permitted for women to go to the mosque?' And here is his answer: 'If she fears disturbing men's minds, it is better for her to pray at home.'[35] After saying that and giving women a distressing responsibility, he cites Bukhari's key Hadith in which the Prophet stresses the fact that the mosques of Allah are not forbidden to women. He concludes by saying that 'the Friday service is not a duty for women.'[36] Finally, just afterwards, he devotes a whole chapter to 'why women should avoid going out'. In it the very fact of going out becomes a dangerous and impious act for a woman; he begins by saying: 'A woman should try to avoid going out as much as she can.'[37]

In such circumstances it goes without saying that access to the mosque is no longer an accepted fact. The custom of excluding women from mosques must have been quite widespread, because Ibn Battuta, who was a near-contemporary of Marco Polo and who travelled in Iran around the beginning of the fourteenth century, was surprised by the amazing number of women who came to the mosque in Shiraz:

> The people of Shiraz are distinguished by piety, sound religion, and purity of manners, especially the women. These wear boots, and when out of doors are swathed in mantles and head-veils . . .. One of their strange customs is that they meet in the principal mosque every Monday, Thursday, and Friday, to listen to the preacher, sometimes one or two thousand of them, carrying fans in their hands with which they fan themselves on account of the great heat. I have never seen in any land an assembly of women in such numbers.[38]

But it is in reading modern authors like Muhammad Sadiq al-Qannuji, the twentieth-century Hindu scholar (died in year 1308 of the Hejira), that one notes the institutionalization of the exclusion of women from such a crucial place as the mosque. In his chapter on 'what has been said on the fact that the Friday service is not a duty for women', he brings out a dubious Hadith which says: 'The Friday service is a duty for all Muslims, with four exceptions: slaves, women, children, and the ill.'[39]

We are certainly a long way from the Prophet's mosque, open to all, welcoming all those interested in Islam, including women. Already showing cracks from the political *hijab* which hides the caliph and distances him from the faithful, the mosque now suffers another betrayal of Muhammad's ideal community: women are declared strangers to the place of worship. Women, who had the privilege of access to the mosque as *sahabiyyat*, Companions of the Prophet, very quickly became the polluting, evil beings they had been in the *jahiliyya*, the pre-Islamic era. From the ashes of that era was reborn a misogyny whose roots reached deep down into archaic fears of femaleness and ignored the Prophet's endeavours to exorcize them by insisting on the necessity for the Muslim man to share everything with his wife. The biography of the Prophet, the *Sira*, always shows him carrying out with his wives the two most important acts of Islam from its very beginning: praying and making war. Not only will there be the fabrication of false Hadith that exclude women from worship. Memory will be custom-tailored to show that the appearance of women in the mosque brings disorder and turpitude. And Nawar, a *jarya* forced by a despot to appear dressed as an imam to lead the prayers, will be the example of this that histories have never failed to mention right up until today.

The appearance of Nawar, a slave singer, at the *mihrab* (prayer niche) of the mosque traumatized the people, and for good reason: she had been sent by a caliph, al-Walid, who was dead drunk, to lead the faithful in prayer in his place.[40] Al-Walid Ibn al-Yazid Ibn 'Abd al-Malik, the eleventh Umayyad caliph who ruled at the beginning of the second century of the Hejira (125/743–126/744), is described by all the historians as the most evil, the most dissolute in Muslim history. Even the refined Andalusian Ibn Hazm, who has left us the marvellous essay on love entitled *Tawq al-hamama* (The dove's necklace), does not hide his aversion for him and loads insulting epithets such as *fasiq* (dissolute) on him. He even put him on his list of 'caliphs who have a reputation for drinking wine' and of those 'who were famous for publicly wallowing in sin'.[41]

I will leave the description of this blasphemous scene of a *jarya* dressed as an imam leading the service to one of the greatest of Islam's historians, Ibn 'Asakir, the author of *Tarikh madinat Dimashq* (History of the city of Damascus). Nawar is the subject of one of the 196 biographies in his volume devoted to women:

Nawar was the *jarya* of al-Walid . . ... She was initiated into the art of song by the great masters of the time, such as Ma'bad and Ibn 'A'isha. She was al-Walid's favourite. It was she whom he ordered to go to lead the prayers in the mosque. While he was drunk, the muezzin had come looking for him to go and discharge his duty [leading the prayers]. He swore that it would be she who led them. She appeared to the public veiled and dressed in the vestments belonging to the caliph. She led the prayers and returned to him . . ... Beyond this we have no further information regarding her.[42]

This shocking event, in which the performance of a woman as imam in a mosque is linked to a caliph who is the incarnation of disorder and evil, is repeated throughout historical literature. Every time al-Walid is mentioned, Nawar is there at his side and leading the stunned faithful. In the thirteenth century Abi al-Hasan al-Maliki described the scene again, mentioning Nawar among 'the famous women of the era of the apogee of Islam'.[43] Nawar is always present. In the twentieth century she is included in 'Umar Kahhala's *Who's Who*-type of book of 'celebrities among women in the Occident and the Orient'. And he obviously had no more information about her than the scene in the mosque.[44] It is needless to add that al-Walid ushered in the end of his dynasty. He himself was swept out of office in year 126 (744) after only a year and two months in power. That year three caliphs succeeded each other, and things went from bad to worse until the seizure of power by the Abbasids a few years later in 750.

The appearance of a woman at the *mihrab*, made even more grotesque and apocalyptic by the fact that it was a *jarya* dressed as a caliph, sounded the death knell of the first Muslim dynasty. But it also shows the omissions and the artificial couplings in the collective memory and confirms that the Friday service as a criterion of sovereignty for women is more than significant. By amplifying outrageous and scandalous scenes, resistance has accumulated throughout the centuries depicting women as alien to the mosque and totally contrary to its nature. But it would be a mutilation of Islam and its historical dynamic to reduce it to such resistance and ignore the counter-resistance. In the present case it would be to reduce it to its misogynistic tendencies. It is not merely because the masters tell the poor, the slaves, or women that they are inferior that they believe it and conform to it. To understand the dynamic of a given civilization, it is necessary to try to understand both the desires of the masters (their laws, ideas, etc.) and the resistance of their supposedly weak, defenceless subjects. We have to free Islam from clichés, go beyond the idealized pretty pictures of the groups in power, scrutinize the counter-resistance, study the marginal cases and exceptions. This is especially necessary for understanding the 'history' of women in Islam, a 'history' doomed, like that of peasants and the poor, never to be reflected in the official discourse. It is time to begin to rewrite the history of the Muslims, to go beyond the Islam of the imam-caliph-president, of the palace and its *'ulama*; to move beyond the Islam of the masters, and doing that means going into the swampy, dark areas of the marginal and the exceptional – that is, the history of dynamic tensions, the history of order thwarted, the history of rejection, of resistance. This is the only history that can give the Muslims back their glorious humanity, by showing them not as obedient automatons, but as responsible beings, able to refuse to obey if ordered to maim themselves, to deprive themselves of the capacity to envisage their own life.

These are the questions that can give us 'another history, which, in its quest for explanations, dares to go to the other side of the mirror'.[45] Islam, a civilization of 15 centuries, which embraces the lives of millions of individuals of different sex, class, and ethnicity, cannot but be a history of complexities, tensions, and rejections. To say today that 'Islam forbids women access to the field of politics' is certainly to speak the truth. But we understand our history a little bit better if we admit that that is one truth among many others. One could, depending on the approach, choose another historical truth by studying the cases of some women who pushed their way into political power. Admitting that there are several historical truths, depending on the point of view of the person speaking, is already a big step forward. This is an admission that Islam and its so-called history are only political weapons, the most dogmatic and efficacious weapons directed at the throat of millions of human beings living in theocracies – that is, the societies ruled in the name of God, but where not everybody has the same right to speak or to rule in God's name.

In this context, the contemporary desire to veil women is really the desire to veil resistance. If you dare listen to women, you will find resistance. If you ignore it, you will have ignored the tensions that are the dynamics of life. In order to take on the present and shape the future, one has to have an active past, a past of beings who always preserved the privilege of being human, of thwarting the plans of the master. We have to discover this past. Studying these queens, whom history has not remembered, means plunging into the living, but also murky, material of our culture. We still have to count how many women fulfilled the criteria of the *khutba* and the minting of coins and can therefore be classed as heads of state. The answer to that question can reveal to us a history that up until now has been covered up – hidden by a veil, the *hijab*, and carefully pushed into invisibility. In addition, are there any historians who are interested in this question and have tried to count these women?

Using the most respected sources of the Muslim heritage, the Turkish historian, Badriye Uçok Un, the author of a book on women rulers in history, identified and studied 16 women who ruled in various countries.[46] According to her, the first was Sultana Radiyya of the Turkish Mamluk dynasty who took power in Delhi in 634/1236. The last was Zaynt al-Din Kamalat Shah, who reigned in Sumatra between 1688 and 1699. Benazir Bhutto would be the seventeenth, and the fact that she is an Asian seems to agree with Dr Uçok Un's theory: the 16 women heads of state she found were Asian, Turkish, Mongol, Iranian, Indonesian, or from the Maldives or other Indian islands; not one was Arab. As a methodical historian Dr Uçok Un chose as criteria the *khutba* and the minting of coins: 'I did not include any woman head of state who did not have money minted in her name or the *khutba* of the Friday service delivered in her name.'[47] That no sovereign included was an Arab woman is explained by the fact that the Arabs opposed their access to the throne and women could only reach the throne at the end of the Arabs' supremacy, that is, at the time of the fall of the Abbasid caliphate.

Athough it is true that two Mamluk queens, Radiyya and Shajarat al-Durr, owed their position to the conquest of power by the slaves who formed a military caste at that time, it would be ridiculous to deduce from that a tendency towards democracy on the part of the Mongols. The Mongols exterminated masses of people with disconcerting ease; rape and the enslavement of whole cities accompanied invasion by these nomads. At all costs we must avoid making impossible comparisons, projecting on to historical events of the thirteenth and fourteenth Muslim centuries our need as Muslims to further our claims of a democratic relationship between the governed and the governors. It is in this spirit that the following chapters about women who reached the throne should be read, with a vigilant, critical, if possible ironic attitude, never pontificating nor eulogizing, and still less indulging in sentimental dreams of glory. At the risk of disappointing some feminists who want to lull us with dreams of democratic matriarchies at the dawn of civilization and superpowerful women in past realms, I examine the sultanas with humour and a bit of irreverence.

The important thing is not unusual, uncommon ancestors, but very human ancestors who in difficult situations succeeded in thwarting the rules of the masters and introducing a little responsibility and freedom. Moreover, these women acquired power in differing contexts, and we should not bunch them into one superwoman model as in American comic strips. On the contrary, we should avoid generalizing; we should take full note of nuances and enrich our approach by not neglecting what are called the details.

The aim of this book about the Muslim queens is not to describe superb ancestors without faults, endowed with extraordinary abilities, and above all invincible in power games, whether they be political or amorous. As difficult as our present situation is, I do not believe that a woman, either yesterday or today, needs to be perfect, superb, and marvellous in order to enjoy all her rights. It is this very idea that has led women to believe that they have to be exceptional in order to be the equal of men and have the right to their privileges. We are not going to be put off by the fact that the queens we are about to study had ordinary, ambitious, or twisted personalities, that they committed blunders, underestimated certain factors, and most of the time failed lamentably. What makes humans great is trying to make the best out of their ordinariness or their defects and defying their lot and the power systems that support it. It is their ordinariness and their humanity that move us when we look at the lives of these queens, just as in contemplating our own. Combative these queens always were, but triumphant rarely.

6
Fifteen Queens

Who are those women whom history has recognized since indisputably they had the symbols of sovereignty, the *khutba* and the minting of coins? In what conditions did they acquire power? Did they have extraordinary abilities, stunning beauty, overwhelming charm, unparalleled intelligence? Were they princesses of the blood or women of the people who climbed the sacred hierarchy to arrive at summits officially reserved to men? Did they dream of democracy and power equally shared among different members of the community, or were they upstarts who thought only of their own interests? Nowadays we hear all over the place those feminist theories that sound like advertising slogans, asserting that if we were governed by women all violence would disappear from the political scene. Were our 15 Muslim queens pacifist or bloodthirsty? Did they recoil from using assassination or murder on finding a rival in their path? Finally – last but not least – were they romantic? Did they fall in love like you and me, foolishly, pathetically, or did they have hearts of stone, unfeeling and cold?

The surest path to the throne is certainly marrying a man who holds one. While according to the law of polygyny, 'normal' Muslim women must be satisfied with a quarter of a husband, these queens (with the exception of Sultana Radiyya, who was single when she acceded to the throne) all had at least one husband at their feet; some had another after the death of the first, and some of them even managed to have three with amazing ease. Rather than some mysterious beauty secret, adornment, or perfume, political power seems to be one of the most effective means of seduction for a woman, beginning with the Mamluk sultanas, Radiyya and Shajarat al-Durr.

THE MAMLUK SULTANAS

The similarities in the careers of these two sultanas are strange indeed. Both of them were Turks, enthusiastically borne to power by their supporters and stoutly defended by them against their enemies, and they both ended in the same fashion, abandoned by their armies, deserted, and finally savagely murdered, partly because of their tumultuous love life.

Their careers began at almost the same time. Radiyya took power in Delhi in 634/1236, and Shajarat al-Durr mounted the throne of Egypt 14 years later in 648/1250. Both of them gained their thrones thanks to the military power of the Mamluks, those former Turkish slaves who for centuries served the palaces that had enslaved them, but eventually succeeded in supplanting their masters. Radiyya took the throne of her father, Sultan Iltutmish, king of Delhi; and Shajarat al-Durr took over the throne of her husband, Malik al-Salih, and last Ayyubid sovereign. The Ayyubid dynasty had been founded a century earlier by Salah al-Din Ibn Ayyub, the famous Saladin, hero of the Crusades. Radiyya's first act of sovereignty was to have coins minted in her name with the following inscription very much in evidence on thousands of coins:

Pillar of Women
Queen of the Times
Sultana Radiyya Bint Shams al-Din Iltutmish[1]

She chose two titles. The first was *Radiyya al-dunya wa al-din*, which, through a play on the meaning of the word *radiyya* (coming from the root word *rada*, benediction), can be translated as 'the blessed of the earthly world and of the faith'. The second was *Balqis jihan*, Balqis being the Arabic name of the queen of Sheba,[2] and *jihan* being a title of nobility. On one of her coins which has come down to us she had struck the following inscription, calling attention to her allegiance to the Abbasid house:

In the Time of Imam al-Mustansir
Commander of the Faithful, Mighty Sultan
Splendour of the World and the Faith

Malika Iltutmish, Daughter of Sultan Iltutmish
She who Brings Glory to the Commander of the Faithful[3]

Imam al-Mustansir, the 36th Abbasid caliph (623/1226–640/1242), held the almost magical power of dispensing spiritual legitimacy to sultans who could gain earthly power only through military force. And this was the case with the father of Radiyya, Iltutmish, one of the Turkish slaves who as general of the army founded the Muslim state of India in 626/1229.

Shajarat al-Durr had no reason to limit her titles. The formulaic prayer that the believers in Egypt psalmodized during her reign, which lasted only a few months, was:

May Allah Protect the Beneficent One
Queen of the Muslims
The Blessed of the Earthly World and of the Faith
The Mother of Khalil al-Musta'simiyya
The Companion of Sultan al-Malik al-Salih[4]

For Shajarat al-Durr to introduce the name *al-Musta'simiyya* into her titles was more than a gesture of allegiance to Caliph al-Musta'sim, the 37th Abbasid caliph, who refused to acknowledge her. It was a pathetic admission of her weakness, a desperate attempt to gain his goodwill. Many historians see the emergence of women on the political scene as a sign of coming apocalyptic upheavals in the Muslim world. And the reign of Shajarat al-Durr heralded the end of the Abbasids and the destruction of Baghdad by the Mongols (1258), which brought about a fundamental redistribution of power in the empire, swept the aristocrats out of office (notably Caliph al-Musta'sim), who was to be the last of his dynasty), and gave the slave armies, the Mamluks, their chance. They gained power in several countries and would keep it for more than two centuries in Egypt and Syria. They deserved the thrones they conquered, as they were elite armies and the only ones who resisted Genghis Khan and succeeded in repelling his attacks. It was the Mamluk armies that conducted the battles against the Crusaders and later against the Mongols. They were the only ones who succeeded in defying the sons and grandsons of Genghis Khan, while everywhere – north, south, east, and west – palaces and sovereigns, troops and fortresses fell before their advance.

Sold as slaves while children, the Mamluks were raised in military schools, from which they emerged well trained in the martial arts and invincible on the field of battle. In the thirteenth century, in both Delhi and Cairo, the power of Islam and its renown were tied to the Turkish military caste.[5] In Asia Iltutmish, Radiyya's father, who began his career as a military slave serving generals in the employ of the sultans of Ghaznah, conquered new territories for Islam. In Africa the Bahri Mamluks (sea-going Mamluks), who worked for the sultans of the Ayyubid dynasty, were the bane of the Crusaders.[6] They thought of taking power only after the death of Sultan al-Salih Ayyub, the husband of Shajarat al-Durr. She was Turkish like them, and was no stranger to power. During the lifetime of her husband she took a lively interest in what went on in high circles, especially within the army. The army was impressed by the first decisions she made in the hours following the sultan's death, decisions which guaranteed the Mamluk army yet another victory.

Firstly Shajarat al-Durr negotiated with the army commanders to keep the death of her husband secret, a necessary condition, according to her, to avoid all danger of political unrest. Then she planned with them how to confront the most urgent problem: defeating the French. Under their king St Louis, the French were conducting a siege of Egypt that lasted from 647/1259 to 649/1260. Once victory was achieved, the Crusaders defeated, and their king imprisoned, Shajarat al-Durr turned to the problems of the succession. Her husband had a son, Turan Shah, who was absent from Cairo at the time of his father's death. She began by sending emissaries to him to advise him of what was happening in the palace and on the battlefield and to request his return to Cairo. Once he had returned, she entrusted power to him. But Turan Shah showed himself incapable of leading the troops. He alienated the officers and, unlike his father, was unable to earn their respect. The conflict between the Ayyub prince, Turan Shah, and the Turkish officers grew worse, and they plotted and carried out his assassination (648/1250). It was after this that the Mamluks decided to put Shajarat al-Durr on the throne.

However, once enthroned, she had to face the opposition of the Abbasid caliph, who refused to recognize her, and this compelled the army to reconsider its decision and to withdraw support from the queen. The Bahri Mamluks of Egypt, who had finally decided to take power and create their own dynasty rather than continue to serve others, needed more than anything the blessing of the caliph of Baghdad. And so, despite their admiration for Shajarat al-Durr, they deposed her after a few months. But one should not underestimate the tenacity of this ex-slave, who had succeeded in playing the politics of the harem to become the favourite in the palace of the Ayyubids. As soon as she found out the name of the general chosen by the army to present himself to the caliph as candidate for the sultanate of Egypt, Shajarat al-Durr determined to marry him. Named 'Izz al-Din Aybak, he was the most powerful of the Mamluk generals. The army trusted him, and the caliph gave him his approval. Shajarat al-Durr married him and once more succeeded in pushing her way on to the political stage. Yet, despite her abilities, she met resistance.[7] Her main concern was to avoid returning to the bleak shadows of the harem. In order not to fall back into the anonymity of female space, she saw to it that in all the mosques of Cairo the *khutba* was said in her name and that of her husband.[8] She made certain that coins were minted in the names of the two sovereigns, and that no official document left the palace without their two signatures.[9]

The word *Mamluk* comes from the Arabic word *malaka* (to own) and means *slave*, a thing owned. Mamluks were white slaves in contrast to *'abd*, another Arabic word meaning *slave*, but which was customarily applied to black slaves. The Mamluks, Turks from the Asian steppes, were captured by slave merchants who sold them to the sultans. After a rigorous military education, they were in principle freed and integrated into the military caste of the palaces. Cairo became famous for its military schools, which were located in twelve barracks in the citadel. Officers would add to their own name the name of the barracks in which they had been trained. Along with the military instruction, they received a very comprehensive religious education, intended to develop in them an identification between success in their career and the defence of Islam. Eunuchs played an important role in the education of the trainees, one of their functions being 'as a buffer between the young and adult Mamluks to prevent pederasty'.[10] Freed at the end of the period of apprenticeship, the Mamluks were named to important posts in the military hierarchy and presented to the sultan at a ceremony which marked their entry into the military elite, one of the most powerful aristocracies of the Muslim world.[11] For a young Turk from the steppes, where life was hard and poverty the lot of most, to be able to aspire to a career as a Mamluk seemed like a gift from Heaven, and only those who fulfilled certain criteria achieved it. One had to

be fair-skinned; to be (in most cases) an inhabitant of the area stretching to the north and to the north-east of the lands of Islam;

to be born an infidel; to be brought into the Mamluk Sultanate as a child or young boy (preferably at the age of puberty); and to be bought, brought up and manumitted by a patron who was a member of the military aristocracy.[12]

Recruits were required to be born an infidel because in principle a Muslim cannot be made a slave.[13] This requirement barred many young children from the Asian steppes whose parents had become Islamicized, so the parents often had recourse to fraudulent subterfuges to conceal this fact. Islam, which emphasizes the equality of all before God, was taken at its word by the Turkish slaves, who applied it to the letter. They defended Islam against all its enemies, including the Crusaders and the Mongols, but they did it by installing themselves comfortably on the thrones and giving themselves all the titles reserved for the great and powerful. The case of General 'Izz al-Din Aybak, Shajarat al-Durr's second husband, a Mamluk officer proclaimed sultan by the army of Egypt, is a good illustration of this political revolution which shook the palaces and the empire in many regions. It was in the wake of the Mamluk army of India that Radiyya had taken power in Delhi a few decades before.

Radiyya climbed the ladder to power in quite different circumstances; unlike Shajarat al-Durr, she was not a slave but the daughter of a sultan. Her father had arrived in India as a slave, and his rise to become sultan in an India that lived within a rigid caste system was excellent propaganda for Islam. Islam appeared as a democratic religion, a religion that broke down hierarchies, that toppled the masters and permitted slaves, if they had ability, to take the place of those who ruled. Having come to Delhi as the slave of a general of Ghaznah sultans, Iltutmish put all his energy into planting the Islamic standard on Indian territory. His success was so rapid that the sultan, Qutb al-Din Aybak, impressed by his bravery, married him to his daughter. At the death of Aybak in 607/1211, Iltutmish took power and declared himself independent of the Ghaznah masters. He has a secure place in history as one of the greatest slave kings who founded Muslim sovereignty in India.[14] Once earthly power had been acquired, the problem of legitimacy still remained. Muslim democracy has its limits. In order to become sultan, a slave had to get himself freed by his master.[15] This was what the *'ulama* demanded of Iltutmish. Ibn Battuta describes the scene in which after the death of his master Iltutmish presented the document declaring him free, without which he would not have been legally in a position to take power:

The jurists headed by the chief justice, Wajih-ud-din al-Kashani, came to him and sat before him; the chief justice sat by his side as usual. The sultan understood what they wanted to speak to him about. He lifted a side of the carpet on which he was sitting and took out for them the charter of his manumission. It was read by the chief justice and the jurists, and all of them took the oath of allegiance to him. So he became an absolute monarch and reigned for 20 years.[16]

One can imagine the effect of such a scene on the untouchables of Delhi and on all the people of the inferior castes.

It was still necessary to get the approval of the Abbasid caliph, as the Mamluks were Sunni. In 626/1229 Iltutmish sent an official request to the caliph of Baghdad, al-Mustansir, asking him for recognition. The caliph responded by sending a mission which was received in Delhi with great pomp and which officially consecrated him as sultan of India. Iltutmish had coins struck on which his allegiance to the Sunni caliph of Baghdad was acknowledged and celebrated with the following inscription: *Nasir amir al-mu'minin* (He who brings glory to the commander of the faithful). This allegiance led to an assassination attempt on him by a Shi'ite sect, the Isma'ilis, who were then very active in India and famous for spreading unrest. They tried to kill Iltutmish while he was leading prayers in the mosque. Their attempt failed, and Iltutmish, more Sunni than ever, conquered still more territory, surrounded himself with *fuqaha* (religious scholars) and with *'ulama*, and died of natural causes in Delhi in 633/1236, full of glory after a reign of 26 years.[17] He had chosen Radiyya as the heiress presumptive, although he had three children. The fact that Iltutmish's children were not all from the same mother complicated the succession; animosities between the two half-brothers and the half-sister were reinforced and fed by intrigues by the mothers from within the harem. One of the half-brothers, Rukn al-Din, who was not at all happy at his father's choice of Radiyya as heiress presumptive, was the most avid for power. His hatred for Radiyya and his half-brother broke into the open after the death of his father and drove him to combat the former and kill the latter.

Iltutmish, the slave whose personal abilities won him promotion, had no problem with recognizing a woman's worth. In his eyes, merit and justice went together; this was the essential point in his understanding of Islam, and as he was very pious, everything else, including difference between the sexes, was irrelevant. Compared to Rukn al-Din's weak character, Radiyya's talents marked her as the obvious successor. Pressed for an explanation of his choice by the amirs of his entourage, who found it surprising, Iltutmish gave a response that was astonishing in its simplicity: 'My sons are incapable of leading, and for that reason I have decided that it is my daughter who should reign after me.'[18]

Nevertheless, after Iltutmish's death the princes and viziers tried to push Radiyya aside in favour of her half-brother Rukn al-Din. Rukn al-Din first attempted to seize power by killing Radiyya's other half-brother, thinking thus to intimidate her and send her back to the oblivion of the harem. But he got a big surprise. Not only did Radiyya not hide herself behind her veils; she recaptured power by appealing directly to the people of Delhi, using a tactic created by her father in combating injustice:

> He [Iltutmish] ordered that everyone who was oppressed should wear a dyed garment, while all the inhabitants of India wear white clothes. Whenever the sultan held a court of justice and whenever he marched on horseback, as soon as his eyes fell on a person wearing a dyed garment he forthwith looked into his case and obtained justice from the person who had oppressed him.[19]

And to hasten the administration of justice and allow the oppressed to ask for help, he decided to have a bell installed at the palace:

> So he set up two marble statues of lions on two towers at the gate of his palace, and round their necks were two iron chains with a huge bell. The oppressed person would shake the bell in the night and the sultan on hearing the sound would instantly look into his case and administer justice.[20]

Radiyya was clever enough to have recourse to the custom established by her father and familiar to the people. She herself put on the coloured garments of the victims of injustice to go among the people to proclaim her charges and call on their help to avenge the death of her half-brother and depose Rukn al-Din, who was now threatening her with death. She waited until Friday and the gathering of the faithful in the mosque to put her plan into action in order to assure maximum publicity for her act. When Rukn al-Din emerged from the palace to go to the adjoining mosque where the service was taking place, Radiyya mounted the balcony dressed in the coloured garments of a victim and began to speak:

> She presented herself to the army (*an-nas*) and addressed them from the roof saying, 'My brother killed his brother and he now wants to

kill me.' Saying this she reminded them of her father's time and of his good deeds and benevolence to the people. This led to a revolt and they proceeded against Sultan Rukn ud-din at the time when he was in the mosque. He was arrested and taken to her. She said that the murderer should be killed; and he was killed in retaliation for his brother's death . . ... The army (*an-nas*) agreed to appoint Raziya as ruler.[21]

According to Ibn Battuta, one of the oldest sources on Radiyya, her first act once in power was to unveil: 'She ruled as an absolute monarch for four years. She mounted horse like men armed with bow and quiver; and she would not cover her face.'[22] Other sources say that she 'cut her hair and dressed like a man, and in this fashion mounted the throne.'[23] These sources say that she decided to dress like a man not only in order to lead military campaigns, but also to keep her contact with the people: 'She walked in the suqs [souks] dressed like a man, and she sat among us to listen to our complaints.'[24] In any case, Radiyya carried out her duties with great competence and was judged a very good administrator by all the historians. Only one thing was held against her: she fell in love with someone inferior to her. This love story brought on her fall, but with unexpected repercussions, just as in good Indian films.

Radiyya, the spinster queen, had such a high evaluation of the abilities of one of her equerries, Jamal al-Din Yaqut, an Ethiopian slave, that she promoted him too rapidly for the taste of others, and it began to be suspected that she was in love. Yaqut's title was 'Amir of horses' (*amir al-khayl*). Too rapidly she named him 'Amir of amirs' (*amir al-umara*), and many of the amirs did not appreciate the fact that they, in place of the horses, were now to be commanded by him. The angry amirs 'began to spy on him to learn the reasons for his speedy rise, and they noted that she took great pleasure in being in the company of Jamal al-Din and often assigned him certain tasks that he was supposed to carry out.'[25] Even worse, they began to spy on the slightest movements of the sultana and her equerry and one day observed that when she was mounting her horse, he made a shockingly familiar gesture: 'He slid his arms under her armpits in order to hoist her up on to her mount.'[26] The report spread through the city that the 'Pillar of Women, Queen of the Times', Sultana Radiyya, had violated ethical behaviour and let herself be touched by her slave. Her enemies had succeeded in their aim: 'She was accused of connections with an Abyssian slave of hers. The army (*an-nas*) agreed to depose her and have her marry.'[27] Despite Islam the India of the caste system won out. The religious authorities and the princes leagued against her, and an army was raised with the governor, Ikhtiyar al-Din Altuniyya, at its head. Radiyya, fearing a siege, left Delhi with her army to engage in battle against Altuniyya. But she lost the battle and became his prisoner. And then came the unexpected turn of events: Altuniyya fell in love with his prisoner. He freed her, married her, and departed with her and a great army to reconquer Delhi and retake the throne of his beloved.[28] But Radiyya was already marked out as fortune's victim. She and her husband lost the battle, their army was routed, and Radiyya fled. Ibn Battuta describes Radiyya's end, an end that reads like something out of the *Arabian Nights*:

Raziya's troops suffered a defeat and she fled. Overpowered by hunger and strained by fatigue she repaired to a peasant whom she found tilling the soil. She asked him for something to eat. He gave her a piece of bread which she ate and fell asleep; and she was dressed like a man. But, while she was asleep, the peasant's eyes fell upon a gown (*gaba*) studded with jewels which she was wearing under her clothes. He realized that she was a woman. So he killed her, plundered her and drove away her horse, and then buried her in his field. Then he went to the market to dispose of one of her garments. But the people of the market became suspicious of him and took him to the *shihna* (police magistrate) . . .. There he was beaten into confessing his murder and pointed out where he had buried her. Her body was then disinterred, washed, shrouded, and buried there.[29]

Ibn Battuta concludes by saying that, at the time of his travels in the fourteenth century, the people had made her a saint: 'A dome was built over her grave which is now visited, and people obtain blessings from it. It lies on the bank of the great river Jun [Jumna] at a distance of one parasang . . . from the city.'[30] Radiyya's tragic end prefigures that of the Mamluk queen who followed in her steps a decade later.

Shajarat al-Durr also came to a tragic end, but a much less innocent one. Amorous passion turned her into a jealous murderess. For her, love and monogamy went hand in hand, but this was not true of her second husband, 'Izz al-Din Aybak, a military strong man. By marrying him she gave him a kingdom. 'Izz al-Din divorced his former wife, Umm 'Ali.[31] His marriage with Shajarat al-Durr was not simply a political contract. There was something else, and that something else is called love. For Shajarat al-Durr love enjoined fidelity. She had even exacted fidelity from her first husband, Malik al-Salih, when she became his favourite. Shajarat al-Durr was endowed with extraordinary beauty and great intelligence: she 'had a brain that she used with great effectiveness for understanding the affairs of the kingdom'.[32] She read a great deal and loved to write as well.[33] What was her surprise when she learned that her new husband, a Mamluk by birth and a Turkish slave like herself, intended to marry the daughter of a king, the atabeg of Mosul, Badr al-Din Lu'lu'. Humiliated and mad with jealousy, she turned her thoughts to murder and came up with a very elaborate plot. She chose a time of pleasure, a visit to the *hammam*, the Turkish bath. It was 12 April 1257 (23 *rabi'* 655): 'When 'Izz al-Din Aybak entered the *hammam*, Shajarat al-Durr had planned everything and given instructions to his *jawari* and servants. They surrounded him and killed him in the bath.'[34] The murder of Aybak threw the army into turmoil. Although a part of it remained loyal to Shajarat al-Durr, she was brought to the Burj al-Ahmar (Red Fort) and killed that same year; her half-nude body was thrown over a cliff. It remained there 'for some days before it was buried'.[35] One can still visit the tomb of Shajarat al-Durr in Cairo. She was buried in the courtyard of a school that she had founded and is known today as Jami' Shajarat al-Durr, the mosque of Shajarat al-Durr. The visitor with a bit of time to spare can decipher on the dome of the mosque a long inscription that recalls her reign and its greatness; there one will find the title she held so dear: *'Ismat al-dunya wa al-din* (the Blessed of the earthly world and of the faith).[36]

Thus ended the political career of Shajarat al-Durr, a woman who succeeded in sharing power with an aristocratic first husband, who reigned officially for 80 days without the authorization of the caliph and without a husband, and who then seemingly managed to reconcile love and power. Her second husband, a man of her own class and origin, shared rule of the kingdom with her and her name was coupled with his at the Friday prayer service; finally, however, she succumbed to the demon of jealousy. The happiness and the reign shared by Shajarat al-Durr and 'Izz al-Din Aybak had lasted seven years, and without his decision to take another wife it would have lasted still longer.[37] This tale reminds us, among other things, of the link beween despotism and polygyny. When a woman, especially a slave, accedes to the throne, the veil covering this link is torn away and the truth revealed: the equal sharing of power between a man and a woman inevitably imposes monogamy on the man as a rule of amorous behaviour. Try as one may to separate them, amorous behaviour and political behaviour nevertheless draw their principles from the same sources.

THE MONGOL KHATUNS

As is well documented by the historian Badriye Uçok Un, after the Mongol invasion the thrones of Muslim states were occupied by an impressive number of women with the privileges of the *khutba* and coining of money. In almost a majority of the cases, this occurred with the blessing of the new masters, the Mongol princes. It is true that the latter seemed to have fewer problems than the Abbasid caliphs in entrusting the governing of states to women. First of all there were the two queens of the Kutlugh-Khanid dynasty, Kutlugh Khatun (also called Turkan Khatun in the documents) and her daughter Padishah Khatun (whom one sometimes finds under the name of Safwat al-Din Khatun).[38] During the thirteenth and four-teenth centuries the Kutlugh-Khanid dynasty reigned over Kirman, a Persian province situated to the south-west of the great central desert, the Dasht-i Lut.[39]

The dynasty came into being in the wake of Mongol conquests. The Mongol ruler Hulagu, one of Genghis Khan's descendants and heirs, had received Persia and Mesopotamia as his share of the inheritance. Theoretically he was also allotted Syria and Egypt. But whereas Baghdad proved easy to conquer, Syria and Egypt were valiantly defended by the Mamluks, and the defeat inflicted on Hulagu's army at 'Ain Jallut in 657/1260 put a halt to Mongol advance into Syrian territory and fixed the boundary between the two powers for good.

Henceforth the venerable caliphate of Baghdad was dependent on the Ilkhan dynasty created by Hulagu. Many local military chieftains took advantage of the Mongol invasion to consolidate their power, among them Barak Hajib. When the Mongols invaded Kirman and put an end to the Seljuk dynasty, Hulagu gave the reins of power to Barak Hajib, who became the uncontested ruler of Kirman. In exchange for his military aid in the region, Barak Hajib demanded a title; the Mongols gave him the title of Kutlugh Khan, and he agreed to pay them an annual tribute. Once his power was militarily established in 619/1222, he provided himself with the other titles he felt the need for. The caliph of Baghdad gave him the title of sultan, although his conversion to Islam was rather late and he had spent a good part of his life as a pagan.[40] At his death Barak Hajib left his heirs an impressive number of Arab and Mongol titles: *Nasr al-dunya wa al-din* (Triumph of the earthly world and of the faith), Kutlugh Sultan, etc. Relations between Kutlugh Khan and the Mongols were strengthened by repeated visits by the princes of Kirman and by marriages. Barak Hajib had a son, Rukn al-Din, and four daughters. One of the latter was Kutlugh Turkan, who was married to his cousin Qutb al-Din. After Barak's death in 632/1234, first his son took power; then his cousin, Qutb al-Din, Turkan's husband, acceded to the throne in 650/1252. At the death of Qutb al-Din in 655/1257, his son being under-age, the notables of Kirman requested the Mongol court to entrust the government to his widow, Kutlugh Khan, who then reigned for 26 years until 681/1282.[41] She cleverly kept in the good graces of the Mongol court by sending her son Hajjaj to fight in Hulagu's army and by marrying her daughter Padishah Khatun to Abaka Khan, Hulagu's son. This marriage was doubly astonishing, because one of the partners was Muslim and the other Buddhist, and because Padishah had been deliberately raised as a boy among the boys in order to deceive the Mongols, who subjected the princesses of their 'colonies' to obligatory marriage.[42] The Kutlugh-Khanids apparently had no desire to ally themselves to the court of Hulagu through marriages, but in this case political opportunism decided otherwise. Officially confirmed in her title by Hulagu seven years later in 662/1264, Kutlugh Turkan bore the title of *'Ismat al-dunya wa al-din*, and she had the right to have the *khutba* proclaimed in her name in the mosques.[43]

Turkan's power was at its height when, as usual, a pretender to the throne appeared on the scene and prevented her from savouring her triumph. He was one of her stepsons, Suyurghatamish, the son of her dead husband, who could not accept the idea that his stepmother should inherit the throne. Suyurghatamish stirred up trouble in the kingdom to such an extent that in order to restore peace she was forced to include his name, along with hers, in the *khutba*. But Turkan played one of her winning cards, her relation with the Mongol courts: she 'complained to her daughter Padishah Khatun and received a *yarligh* forbidding her stepson to meddle in the affairs of Kirman'.[44] Only the end of Turkan Khatun's reign, which 'brought prosperity to Kirman', was clouded by a chill in relations with the Ilkhan court upon the death of Abaka, her son-in-law, which occurred several months before her own death in 681/1282.

Abaka's brother and successor converted to Islam and took the name of Ahmad Teguder. This created some consternation among the Mongols, who until then had been either Buddhists, Nestorian Christians, or Shamanists, but until then not Muslims. Even though the Mongol conquerors of Persia had immediately fallen under the spell of the conquered civilization and had readily adopted Persian customs, the decision of an Ilkhan sovereign to convert to Islam was nevertheless a shock to the court and the princes. Ahmad Teguder did not last long; he was dethroned two years later in 683/1284 by Abaka's son Arghun, whose Buddhist faith was beyond suspicion. During his short reign, Ahmad Teguder presented Turkan Khatun with her greatest crisis by installing her stepson and rival Suyurghatamish on the throne of Kirman. Turkan went to the capital of the Mongol court at Tabriz to plead her case, but Ahmad was unyielding. Turkan Khatun died a year later without regaining her throne.[45] But she was avenged a few years later when through a second marriage her daughter Padishah Khatun regained both her place at the Mongol court and the throne of Kirman which her mother had lost.

Padishah Khatun was not content just to be beautiful; she astonished the Ilkhan princes with her gift as a poet, and no one was surprised when, after being widowed, she married Gaykhatu, the fifth ruler of the Ilkhan dynasty, who succeeded to power in 690/1291 and who was one of the sons of her former husband. This marriage, shocking according to the Muslim *shari'a*, was not at all shocking according to Mongol customs. Padishah Khatun lost no time and demanded that her new husband, Gaykhatu, give her the throne of Kirman as proof of his love for her. Gaykhatu acceded to her demand, and Padishah Khatun came to Kirman as head of state. One of her first acts was to arrest her half-brother Suyurghatamish and throw him in prison. Then, when he tried to escape, she had him strangled. After this very sisterly act, Padishah Khatun took the title of *Safwat al-dunya wa al-din* (Purity of the earthly world and of the faith) and became the sixth sovereign of the Kutlugh-Khanid dynasty – not only officially but also unchallenged. She had money coined in gold and silver in her name. Some coins still exist in a museum in Berlin and bear the following inscription: *Kikhan Padishah Jihan Khadawand 'Alam Padishah Khatun.*[46] *Khadawand 'Alam* means 'Sovereign of the world', and is made up of a first word in Turkish meaning 'sovereign' and a second in Arabic meaning 'world'. It is interesting to note that – at least in the inscription on the coins – she only laid claim to the world here below and made no reference to the faith (*al-din*) and therefore to the Beyond, which is rare among Muslim sovereigns, be they men or women. She reigned over Kirman until the death of her husband in 694/1295 and the accession to power of his successor Baydu. He was more inclined to listen to her enemies and to support the clan that still sought to avenge the killing of Suyurghatamish; this clan was led by a woman, Khurdudjin, the widow of Suyurghatamish, who was not just anybody – she was a Mongol princess of royal blood, a descendant of Hulagu. The grieving, vengeful widow demanded of Baydu, the new ruler, that he put to death Padishah Khatun.[47]

Thus, with the support of the Mongols, one queen succeeded another on the throne of Kirman. During his journey through the Mongol Empire in the first part of the fourteenth century, Ibn Battuta, the rather conservative Moroccan, was very surprised by the great respect he found accorded women under the rule of Abu Sa'id Behadur Khan, the ninth sovereign of the Ilkhan dynasty, who ruled in Baghdad between 716/1316 and 736/1335. And one can deduce from his observations that women were treated differently in Tangier, his native city. Ibn Battuta, who was a qadi (that is, a religious authority entitled to make rulings on the role of women), scrupulously took note of what he observed: 'Among the Turks and Tatars their wives enjoy a very high position; indeed, when they issue an order they say in it "By command of the Sultan and the Khatuns". Each khatun possesses several towns and districts and vast revenues.'[48] But it was the special attention and deference that the sovereign accorded to women in public during state rituals that fascinated Ibn Battuta, who had never seen such a thing in Tangier. He had an opportunity to see this with his own eyes when he accompanied Abu Sa'id Behadur Khan, his Mongol host, on a tour. He wanted to see 'the ceremonial observed by the King of al-Iraq in his journeying and encamping, and the manner of his transportation and travel'.[49] And what does he report? Women were not at the rear; they were very visible at the head of the procession:

Each of the khatuns rides in a waggon, the tent that she occupies being distinguished by a cupola of silver ornamented of wood encrusted with precious stones . . . . Behind the khatun's waggon there are about a hundred waggons . . . . Behind these waggons [again] are about three hundred waggons, drawn by camels and oxen, carrying the khatun's chests, moneys, robes, furnishings and food.[50]

Even among the musicians who accompanied the troops, those of the khatuns played a leading role: 'When the moment of departure comes, the great drum is beaten, followed by the beating in succession of the drums of the chief khatun, who is the queen, and of the other khatuns, then of the vizier, then of those of the amirs all at once.'[51]

Ibn Battuta, who was very well versed in the *shari'a*, was also impressed by the protocol and rituals of another court, that of Sultan Muhammad Uzbeg Khan, the Mongol sovereign of the Golden Horde (1312–41). In order to give his reader a general framework, he first describes the greatness of this sovereign: 'This sultan is mighty in sovereignty, exceedingly powerful, great in dignity, lofty in station, victor over the enemies of God . . .. He is one of the seven kings who are the great and mighty kings of the world'.[52] He continues by describing a ceremonial audience:

> He observes in his [public] sittings, his journeys, and his affairs in general, a marvellous and magnificent ceremonial. It is his custom to sit every Friday, after the prayers, in a pavilion magnificently decorated, called the Gold Pavilion. It is constructed of wooden rods covered with plaques of gold, and in the centre of it is a wooden couch covered with plaques of silver gilt, its legs being of pure silver and their bases encrusted with precious stones. The sultan sits on the throne, having on his right hand the khatun Taitughli and next to her the khatun Kabak, and on his left the khatun Bayalun and next to her the khatun Urduja. Below the throne, to his right, stands the sultan's son Tina Bak, and to his left his second son Jani Bak, and in front of him sits his daughter It Kujujuk.[53]

Seating the khatuns in such a prominent position during the Friday ceremony was in itself astonishing enough to a Sunni, but this king, one of the most powerful in the world, stands up upon the arrival of each one. The astounded Ibn Battuta takes careful note of all the details: 'As each of the khatuns comes in the sultan rises before her, and takes her by the hand until she mounts to the couch . . .. All this is done in full view of those present, without any use of veils.'[54] Ibn Battuta was so astonished by the respect and consideration shown to these women, whom the Mongols exhibited at their side unveiled during the religious ceremonies, that he devoted several chapters to them in his books: 'Account of the Khatuns and their Ceremonial'; 'Account of the Principal Khatun'; 'Account of the Second Khatun who comes after the Queen'; and finally accounts of the third and the fourth khatuns.[55]

Ibn Battuta was right to emphasize the difference between the man/woman relations among the Mongols and those in the Sunni tradition that he, an Arab, knew so well. Despite their Islamicization, the Mongols never went as far as making concessions in matters concerning women. Gradually, little by little, the initially unacceptable idea of the conversion of the Mongol sovereign to Islam, which cost the ill-fated Ahmad the throne, became a common-place beginning with his fourth successor, Ghazan, the seventh of the line (694/1295 to 703/1304).[56] And he, even while embracing Sunni Islam, held out against pressure, and his conversion 'did not completely suppress old Mongol traditions, such as the respected public status of women'.[57] Apparently many queens and princesses knew how to take advantage of this goodwill, hitherto unknown in the political life of Arab Islam.

The third queen to ascend the throne in the manner of Padishah Khatun – that is, through marriage to an Ilkhan prince – was Absh Khatun, who ruled the Persian realm for a quarter of a century from 662/1263 to 686/1287. She was the ninth sovereign of the Persian dynasty of the Atabeks, which was known as the Sulghurid dynasty, from the name of its founder, Sulghur, chief of a Turkoman tribe which migrated to Iran. The Sulghurids remained in power for about a century, from 543/1148 to 686/1287. Their capital was Shiraz, and Absh Khatun was the last sovereign of the dynasty. Like Padishah Khatun (who was her aunt), she was married very young. Her husband, Manku Timur, was one of Hulagu's sons.[58] Hulagu was unhappy with the way things were going in the Persian realm, which was under his dominion, so he sent an army against Seljuk Shah, which defeated and killed him. His daughter-in-law, Absh Khatun, was dispatched from Urdu, the Ilkhan capital, where she was living with her husband, to Shiraz, the capital of her native country. There she was received with great pomp on the orders of Hulagu.[59] As in the case of Padishah Khatun, the Friday *khutba* was proclaimed in her name and coins were struck in her name.[60] The Mongols made use of alliances, and especially of daughters-in-law from sovereign states, as a means of consolidating their domination. The existence of Ilkhan daughters-in-law/heads of state was thus a tradition that appeared in all the dynastic family trees of these states – something inconceivable under the Abbasids, where there are never any women's names.

The fourth woman to come to power under the same conditions was Dawlat Khatun, the fourteenth sovereign of the Bani Khurshid dynasty, which governed Luristan for almost four centuries beginning in 591/1195. Luristan is situated in south-western Persia and was under Mongol domination like the rest of the area. After the death of her husband 'Izz al-Din Muhammad, Dawlat Khatun acceded to the throne in 716/1316.⁶¹ An especially poor administrator, 'who was not successful in managing the affairs of state', she abdicated in favour of her brother-in-law 'Izz al-Din Hasan.⁶² Quite different was the Mongol queen Sati Bek, who had such an appetite for power that she made use of three successive husbands to maintain herself in power.

When Sati Bek came to power in 739/1339, the political scene was completely different from what it was when Hulagu created the dynasty: Ilkhan princes and princesses were killing each other, and the past greatness was replaced by an unheard-of display of palace intrigues and interfamilial assassinations. Sati Bek's marriage choices were all extremely calculated. Her first husband, Amir Tchoban, grandson of one of Hulagu's generals, was commander-in-chief of the armed forces. After his death she chose for her second husband Arpa, an Ilkhan sovereign who briefly acceded to the throne in 736/1335. She finally ascended the throne as official head of state during the year 1339. During that period the *khutba* was proclaimed in her name and she hastened to have coins struck bearing the following inscription: *Al-sultana al-'adila Sati Bek Khan khallad Allah mulkaha* (The just sultana Sati Bek Khan, may Allah perpetuate her reign).⁶³ Allah did not grant her wish, and her reign lasted only nine months. She had to cede power to Sulayman Amin Yusif Shah. But the lust for power still burned fiercely in her, and what better way to satisfy it than to try to seduce Sulayman Amin, the hero of the hour? He did not resist and became her third husband.

Another Mongol queen received highest honours and ruled in Baghdad. She was called Tindu and belonged to the Jallarid dynasty, a branch of the Ilkhan dynasty which governed Iraq during the fourteenth and fifteenth centuries, from 714/1336 to 814/1411. Very beautiful, Tindu was the daughter of King Awis, one of the greatest Mongol sovereigns. But times had changed. The Mongols were no longer the invincible invaders of the region; they were now well-established rulers whose fighting spirit on the battlefield had been lost. Awis, who governed Iraq, could only defend it by seeking alliances in the region against a new military power, that of Tamerlane, who came out of the steppes, like Genghis Khan before. Awis's allies against Tamerlane were the Mamluks of Egypt, the former enemies of the Mongols. It was from them that he sought aid and support, and Tindu's first marriage was more a political alliance than anything else. Her first husband was al-Zahir Barquq, the next to last Mamluk king of Egypt (784/1382 to 791/1389). He had been struck by her beauty during a journey that she made with her uncle, and asked for her in marriage; this was welcomed because Iraq was having difficulty repelling the repeated attacks of Tamerlane's armies. In exchange for Tindu, who was to remain in Cairo, Baghdad received the support of the Egyptian armies. But Tindu, who was very attached to her homeland, did not like life in Cairo. Barquq, who loved her very much, finally let her return to Iraq. As a second husband she married her cousin Shah Walad, and after his death she acceded to the throne in 814/1411. She remained in power for eight years until her death.[64] Hanbali relates that, 'The *khutba* was said in her name from the pulpits and money was coined in her name until her death in 822. Her son took power after her.'[65]

According to Badriye Uçok Un, there is supposed to have been a last Mongol queen, Sultana Fatima Begum, whom the Russians know under the name of Sultana Sayyidovna and who ruled the Ilkhan kingdom of Qasim in Central Asia between 1679 and 1681.[66] We know that Batu, one of the grandsons of Genghis Khan, 'succeeded in subjugating large parts of Russia in the years 1236 to 1241. Only the north west (with Novgorod at its centre), was spared . . . .. The new state was called the "Golden Horde" by the Russians and thus also in Europe.'[67] The Tatar domination lasted two and a half centuries, and one of its consequences was the Islamicization of whole areas of Russia.[68] Sultana Fatima Begum is supposed to have been the last sovereign of the Qasim dynasty. But except for the mention of her by Dr Uçok Un, I could not find any reference to this queen in any of the works in Arabic that I consulted, in which mention would have been made of her right to having the *khutba* said in her name and money coined in her name. So I merely cite her without counting her among the women heads of state. This reduces to six the number of Mongol queens who meet my criteria.

This rise to power of women in the Mongol Empire is all the more remarkable considering the almost total absence of queens on the political scene before the taking of Baghdad in 1258. However, it must be kept in mind that among the Mongols this privilege applied only to women of the aristocratic class and that the local populations were treated with little consideration. How is one to explain how a people can be so violent and at the same time accord a pre-eminent place to women on the political scene? The answer to that question would require another book, which would lead us into the dark areas of the very fascinating links among the various societies' complex laws that govern that fundamental triad – power/ violence/sex. Meanwhile, we can take a quick look at a third group of women heads of states, those of the island kingdoms of South-East Asia, another Muslim culture with other possibilities and other models of behaviour.

THE ISLAND QUEENS

Seven sultanas reigned in the Indies: three in the Maldives and four in Indonesia. The first, Sultana Khadija, daughter of Sultan Salah al-Din Salih Albendjaly, reigned from 1347 to 1379. Luckily for us, Ibn Battuta travelled in the Maldives during her reign, and fell completely under her spell:

> One of the wonders of these islands is that its ruler (*sultana*) is a woman named Khadija . . .. Sovereignty was exercised first by her grandfather, and then by her father. When the latter died her brother Shihab-ud-din became king. He was still young and the vezir 'Abdal-lah son of Muhammad al-Hazrami married the mother of Shihab-ud-din and overpowered him. And it was he who married also this Sultana Khadija after the death of her husband, the vezir Jamal-ud-din.[69]

After describing the power struggles which resulted in her brother being deposed and then put to death, Ibn Battuta describes the circumstances of Khadija's enthronement:

> The only survivors from the ruling house were his three sisters . . .. The inhabitants of the Maldive islands preferred for sovereign Khadija and she was the wife of their orator (*khatib*) Jamal-ud-din who became vezir. He took over the reins of power . . . but orders were issued in the name of Khadija only. The orders were written on palm leaves with a bent piece of iron similar to a knife, while paper was not used except for writing the Qur'an and books of learning.[70]

Was the *khutba* proclaimed in the name of Sultana Khadija? We can count on Ibn Battuta to record the formula meticulously:

> The orator (*khatib*) mentioned the queen (*sultana*) in the Friday prayer and also on other occasions. 'O my God!' says he, 'help Thy

female slave whom Thou in Thy wisdom hast chosen from all creatures and made an instrument of Thy grace for all Muslims – verily,
that is, Sultana Khadija, the daughter of Sultan Jalal-ud-din, *bin*
Sultan Salah-ud-din.'[71]

After the death of Sultana Khadija, who reigned for 33 years,
her sister Myriam succeeded to the throne. She remained there until
785/1383, her husband also occupying the post of vizier. After
Sultana Myriam, her daughter, Sultana Fatima, ascended the throne
and ruled until her death in 790/1388. So, for forty years the Muslims
of the Maldive Islands were governed by women. Ibn Battuta, who
held the office of qadi, did not long resist the charm of the women
of the islands. He described his marriage to the stepmother of the
sultana:

> The *qazi* and witnesses were summoned, and the marriage was sol-
> emnized, and the grand vezir paid the dower. After a few days she
> was brought to me. She was one of the best women and her society
> was delightful to such an extent that whenever I married another
> woman she showed the sweetness of her disposition still by annointing
> me with perfumed ointment and scenting my clothes, smiling all the
> time and betraying no sign of ill humor.[72]

Ibn Battuta was so enchanted with the royal treatment given him
by his wife that he did not hesitate to have four. He married
often during his journeys through the Muslim world, which lasted
practically his whole life, but the memory of his domestic happiness
with the Maldive women was particularly sweet. One detects some
regret that he could not bring one back with him to Tangier:

> The women of these islands never leave their country, and I have
> seen nowhere in the world women whose society was more pleasant.
> A woman in these islands would never entrust to anybody else the
> serving of her husband; she herself brings him food and takes away
> the plates, washes his hands and brings him water for ablutions and
> massages his feet when he goes to bed.[73]

However, there was one thing that intrigued him:

> One of the customs of the country is for the women not to dine with
> their husbands and the husband does not know what his wife eats.
> In these islands I married several women; some of them dined with
> me after I had tackled them, but others did not. And I was not able
> to see them eat and no device on my part was of any avail.[74]

The only fault he found in the Maldive women – especially in his role as qadi – was that they went about half-naked:

> The women of these islands do not cover their heads, nor does their queen and they comb their hair and gather it together in one direction. Most of them wear only a waist-wrapper which covers them from their waist to the lowest part, but the remainder of their body remains uncovered. Thus they walk about in the bazaars and elsewhere. When I was appointed *qazi* there, I strove to put an end to this practice and commanded the women to wear clothes; but I could not get it done.[75]

Ibn Battuta was too intelligent not to see the link between the sensuality of the women believers and their walking around half-naked. In his capacity as qadi he insisted on a compromise. The women believers could walk about half-nude, but in the audience hall of the tribunal where he administered the *shari'a* they would have to show a minimum respect for appearances: 'I would not let a woman enter my court to make a plaint unless her body were covered; beyond this, however, I was unable to do anything.' With the archness so typical of a native of Tangier, Ibn Battuta notes later on that their half-nude state suited the Maldive women much better: 'I had slave girls whose clothing was like that of the women of Delhi and who covered their heads. But far from being an ornament it looked like a disfigurement since they were not used to putting it on.'[76] All things considered, the qadi was ready to make concessions about the pertinence of the *shari'a* regarding the veil for women when it interfered with something as serious as aesthetics, especially in such a sensual environment as that of the islands. But not all the islands resembled each other, nor did their women. During his stay in Indonesia, he was not so impressed by the women. And yet, even there, women were destined to take power, although it is true that it happened some centuries after Ibn Battuta's stay in the Far East.

Four princesses succeeded each other in Indonesia in the state of Atjeh in the second half of the seventeenth century (from 1641 to 1699). The province of Atjeh, located in the most northerly part of the island of Sumatra, was the first region of Indonesia to see the establishment of a Muslim kingdom. As early as 1292 Marco Polo, who passed through there, mentioned the existence of a Muslim sovereign.[77] These four queens are on H. Djajadiningrat's list of 34 sovereigns who ruled over Atjeh from the sixteenth century to the beginning of the twentieth century. Sultana Tadj al-'Alam Safiyyat al-Din Shah (1641–75) was the fourteenth sovereign of the dynasty; Sultana Nur al-'Alam Nakiyyat al-Din Shah the fifteenth (1675–8), 'Inayat Shah Zakiyyat al-Din Shah the sixteenth (1678–88), and Kamalat Shah (1688–99) the seventeenth. They reigned despite the fact that their political enemies had imported from Mecca a *fatwa* that declared that 'it was forbidden by law for a woman to rule'.[78]

Despite decrees from Mecca, opposition from the caliphs, and the opportunism of political men, 15 Muslim women sovereigns ascended the thrones of Muslim states between the thirteenth and seventeenth centuries, holding all the official insignia of sovereignty. The first two, Radiyya and Shajarat al-Durr, were Turks belonging to the Mamluk dynasty. Six sultanas came to the throne when Mongol princes replaced the Abbasid Arab caliphs at the head of the Muslim Empire. And seven others were Islamic rulers in the Maldives and Indonesia. The historian Uçok Un found no true Arab sultana. Women were only able to accede to power when the Arabs were defeated: 'It was only with the end of the Abbasid state, which was a major obstacle to women's acceding to the leadership of states, that women were able to take their seat on a throne.'[79] The disappearance of the Abbasid state 'opened the road to them and finally permitted them to come to power.'[80]

In her explanation of this, Dr Uçok Un constructs a vision of the world that is coherent, convincing, and so simple that it seems irrefutable. But her explanation rests on a factor that is at the very least disquieting – race. She finds that the Arabs showed avowed misogynistic behaviour, while the Turks, Mongols, Indonesians, and Asians in general seem almost feminist. The fact that all the women who managed to reach the throne, 'except for those in the Indian Islands, [were] Turks or Mongols is clear proof of the importance that these cultures gave to women in public affairs.'[81] The problem with theories based on race is that it only requires the finding of one exception to make them vanish like soap bubbles. What if we succeeded in finding one Arab woman head of state? If we unearthed one or two Arab queens, we would be confronted by another question: Why have they been wiped out of history? Why does no one want to remember that there have been Arab women heads of state?

It is understandable that a non-Arab like the historian Uçok Un, who wrote in the 1940s at a time when the Arab world was just beginning to emerge from a long period of Ottoman domination, could advance a colonizing theory that gives the Ottomans the best role. Nevertheless, there have been Arab queens, and, incredible as it may seem, they have been consigned to oblivion. What do they represent that is so dangerous, so deeply disturbing that it was decided to bury them in the depths of the unconscious?

PART III

The Arab Queens

7
The Shi'ite Dynasty of Yemen

———••✦✦✦✦✦✦✦✦••✦•✦——

Yemen is exceptional in the Arab world, not because many women exercised political power there, but because two of them, Malika Asma and Malika 'Arwa, enjoyed the privilege and unquestioned criterion of a head of state: the *khutba* proclaimed in their name in the mosques. No other Arab woman had this honour in any Arab country after the advent of Islam.

Asma Bint Shihab al-Sulayhiyya, who died in 480/1087, governed Yemen with her husband, 'Ali Ibn Muhammad al-Sulayhi, founder of the dynasty that bears his name. Asma claimed the attention of the historians not only because she held power, which, as we shall soon see, was not as rare as one might think, but first and foremost because she 'attended councils with her "face uncovered" ' – that is, unveiled; and then because 'the *khutba* was proclaimed from the pulpits of the mosques of Yemen in her husband's name and in her name.'[1]

The second queen is 'Arwa Bint Ahmad al-Sulayhiyya, who also had the right to have the *khutba* pronounced in her name, which was the unquestioned criterion of a head of state. She was the daughter-in-law of Asma, the wife of her son al-Mukarram, who carried on his father's tradition and shared power with his wife. 'Arwa held power for almost half a century (from 485/1091 to her death in 532/1138).[2] The two queens bore the same royal title: *al-sayyida al-hurra*, meaning 'The noble lady who is free and independent; the woman sovereign who bows to no superior authority'. We know the precise wording used by the believers all over Yemen when the *khutba* was said in 'Arwa's name: 'May Allah prolong the days of al-Hurra the perfect, the sovereign who carefully manages the affairs of the faithful.'[3]

As we have seen, it frequently happened that women took over political power from the men with whom they shared their life. But it is exceptional in the Arab part of the Muslim Empire that the *khutba* should be preached in their name. So what is the secret behind the privilege enjoyed by these queens of Yemen?[4]

The most fascinating historical fact about Asma and 'Arwa, who effectively passed power from one to the other during a good part of the century-long reign of the Sulayhi dynasty, is the complete amnesia that afflicts people today. No one remembers them! No one has ever heard of them! A colleague of mine, a historian who specializes in the Middle Ages, whom I consulted at the beginning of my research for information on this subject, was very sceptical. Arab women heads of state? Are you not mistaken about the area? When I recited to him the form used when the *khutba* was proclaimed in 'Arwa's name, he asked me with disconcerting conviction: 'Didn't you read that story in the *Arabian Nights*?' Still more surprising is that this amnesia affects even Western historians, who seemingly should not be at all threatened by the Arab woman/power connection. With an assurance that recalls to mind the ayatollahs, Bernard Lewis affirms that 'there are no queens in Islamic history, and the word "queen", where it occurs, is used only of foreign rulers in Byzantium or in Europe. There are a few instances where Muslim dynastic thrones were briefly occupied by women, but this was perceived as an aberration and condemned as an offense.'[5]

This type of categorical statement by brilliant Islamic scholars of the stature of Bernard Lewis confirms just one thing: Muslim women in general, and Arab women in particular, cannot count on anyone, scholar or not, 'involved' or 'neutral', to read *their* history for them. Reading it for themselves is entirely their responsibility and their duty. Our demand for the full and complete enjoyment of our universal human rights, here and now, requires us to take over our history, to reread it, and to reconstruct a wide-open Muslim past. This duty, moreover, can turn out to be no drab, disagreeable task, but rather a journey filled with delight. And what is even more important, excursions into our past can not only divert and instruct us, but also give us precious ideas about how to find happiness in life as a woman, a Muslim, and an Arab – those three characterizations that they try to pin on us as a maleficent triad, an abyss of submission and abnegation in which our own wishes must inevitably be drowned. The journey into the past in search of these forgotten queens invites us to take another look at what was inculcated into us in our adolescence, such as the idea that in order to please men one has to swoon away in a pretty gesture of submission and constantly show that one is frail and defenceless. Any show of our strength and power would supposedly be immediately punished by the unconditional withdrawal of their love. The history of the Yemeni queens tells us that that is all rubbish. The pleasures of love can be combined with the conquest of power. Asma and 'Arwa, as women, were actively involved in the transformation of their own lives and that of their community and the world around them.

The Yemeni historians, modern as well as ancient, do not refer to the reigns of these *malikaat* (queens) as 'scandalous', but rather as prestigious and, above all, prosperous moments in their history. A contemporary Yemeni, 'Abdallah al-Thawr, clearly affirms that the reign of Malika 'Arwa was a particularly beneficent and peaceful period in the history of Yemen. 'It is enough for an honest historian to compare the reign of the imams . . . to the relatively very short period of the reign of a Yemeni woman who held fast to her principles, loved her people, and was faithful to them, namely Sayyida 'Arwa Bint Ahmad al-Sulayhiyya,' he confesses in reflecting on the recent history of San'a, which was governed by imams from 1000/1591 to 1343/1925. In fact the imams did not lose power completely until the recent revolution and the establishment of the republic in 1969. He notes that 'Arwa 'left monuments, buildings, roads, mosques – far more things than a long period of power by the imams was able to accumulate'.[6] The determining factor in the historical amnesia seems to be geocultural: not all the Arabs forget the same things. What they forget depends on the national context, on regional memory. The Yemeni historians seem to have fewer memory gaps on the subject of women and power than do the others. On the contrary, they are proud to claim that they had women rulers in the past. This little detail indicates the special regional memories in the Muslim world in general, and the particular Arab memories in the various regions. The Indonesian Muslim memory is certainly different from the Moroccan or Senegalese Muslim memory. And, among the Arabs, it will be fascinating to explore what events and which historical persons constitute the landmarks and key persons of regional cultural identity. If the modern Yemeni historians have no problem in proudly claiming a woman sovereign as a great head of state and affirming, after an analysis of the facts, that she was politically much more competent than a number of imams, why do other Arab historians have trouble in doing so? What is special about the relationship of the Yemenis to women as a basic element of their history? Is it the pre-eminence of the female element in the ancient cults and religions? Is the memory of the legendary queen of Sheba as persistent as the bewitching perfumes of the region? Is it the fact that back at the dawn of time the Shebans practised polyandry? Trying to answer these questions would certainly lead us along paths full of surprises, but too far from our current objective, which is to clarify the reasons for the amnesia. Why does an *hijab* veil the recollection of the queens Asma and 'Arwa? What ghosts, what phantoms, what thoughts, what anxieties would their memory awaken?

I am led to believe that the fearful ghost that the memory of Asma and 'Arwa rouses is that of *shi'a* – meaning political dispute linked to a very particular violence, violence in the name of Allah. This is a dispute which destabilizes political power at its most fundamental point, its legitimacy, which is by nature sacred – and all this in the name of religion. For centuries *shi'a* shook the foundations of Sunni Islam in its claim to be a totalitarian orthodoxy, its dream of a powerful empire in which unity and prosperity went hand in hand and were inconceivable in any other way. The sudden irruption of Shi'ite Islam on to the international scene with the accession of Imam Khomeini to power during the 1970s led to the Iran–Iraq war which, perhaps with modern missiles but also with feelings as old as Islam itself, killed thousands of Muslims. The aftermath may not be the best time to stir up certain memories; amnesia is exactly what is wanted by all those who do not want to probe into this problem. And the problem is the development of democracy in Islam. The Sunni–Shi'ite conflict is nothing but a long, sad, aborted dialogue on the question of representation and power. Aborted dialogue always sweeps the frustrated disputants into a violent blood bath. Therefore one can understand their deliberate attempt to heal wounds by taking refuge in forgetfulness so as to avoid thinking about history and the failed dialogue between Sunni and Shi'ite, for it reflects credit on no one. But today, for us as Muslim men and women, remembering the price paid in blood for failed dialogue by our ancestors can only benefit us. Today, when fanaticism reigns more strongly than ever, when the spectre of internecine violence hovers over us, today, when the problem of tolerance and difference of opinion is posed in a fundamental way for all nations, forgetting Asma and 'Arwa means wanting to forget the murderous madness caused by the Sunni–Shi'ite conflict for fifteen centuries. This conflict crushed thousands, maybe millions, of Muslims of all races and ranks, since princes and soldiers were its victims, and men and women, adults and children perished in it. Both Asma and 'Arwa were Shi'ites. And this small fact would explain the wide, sometimes abysmal gaps in memory. Starting out in all innocence in search of them in the libraries of Rabat (musty in autumn), I entered a realm which all those not concerned with the memory of a libertarian Islam want to forget. It was a realm in which the population, in search of justice, repudiated the legitimacy of the Abbasids of Baghdad and so of Sunnism. They threw themselves heart and soul into an adventure which at that moment represented a revolutionary alternative – Isma'ili Shi'ism – and they did this by giving power to the Sulayhi family.

The Sulayhis appeared in Yemen, a tyranically governed province of the Umayyad (later Abbasid) empire, as heirs of the promise of revolution and the ideal of national independence. 'Ali al-Sulayhi was able to impose his rule without difficulty, as he was both a Shi'ite imam and a descendant of the prestigious pre-Islamic sovereigns of the realm of Sheba. His family history went back to the Yam clan of the Hamdan tribe, a name which appears in Sheban inscriptions.[7] In many Arab countries with a culture different from that of the tribes of Mecca and Medina, the Prophet's native town and adopted town, Islamicization had come as the invasion of a foreign power. The governors were named and sent by the central power without any input from the conquered population, and this created a gulf of non-communication and frustration between the emissaries of the Muslim capital and the local elites.

Muslim history is, among other things, a chronicle of excesses by the governors and revolts by the local populations, which always systematically took on the look of religious conflict. From the time of the Prophet the Yemeni people resisted by setting up their own prophets in opposition to him. Of these the most famous is Musaylima al-Kadhdhab (Musaylima the liar). After the death of the Prophet Muhammad, Yemen was one of the centres of *ridda*, the apostasy movement, and the first orthodox caliph, Abu Bakr, mobilized his whole army in order to bring this country back to the Muslim faith. Very quickly thereafter the challenge to the central despotism took on the vitriolic aspect of Shi'ism. This development occurred in many regions. Yemen was its pioneer, and had the honour of endowing the Muslim political scene with the 'brains' of Shi'ite subversion, 'Abdallah Ibn Saba, a professional agitator next to whom the devil looks like a rank amateur.

Saba had legendary powers of persuasion when it came to subversion. He is credited with the crime of having launched many heretical ideals in Islam, and, above all, with being the first to come up with the idea of fighting official power initially with propaganda and only later with weapons. According to Tabari, he was 'a Jew from San'a whose mother was black and who was converted to Islam during the reign of 'Uthman'. That puts us in the seventh century during the reign of the third orthodox caliph, when the wrath of the people of Yemen, Egypt, and Iraq was stirred up by the excesses and inefficiency of his governors. In the eyes of Tabari this was assuredly not enough to inspire ideas of revolt. 'Abdallah Ibn Saba is accused of having drawn his ideas not from daily frustrations and injustices, but from books by the enemies of Islam: 'He had read the ancient works and was very learned.'[8]

One of the ideas foreign to Islam that he revealed to his followers was the heretical notion of the return of the Prophet: 'The Christians say that Jesus will return to this world. But the Muslims have even more right to claim that Muhammad will return for it is said in the Koran: "Lo! He who hath given thee the Qur'an for a law will surely bring thee home again" [sura 28, verse 85].'[9] Saba was an innovator : he systematically used the idea of a revolt against official power in the name of 'Ali; and he set the world on fire by thinking up a propaganda model that later became a classic and is still used today. This method was to recruit people into small groups conditioned to oppose the established regime, with totally secret initiation followed by action, including violence if needed.

It is supposed to have been Saba who first had the idea of deposing Caliph 'Uthman and putting 'Ali, the Prophet's cousin, in his place: 'Uthman,' he told them, 'acceded to power when he had no right to, since the Prophet had chosen 'Ali as his successor. So begin by spreading this idea, take action, go right after the reigning princes.'[10] It was thus, according to Tabari and many other Sunni historians, that the idea of *shi'a* (dissension, schism, breakaway) began – in the mind of an ex-Jew from Yemen, 'who became a Muslim and journeyed throughout the Muslim countries with the aim of leading them astray. He went first to Hijaz, then to Basra, then Kufa, and then to Shams [Syria]. He was unable to achieve what he wanted in Shams. The Syrians turned him out. Then he went to Egypt.'[11] And it was in Egypt that he gathered around him a whole flock of followers whom he completely won over to his ideas. Saba's ideas led directly to the murder of 'Uthman and to the first civil war in 36/656, which shattered the unity of Islam by splitting the faithful into Sunnis and Shi'ites: 'Having been seduced by the doctrine of the second coming of the Prophet and of the right of 'Ali to have the authority . . . they declared 'Uthman an infidel. But they kept this belief secret, while publicly preaching the duty to do good.'[12] Thus began the round of violence.

As one might imagine, understanding the *shi'a* phenomenon was, and still is, a vital matter for the Sunnis. The texts about it are legion, and throughout the centuries the most brilliant minds have tried to understand this very powerful and persistent form of political opposition in which violence and religion are intimately linked. Contrary to certain orientalists, who limit themselves to describing the Arabs as fanatics by stupidly condemning Shi'ism, our historians have tried to analyse this movement from a Sunni perspective, and their attempts have not been as narrow-minded as one might expect. It is true that in the writings of modern historians 'Abdallah Ibn Saba still wears his devil's turban, but their approach to Shi'ism is carefully nuanced and has nothing in common with the crude condemnations of the ancient chroniclers.[13] The contemporary historians Ahmad Amin and Abu Zahra, who have access to much more information and a better perspective than Tabari, advance extremely well-considered explanations of Shi'ism. They bring out various reasons for its introduction into Islam, notably the ethnic and regional elements, the class interests, and finally the individual motivations, thereby clarifying the sociological and psychological dimension of Shi'ism. Although *shi'a* had an undeniable attraction for different individuals and groups in various countries, the motivations were not always the same. Like any other political party, the *shi'a* party (*hizb*) brought together authentic activists and some opportunists. Among the Shi'ites and their leaders there were those who hated the central power, initially the Umayyads and then the Abbasids, because they felt themselves to be the object of injustice. Among the Arabs there were those who opposed the Umayyads for purely tribal reasons: since the Umayyads were in power, tribal law required that they be against them. There were also many *muwali* (non-Arabs converted to Islam) who declared themselves Shi'ites because the supremacy of the aristocracy reduced their chances for advancement. Another reason suggested by Ahmad Amin is simply the desire on the part of non-Muslims to destroy Islam, which threatened them and with which they were in competition. This is a desire that one understands very well today when one looks at how news of the Muslim world is reported by Western television.

And finally there is the Persian component of Shi'ism, which questions a fundamental principle of Arab Islam: the principle of the
equality of all.

Many Persians became Shi'ites, Ahmad Amin tells us. In their
culture they were used to the cult of royalty: royalty is sacred; the
blood of kings is different from that which flows in the veins of the
people. This is an idea that is absolutely foreign to Arab civilization,
which without denying the existence of social hierarchies links them
to the power of the strongest and not to a superiority of blood.[14]
When they became Muslims, the Persians took from the Prophet a
Caesarist idea. For them, the descendants of the Prophet were like
the descendants of the ancient kings of Persia, sacred beings. When
the Prophet died, only his descendants, the 'people of his house'
(*ahl al-bayt*), were in a position to replace him. Only the descendants
of his daughter Fatima and 'Ali could lead a community of Muslims;
all others could only be imposters. From this came the incredible
fixation on genealogical descent by the Shi'ite pretenders to power,
a fixation that clashes with the egalitarian message of Islam. This
message stresses that only the quality of an individual's faith can
legitimately be claimed as establishing his or her superiority over
another. Who your father or your mother was becomes an insignifi-
cant question in Sunni Islam – at least in principle. In the eyes of
the Prophet, putting an end to the arrogance of the tribal aristocracy
of pre-Islamic Arabia and curtailing its hegemonic ambitions was a
fundamental part of the religion he professed. By resisting pressure
and appointing slaves to high-level commands in his army, which at
the outset had been made up of bold aristocratic members of the
tribe of Quraysh, the Prophet demonstrated the importance he
attached to the question of establishing a meritocracy as an alternative to the aristocracy.[15] And there we have a fundamental difference between the Sunni meritocratic conception of the political
leader and the aristocratic conception of Shi'ism.

We must halt here for a moment to explore with Ibn Manzur
(born in Cairo in 630/1232 and died in 711/1311), the author of the
Lisan al-'Arab (Language of the Arabs), the etymology of the word
shi'a.[16] Leafing through a thirteenth-century dictionary plunges us
into the deep layers of the language that dictates our more or less
unconscious contemporary conception of the right to differ and of
dialogue in the political arena with someone who does not have the
same ideas. Above all else, the Sunni–Shi'ite conflict raises the
question of democracy – that is, the ability of a Muslim society to

ensure the right to expression and the interests of groups having differing opinions and dissonant visions of people and power.

The word *shi'a* means first of all *firaq*, 'groups that rally to a common idea': 'Every group of people who rally together around an idea are called *shi'a*.' Here also is found the idea of following and of inciting. And every group that rallies around a leader and an idea is called *shi'a* because, Ibn Manzur tells us, 'the root word *shi'a* means both to follow [*taba'a*] and to enforce obedience [*tawa'a*]. Thus one of the words for wife is *sha'at al-rajul*, she being the *sha'a* of a man because she "follows him and gives him her support".' Ibn Manzur expatiates on the association of the word *shi'a* with the idea of a flock (*shay'at al-ghanam*): '*Shi'a* is the sound emitted by the shepherd's pipe, as it is with this instrument that he calls the flock together.'

The second key idea, just as fundamental, is the idea of differing: '*Shi'a* refers to groups that are not in agreement. The *shi'a* are those who see things differently.' This idea of differing was applied at that time to a very specific category: the Jewish and Christian sects:

Allah said in the Koran: *al-ladina farraqu dinahum wa kanu shi'an* [those who split their religion and became sects]. Allah refers here to the Jews and Christians, because the Jews, like the Christians, are formed of groups that declare each other heretical. Even more, the Jews call the Christians nonbelievers and vice versa although at the beginning they received the same message.

In modern Arabic there is an alternative word to *shi'a* for referring to a political group that has a differing vision of things – the word *hizb*. This word also has nothing to do with parliamentary democracy. It carries with it very ambiguous feelings about the right to differ. Like *shi'a*, *hizb* means 'a group united around an idea', with the connotation of differing as necessarily negative and destructive – something that should make us think a bit about the political terminology that we use every day. The word *hizb*, which is used throughout the Arab world to designate a political party in the modern – that is, Western – sense, refers to 'any group in which hearts are united and which initiates a common action'. But in the beginning it was also *al-ahzab*, 'those who gave the title to a sura of the Koran and who were the enemies of the Prophet', *junud al-kuffar* (the armies of the infidels), 'those who are in league against the Prophet and plotted against him'.[17]

The third key meaning expressed in the word *shi'a* is 'setting fire', which implants in our mind the idea of conflict and destruction. It is even the definition of a fanatic, who denies the right to differ. 'Do not use the word *shaya'a*', Ibn Manzur admonishes us, 'to mean "stir up the fire" [*shaya'a al-nar*], that is, to make it flame up by throwing little pieces of wood on it.' In fact, he explains, 'one says *shuyu'* or *shiya'* for the little pieces of wood with which one stirs up the fire.' Finally, he quite logically concludes, by association of these ideas, that *shaya'a al-rajul* means 'to burn a man'.

There is still the fourth key idea: *shi'a* as the dissemination of a secret. This dimension will show us the place of clandestine indoctrination and initiation of the adherents as necessary techniques for the survival of an opposition. The Shi'ite opposition was known for its cult of secrecy and clandestinity for the new recruit as the sole means to guarantee success. 'Ali, the Yemeni sovereign, husband of Asma and founder of the Sulayhi dynasty, is a perfect example of this. He operated for 15 years in the shadows before coming out as an armed opponent confronting the Sunni caliph of Baghdad.

These ideas of secrecy and clandestine operations, that is, a particularly close control of information and its circulation, are characteristic of any opposition in Islam. In order to understand them better let us return to the invaluable pages of Ibn Manzur: '*shi'a*, to disseminate, is used for a piece of news that circulates among the crowd.'[18] Thus, he explains, *al-sha'a* means 'information that everybody knows about'. The same root is used in modern Arabic to designate the dissemination of light: hence, *ashi'a* (rays of light) and *isha'at* (dissemination of false rumours). To say 'divulge a secret', Ibn Manzur reminds us, there is a word formed from *shi'a*: 'If I say *asha'tu al-sirra*, that means that I have revealed it to others.'

In the eleventh century, at the time of 'Ali al-Sulayhi, Shi'ism was no longer a marginalized political opposition reduced to the clandestine activity that had been its traditional place until then. It took on the status of a true official Shi'ite caliphate established in Cairo, with pomp and rituals hitherto never seen among the Sunnis. This was the Fatimid caliphate, the bitter enemy of the Sunni caliphate of Baghdad. 'Ali, the Yemeni sovereign, was a vassal of the Fatimids of Cairo and, as such, determined to undermine Sunnism. But the secrecy aspect of Shi'ism should not be seen just in terms of its historical status as a marginal opposition. It had to do above all else with its vision of the world, its deepest philosophy.

This is what today gives it its incredible skill in the use of the media and the orchestration of strategies in such a way as to make the moguls of European and American advertising look like sheer beginners.

However, can one say that the Shi'ite phenomenon is an Iranian phenomenon? This is an idea that is obviously very dear to the hearts of many people, above all, to Arabs who insist that subversive ideas are non-Arab, foreign ideas and who simplify even further by insisting that Shi'ism is an Iranian phenomenon. There are also some Western journalists who are ignorant of history and only discovered Shi'ism with the Iranian revolution. They have led millions of Westerners to confuse Shi'ism with Iran. However, *shi'a* is above all an intrinsically Arab phenomenon, even though the contribution of non-Arabs – Iranians and others – is very important, especially from the intellectual point of view. In the fourth century of the Hejira (tenth century AD), Khawarizmi drew attention to the fact that the *watan* of *shi'a*, its birthplace, was Iraq.[19] Only the parts of Persia neighbouring Iraq, which were in contact with Arabs who adopted this doctrine, were Shi'ite.[20] The first officially Shi'ite state opposed to the Sunni caliphate of Baghdad appeared in North Africa, and then in Egypt with the creation of the Fatimid caliphate in the tenth century. They were known as Isma'ilis, referring to Isma'il, one of the descendants of Caliph 'Ali, on whom they based their claim.[21]

Isma'ilism, a major branch of Shi'ism that has survived to this day, is the official religion of several groups of Muslims around the world, notably the Druze of Lebanon and various communities in Asia in places like Bombay, Baroda, and Hyderabad in India. One of these communities became famous when their leaders, the Aga Khans, made headlines in the 1940s by their involvement with stars of Western fashion and movies. The marriage of Prince Ali Khan, the son of an Isma'ili imam, to Rita Hayworth in 1949 became a legend that is still material for the media today: 'In the name of 70 million followers of the Aga Khan, the father of Ali, India and Africa offer Rita 16 kilograms of diamonds and precious stones.'[22]

At the end of the tenth century the Isma'ilis dealt a fatal blow to the Sunni Abbasid caliphate of Baghdad by creating a Shi'ite counter-caliphate in Cairo. Its name, the Fatimid caliphate, refers to Fatima, the Prophet's daughter. Paradoxically in a kinship system that in theory is exclusively male, the lineage passed through his daughter because the Prophet left no male descendants, all his sons having died young. In addition, Fatima was married to his paternal cousin, 'Ali Ibn Abi Talib, to whom she bore two sons, Hasan and Husayn.[23] Because of who their mother was, they were regarded as the only ones carrying on the Prophet's lineage and the only ones having the right to lead the Muslims. Some people claim that Fatima had a third son named al-Muhassan, who died young.[24] All claims of descent from the Prophet must go back to the two children born to Fatima and 'Ali, Hasan and Husayn.

After the death of Fatima, 'Ali married eight women.[25] In order to understand 'Ali's importance in Shi'ism, it is necessary to recall his death even more than his descendants. He died a martyr in an assassination that was politically motivated and meticulously planned, after he had been evicted from power by caliph Mu'awiya. After his death, his children and their descendants were persecuted. The name of 'Ali would forever be associated with injustice, political murder of the innocent, and violation of the message of brotherhood and equality among the Muslims. 'Ali became the symbol around which rallied all those who felt their rights denied or who claimed unjust treatment.[26]

Throughout the centuries political challenge of an established regime has been expressed in Islam in terms of claims of *nasab*, filiation, lineage. Claim of descent is then always contested, as it must be, by one's political opponents. The basic idea of Shi'ism is that only 'Ali, because of his closeness to the Prophet, and his descendants can be as legitimate as the Prophet was. For, although all the caliphs since the death of Muhammad claim descent from one single Quraysh ancestor, their degree of closeness to the Prophet's branch varies considerably. The Umayyads only shared two Quraysh ancestors with him; the Abbasids, closer because they descend from his uncle 'Abbas, share four ancestors with him (Quraysh, 'Abd Manaf, Hashim, and 'Abd al-Muttalib). Only 'Ali was doubly close to the Prophet, as his first cousin (the Prophet's father, 'Abdallah, was the brother of Abu Talib, the father of 'Ali), and as his son-in-law, the husband of Fatima and father of her children. This close ancestral link was the basis of the legitimacy of the Fatimids. It was their authority for establishing a counter-caliphate, which could finally bring into being on earth the hope for a just political regime – that of the Shi'ites. Their strategy was straightforward and systematic: first to form an army of adherents by giving them the essential knowledge; then to transform them into soldiers, which followed naturally afterwards. The Fatimid seizure of power illustrates this process to perfection. The first Fatimid generals who worked in the field were not narrow-minded military men who taught recruits the use of arms; they were great scholars of Shi'ite doctrine, who dazzled the newcomers with their extraordinary vision of a world where human life is secretly entwined with the movement and the wisdom of the stars.

The advent of the Fatimid caliphate, first in North Africa (297/909) and then in Egypt a half-century later (358/969) – major dates in the history of Islam – constitutes the most oustanding political event of the fourth century of the Hejira. The founder of the dynasty, 'Ubayd Allah al-Mahdi, known as al-Mahdi al-Fatimi (259/873–322/934), took power in Africa after his *da'i* (the person charged with *da'wa*, indoctrination), Abu 'Abdallah al-Husayn, counselled him to proceed there. Abu 'Abdallah al-Husayn, the real brains of the Shi'ite conversion project, knew what he was talking about: an area was ready to be conquered by force of arms once its population had been imbued with Shi'ite doctrine, carefully distilled and precisely measured out. Abu 'Abdallah al-Husayn was such an expert *da'i*, a propaganda technocrat, that he was given as a surname just simply 'the Shi'ite'. He had begun his fieldwork in Mecca during the pilgrimage, seeking out the fiercely independent Berber delegations, particularly the Ketama tribesmen, warriors who would become the spearhead of the Fatimid armies. 'Where are the Ketama pilgrims?' he asked in the midst of the sea of humanity which in principle came to pray and call upon Allah.[27] When he had spotted them, he introduced himself and entered discussions with their chieftains. Then came the moment when he raised the crucial question: 'Do you bear arms?' And the Ketama chieftains replied with surprise: 'But that is our occupation!'[28] This was a meeting marked by destiny: the Middle East Shi'ite revolution had found its military troops in the Far West of the Muslim world (*al-maghrib al-aqsa*).

Once the contacts had been made in Mecca, the Yemeni arrived in the Maghrib in 280/893 and began to indoctrinate the Berber tribesmen with the idea of the 'expected mahdi' (*al-mahdi al-muntazar*). Abu 'Abdallah al-Husayn was creating an expectation, the need for an imam able to solve all problems. Once his aim was achieved, the *da'i*/missionary sent his messengers to notify al-Mahdi al-Fatimi, who was living in hiding, to come to North Africa, where he would be enthusiastically received – which proved to be absolutely true, both spiritually and militarily. In year 296, the Fatimid appeared in Sijelmassa and announced that he was the one who was expected, the one who was going to save the world[29] and institute the reign of Muslim justice, which the other caliphs had failed to achieve. All the elements of revolutionary prophecy were now present: the transformation of the world was only a matter of months. At Kairouan in 297 the *bay'a*, the official ceremony of recognition of the sovereign, took place. In year 303 he constructed the city of Mehdia in the vicinity of today's Tunis, and declared it his capital.[30]

In 358/969 Egypt was conquered, and it was there that the Fatimid dynasty was to thrive. North Africa was too distant, too isolated, too westerly. Cairo, on the other hand, offered the new dynasty the possibility of being in the centre of things with unparalleled opportunities for branching out. Henceforth the Muslim world had two caliphs: a Sunni in Baghdad and a Shi'ite in Cairo. Many of the local elites, who wanted to set up independent states and did not want to pay taxes to Baghdad, rallied to the Isma'ilis. The Fatimid dynasty remained in power for two centuries, from the tenth century until almost the end of the twelfth century (567/1171), defying Sunnism, conquering its territories, and allowing its antagonists (for example the Sulayhi dynasty of Yemen) to set up independent states challenging its authority. All this was done in the name of the Prophet and his descendants through 'Ali and Fatima.

One can easily imagine that the lineage of these descendants was violently challenged by the religious authorities in Baghdad. Some even went so far as to say that al-Mahdi al-Fatimi was an impostor of Jewish descent. Ibn al-Athir reports this, but, after a chain of reasoning based on historical facts, arrives at the conclusion that the first Fatimid was indeed a descendant of 'Ali.[31] The struggles between the Sunni caliphs of Baghdad and the Shi'ite caliphs of Cairo were not confined to the field of battle, the concern of the military. Like everything that concerns power in Islam, the secular struggles necessarily had to be accompanied by spiritual struggles that took place in the field of religion and involved armies of intellectuals and religious authorities – *'alim* here, *da'i* there.[32] But although this fourth century of the Hejira allowed the Shi'ites, the perpetual outsiders, to create their own caliphate, to realize the dream of a state led by the ideal imam, the expected imam, the dream soon turned to nightmare, as with many revolutionary prophecies. The people of North Africa, who were the first to have the honour and privilege of realizing the revolutionary dream of a Shi'ite state, rapidly became disenchanted. Massacres of Shi'ites, called *al-mashariqa* (the orientals), took place in Mehdia and Kairouan in 408, that is, less than half a century after the appearance of 'Ubayd Allah al-Mahdi, the first avidly awaited imam. The Shi'ites were

massacred to the last man by the *'amma* (the masses). Ibn al-Athir
tells us: 'Many Shi'ites were killed, and a great number were burned
outright and their houses ransacked. The Shi'ites were hunted to
death all over Africa.'[33] The Sunnis were reinstalled in power
forever on the shores of North Africa. But it was in Egypt that the
dream of the infallible imam led to the atrocities of al-Hakim Ibn
Amri Allah, obliging his sister, Sitt al-Mulk, to save the Muslims
and take power in his place.

We are far indeed from the stereotype of the Shi'ite phenomenon
as a specifically Iranian phenomenon. It was only in the sixteenth
century, with the Safavid dynasty, that Shi'ism was decreed to be
the state religion in Persia. It is true that in the tenth and eleventh
centuries a Shi'ite dynasty had held power in Persia, but, the Buyids
(320/932–447/1055) were never the enemy of the Sunni caliphs of
Baghdad. On the contrary, they showed great respect for them.[34]
It is indisputable that Iraq was the centre of Shi'ism, if only because
of Kufa. This city holds the tomb of 'Ali Ibn Abi Talib, the husband
of Fatima and father of Hasan and Husayn. As the fourth orthodox
caliph, he was assassinated by the first terrorist in the political
history of Islam, who belonged to the sect known as the Kharijites,
literally 'those who quit', dissenters who today would be called
nihilists. 'Ali Ibn Abi Talib – the first victim of organized, clandestine political violence – fell at Kufa, which then became a great
centre of Shi'ism until the fourth century of the Hejira.[35] Another
city, Basra, also became a centre of Shi'ism.[36] As for the Arabian
peninsula, 'in the fourth century it was entirely Shi'ite, except for
the great cities like Mecca, Tuhama, and San'a.'[37] And absolutely
central to the Shi'ite success was the role of Yemen and Yemenis
like Abu 'Abdallah al-Husayn, the brains of the Shi'ite seizure of
power in North Africa, and others like his contemporary, Ibn
Hawshab.[38] And generations later the *da'i* al-Rawahi initiated 'Ali
al-Sulayhi into Shi'ism, using the example of Ibn Hawshab. This
was done when the initiate was still very young and without the
knowledge of his parents, as we shall see. And with 'Ali al-Sulayhi,
who later became the husband of Queen Asma, the three cities
which had eluded the Shi'ites – Mecca, Tuhama, and San'a – fell
into their hands.

The Shi'ism of the time of the Yemeni queens Asma and 'Arwa
was no longer just a dissident movement of scattered sects, attracting
little groups of malcontents and outsiders. It was now a powerful
state, mobilizing all its power from Cairo and in the name of the
Prophet orchestrating the destruction of Sunnism and its caliphate

on an international scale. Following in the footsteps of the Fatimids, 'Ali al-Sulayhi, the husband of Asma and father-in-law of 'Arwa, took power and created a dynasty that reigned in Yemen for a century (429/1037 to 532/1138). From his masters in Cairo he received precise instructions, according to the quasi-militaristic code of the Isma'ilis, on how to manage his political career. He was closely instructed on how much secrecy and how much openness to adopt, the number of persons to confide in at each stage, and the precise moment to assert his authority as a military force.[39]

For 15 years 'Ali al-Sulayhi was seen as an extremely cultivated man whose occupation was to escort groups of pilgrims making the annual pilgrimage from Yemen to Mecca.[40] Rare were those who knew that he was actually the heir to the Shi'ite *da'wa* for Yemen, following a deathbed vow to his shaykh and teacher, *da'i* Ibn 'Abdallah al-Rawahi, one of the 'propagators of the Fatimid cause'.[41] 'Abdallah al-Rawahi had received his *da'wa* from his shaykh, Yusif Ibn Ahmad al-Ashh, who had received his from Harun Ibn Rahim, who had received his from Ja'far, the son and heir of Ibn Hawshab.[42] Etymologically *da'a* means 'to invoke, to call upon, to ask for help', often addressed to the divine. The appeal to the divine is so strong that the word *du'a* means just simply 'worship'.[43] But there is also the idea of persuading, of stirring up, especially in the sense of a call to heresy (*dhalala*). And a *da'i*, concludes Ibn Manzur, is 'a man who calls upon others to follow him in *bid'a* (innovation) or *din* (religion), from which comes another connotation of "espousing something that is not true".'[44]

In any case, for the Isma'ili branch of Shi'ism, the *da'i* is one of the ranks in their secret heirarchy, which had seven ranks, according to Ibn al-Nadim (nine, according to others). Ibn al-Nadim, who seems to be one of the authorities on the subject of Isma'ili literature, devoted a chapter to it in his invaluable *Fihris*, an encyclopedic collection of all the important books written by the Muslims up until his time (the fourth century of the Hejira). According to him, their propagandizing was carried out via seven *balagh*, messages, each contained in a *kitab*, an instruction manual which was given to the initiate as he progressed. The first *kitab* was for the *'amma* (common people), Ibn al-Nadim tells us; the second was for the next level reached; and the third was only given to those who had been in the sect for a year. The fourth *balagh* was for those who had been in the sect for two years; the fifth for those who had spent three years; the sixth for those who had been a member for four years. Finally, a member received the seventh *balagh*, which contained the synthesis and great revelation (*al-kashf al-akbar*).[45] The *kashf* is the unveiling of the secret, the ability to see the *batin*, the meaning within, the hidden meaning beyond appearances.[46] Nothing better summarizes this idea of 'the secret' than the declaration (which became almost an adage) of the great Shi'ite imam Ja'far al-Siddiq, who was sixth in the line of imams: 'Our cause is a secret [*sirr*] within a secret, the secret of something that remains veiled, a secret that only another secret can teach; a secret of a secret that is veiled by a secret.'[47] A notable illustration of this phenomenon can be seen in the more or less clandestine initiation of 'Ali al-Sulayhi, which began when he was still a child by a Shi'ite preceptor to whom his Sunni family sent him to learn the fundamentals of the Muslim faith.

'Ali's father, Muhammad Ibn 'Ali al-Sulayhi, was a qadi (judge), very well versed in religious doctrine. He practised his profession on the Massar mountain in Haraz province and was one of the most prominent of its notables. As such, he was visited by local religious personalities, who came to pay him homage. One of his visitors, the Shi'ite *da'i* Amir Ibn 'Abdallah al-Rawahi, who visited him because of 'his piety and his learning', showed a particular interest in 'Ali, then still a young child, whose great promise he perceived. The sources differ on the religious affiliation of 'Ali's father. According to Ibn Khallikan he was Sunni.[48] According to Ibn Imad, the dyed-in-the-wool anti-Shi'ite Hanbali historian (the Hanbalis were known for their strictness), the qadi held 'perverted beliefs', which in his vocabulary meant Shi'ite beliefs plain and simple.[49] In any case, during these visits Al-Rawahi showed such pleasure in talking to the qadi's child that the youngster was entrusted to his care for instruction. He became 'Ali's tutor. Among the key messages that he imprinted on the child's mind was that Yemen was just waiting for him, 'Ali, the predestined hero, to lead it to a marvellous future. Al-Rawahi was convinced that 'Ali was an exceptional being who had been portrayed in a very precious ancient book, *Kitab al-suwar*, that made it possible to know the future and foresee coming events.[50] This treasured book was only one among several that were part of al-Rawahi's library, which, as trustee of the Shi'ite mission, he was supposed to pass on to the one who would carry on his secret work.[51] And he was absolutely convinced that no one was worthier of the task of propagating and defending the Shi'ite faith in Yemen than 'Ali, the child with the prodigious intellect. Al-Rawahi revealed nothing of his ideas and projects to the father, who suspected nothing. But one day al-Rawahi, having a foreboding of his impending death and eager to make arrangements for his successor, decided to confide his secret to 'Ali. He revealed to him his true identity, informing him that he was the *da'i*, the missionary-trustee of the Shi'ite *da'wa*; he told him about his *madhab* (school, doctrine) and began 'to initiate him although he had not yet attained the age of puberty'.[52]

The child was worthy of his master's confidence. He guarded the secret well and confided in no one, not even his own father. Shortly before his death, al-Rawahi designated him as the *wasi* (heir of his mission) and inheritor of his library.[53] 'Ali began to study the books, and 'with his great intelligence he became very well versed in the doctrines of the Isma'ilis.'[54] His hierarchical superior was the Shi'ite caliph in Cairo. He had to report his political projects to him. Very soon 'Ali's reputation as a brilliant scholar, with wide knowledge of Shi'ite doctrine, got around the whole country. Yemen, divided by religious conflicts, was awaiting its imam, the saviour whom the ancient books had promised. But 'Ali did not succumb to the vanity of celebrity. His instructions had been to begin his work in secret. He would know, as events unfolded, when he should come out of the shadow and proclaim his dreams and intentions to the world.

What was he to do while awaiting his destiny? What occupation should one pursue when one is the son of a qadi and extremely well versed in religious doctrine, and when one is charged with a mission that requires contact with the greatest number of people? There was one occupation to fit all the requirements – escorting groups of pilgrims to Mecca. This work demanded both intellectual and military abilities, because the leader had to conduct the caravans from Yemen safely to Mecca along very hazardous routes. 'Ali's job as guide of annual groups of pilgrims to Mecca was made to measure. It was a prestigious occupation, a more than adequate means of subsistence, and above all a unique opportunity to meet people and chat with them during the long starry nights on the journey to the holy sites.[55] For 15 years 'Ali secretly carried out 'propaganda for the Fatimid Isma'ili caliph al-Mustansir, who held Egypt'.[56] The pilgrimage is the ideal place for a propagandist. It is an enormous assemblage of leaders from many countries, and affords a unique occasion for exchanging information, drawing up contracts, and forming alliances with all parts of the Muslim world.

It should not be forgotten that this is the way Islam began four centuries earlier. Muhammad, a Meccan of the Quraysh aristocracy, in the prime of life, barely in his forties, sought a hearing for his new message, an audience for his new religion in the crowd of pilgrims who were celebrating the pagan rites around the Ka'ba. Where would one find supporters for a message destined to revolutionize the world if not in the huge crowd of pilgrims from everywhere as they came together in the confines of the Ka'ba, the heart of Mecca, the holy place where the divine has manifested itself since time immemorial? Thus it has been since the time of the Prophet; thus it was in the time of 'Ali al-Sulayhi centuries later; and thus it still is, as witness live-televised events such as Iranian pilgrims battling Saudi security forces, which from time to time remind us that in Mecca at least nothing is more political than the sacred. And this close link between the political and the sacred in the Arab world dates from before Islam. Al-Baghdadi (died in year 245 of the Hejira, the ninth century), one of the rare Arab historians who wrote about the pre-Islamic religions in his invaluable book *Kitab al-mukhabbar*, reminds us that the pilgrimage to Mecca was part of the traditions that existed in the *jahiliyya* and was retained by Islam: 'They [the Arabs before Islam] made the pilgrimage; they made the circuits around the *bayt* [the sanctuary of the Ka'ba] for a week; they touched the black stone and continued their march between Safa and Marwa.'[57] The only difference is that before Islam, during the pagan pre-Islamic era, each group of Arabs made the circuit around the Ka'ba while calling upon a specific god or goddess. The idea of the Muslim Prophet was that all the pilgrims make the circuit calling upon one single God – Allah. His dream of Arab unity and strength was necessarily connected to religious unification: to worship the same God and thus have the same leader. This was a threatening revolutionary idea that resulted in his being persecuted as a danger to polytheistic Mecca. And where was he to find allies if not there, at the place of worship, where people gathered by the thousands? The Prophet Muhammad took to awaiting the annual pilgrimage in order to propose his new religion to the pilgrims, who were usually tribal leaders from all over Arabia. It was only after several failed attempts that he persuaded the party from Medina to agree to sponsor his cause and invite him to come and preach his new religion in their city. The move from Mecca to Medina is called *al-hijra* (known in English as the Hejira), and this became the beginning of the Muslim calendar, which starts in the year AD 622, the year when the people of Medina received the Meccan Prophet after he had been driven out of his native city by those in power.[58] The incredible success of the Prophet of Islam is in itself a lesson in political strategy, in which everything took place around the most eminently sacred site, the sanctuary of the Ka'ba.

So 'Ali al-Sulayhi was in no way an innovator. If the Yemeni *da'i* spent 15 years doing discreet propaganda work, hidden behind his job as a guide for pilgrims, it was because he was preparing a masterly coup. This was to follow up the conquest of Yemen for the Isma'ili Shi'ite cause, which was incarnated in the Fatimid sovereign of Egypt, with the conquest of Mecca. It is obvious that his personality made a big impression through 'his determination, his intelligence, his courage, and his eloquence'. 'Ali, the man who would dazzle Queen Asma, already shone as a spiritual leader. 'It was said that this man was going to conquer Yemen, but he "hated those rumours".'[59]

It was not until the year 429 that he thought the moment had come when he 'should unveil his mission, after having asked authorization from Caliph al-Mustansir, which was granted.'[60] We have seen that the hierarchy of Isma'ili Shi'ism is extremely precise, with each grade having to refer matters to its superior. As *da'i*, 'Ali al-Sulayhi took his orders from the supreme authority, who was the imam in person, and according to the Shi'ite hierarchy that was none other than the Fatimid sovereign of Egypt. Moreover, under the Sulayhis the *khutba* in the mosques of Yemen was proclaimed first in the name of the Egyptian caliph, al-Mustansir (428/1036–487/1087), and then in the name of the Yemeni sovereigns and their spouses. Once authorized to reveal his mission and its military objectives, 'Ali 'embarked on the conquest of the country and toppled the fortresses one after the other with incredible speed'.[61] He made San'a his capital, but it was his occupation of Mecca in 455/1064 that gained him international fame.[62] Among the outstanding events of year 455/1064, Ibn al-Athir mentions the conquest of Mecca by 'Ali al-Sulayhi, the sovereign of Yemen, who had conquered it, re-established order, and governed it well: 'He put an end to injustice, reorganized the supply system, and increased the acts of beneficence.'[63] In the space of a few months he demonstrated his qualities as a statesman and soldier, to the great delight of his compatriots.

Torn by dissension and clan rivalries, Yemen had need of a national hero with whom it could identify and in whom it could recognize itself with pride. 'Ali al-Sulayhi was the perfect Arab hero – with physical vigour and endurance, confidence in himself, and fearlessness, allied to that intellectual agility so characteristic of learned people who are loved and as a result feel no need to be conspicuous and try to outshine others. Raised by his Shi'ite masters with the idea that the people's happiness depended on the success of his enterprise, 'Ali had that intense manner of silent attention combined with detachment of the true political leader. Such a leader is there to receive us and not harangue us, to listen and not just give orders, to synthesize our ideas and problems and not depreciate them; his charisma is enchanced by the brilliance of those around him, not by their self-effacement. We see ourselves in such a leader, and he enchants us. The citadel at San'a soon became a gathering place for all the chiefs of the rival clans, invited to come and sit together and voice their opinions. In fact, following an ancient Yemeni custom, which would survive until the proclamation of the Republic of Yemen in 1969, 'Ali kept all the conquered princes at his side.[64] He constructed palaces in San'a for them, close to his own, and thus made them participate in the running of the country – a peaceful way of neutralizing political opponents that one scarcely finds on the contemporary Arab scene.[65] In under three years Yemen was transferred from a zone of internal discord and divisions into a prosperous country where the safety of the roads assured and reflected the country's prosperity.

In 458/1066 'Ali decided to undertake a journey that was dear to his heart, a journey that would be the crowning event of his career: a pilgrimage to Mecca with all the pomp and ceremony that would recall to Muslims the grandeur of their ancestors, when in the time of the Prophet he and his Companions saw advancing toward them in the dusty streets of Medina the delegations from San'a, come like all the others to swear the oath of allegiance. The sovereigns of Yemen stood out from all the others with their crowned heads and cloaks of fabulous weaves, and with their gold-harnessed mounts. And what better place, for a Muslim head of state who wanted to exhibit his power on the international scene, than Mecca with its huge crowds? The pilgrimage drew the common people, it is true, but at this time in history the caravans of pilgrims often had the look of an official cortege and in some years were led by the heads of state themselves or their heir apparent. They consisted of enormous retinues that spent whole weeks *en route* and as a result required painstaking organization, not just of supplies, but also of diplomatic and sometimes military arrangements to ensure security during the crossing of various territories that were not always friendly. As a matter of fact, the safe and sound arrival of the caravan of a given country in Mecca was in itself proof of its military power and prosperity. The Fatimids out-manoeuvred the caliphate of Baghdad by sowing turmoil and civil wars in the provinces that the caravan from Iraq was traversing, and this impeded its arrival in the holy city on the day of the *'id* (feast day). The pilgrims thus knew that something grave had taken place. It was at Mecca that subversives declared their revolt, and it was at Mecca that reconciliations were made official. Heart and mirror of a Muslim world where fraternity was supposed to reign, Mecca reflected the least tremblings of trouble and reverberated with its problems, its unrest, and its stresses.

'Ali was convinced that the year 458/1066 was the year of his greatest happiness and achievement. What he did not know was that the stars had decided that that year would also be the year of his tragic death – as unexpected as the premonition of misfortune in those moments of euphoria when we feel giddy with success. He had forgotten about hate and those who made a career of it. He had forgotten the Banu Najah, the masters of Zubayd, the only principality which still resisted him, one of the few where he had resorted to political murder. The Banu Najah were a family of former Ethiopian slaves who pursued a pitiless vendetta against the Sulayhis.[66] The history of Yemen has always been marked by Ethiopian invasions, and the comings and goings between the two countries, whether it be armies or merchants, go back to the dawn of time. Moreover, a large part of the Sulayhi army was made up of Ethiopian soldiers. The Banu Najah had never forgotten the murder of their father, ordered from San'a by 'Ali – a murder accompanied by the sweet smile of a charming and talented *jarya*, carefully chosen from among hundreds of candidates and dispatched by 'Ali to Zubayd with the order to seduce and poison him. The *jarya* arrived in the city of the Banu Najah with nothing in her baggage but a lute and a vial of poison hidden among some poems to be sung. Her success in reaching the bed of the chief was never in doubt.[67] Zubayd awoke one morning grief-stricken by a death that had struck the palace at its very core. The sons of the poisoned sovereign, especially Sa'id Ibn Najah, pledged themselves to revenge. The higher the Sulayhi star rose, the easier was the task of keeping watch on it.

When 'Ali left San'a with his wife Asma at his side to head for the holy city, Sa'id Ibn Najah already knew what route he would take. But this time the caravan was more impressive than in previous times. 'Ali was no longer at the head of a modest group of simple pilgrims. He was leading a splendid caravan of princes and notable horsemen, which was evidence both of his dazzling rise and of the military objectives of his journey: to reaffirm that Mecca was more than ever within the Shi'ite orbit. The fate of the holy place, site of the struggles between Baghdad and Cairo, between Sunnis and Shi'ites, fluctuated between the fleeting triumph of the one and the short-lived defeat of the other. The Yemeni leader wanted to repeat in Mecca what he had accomplished three years before – have the *khutba* pronounced in the name of the Fatimids of Egypt and make himself admired as the military and spiritual leader capable of such a miracle.[68]

'Ali's caravan was made up of a thousand horsemen of whom a hundred were of the Sulayhi family, a force of 5,000 Ethiopians, and all the Yemeni princes whom 'Ali had conquered during his battles for the unification of Yemen and who had lived since then at his side in the palace at San'a.[69] As a security measure and to make them participants in his schemes, 'Ali had demanded that the latter accompany him to Mecca. Asma, his wife, was on the journey, and, as protocol dictated, she was accompanied by her own court, hundreds of *jawari* clothed in rich garments.[70] 'Ali had designated al-Mukarram, his son who was married to 'Arwa, to take his place during his absence.[71] The caravan began its journey with a great show of luxury and power, and the news spread throughout the country that the Sulayhi was *en route* to Mecca.

Many Sunnis must have thought about the Karmatis as they watched the glittering caravan of 'Ali and Asma pass by. The Karmatis were the sowers of death and destruction whose name has become synonymous with blasphemy. They were an extremist Shi'ite sect which had attacked pilgrims a century earlier in 317/930, an attack that no Muslim will ever forget despite the passage of time. The Shi'ites, and especially 'Ali always had great trouble dissociating themselves from the memory of the Karmatis, who had been officially disavowed by the Fatimids. But any Shi'ite caravan, displaying force and power, revived the horrifying memory of the Karmatis entering Mecca, profaning the sanctuary of the Ka'ba, stripping it of its *kaswa* (precious veils), and carrying off the famous Black Stone.[72] Although it is true that all this happened generations before 'Ali and Asma, one of the most striking characteristics of traumatizing events is that the passage of time never dulls them: 'That year no one completed the ritual of the pilgrimage. The dead were estimated at 30,000, and just as many women and children were taken as prisoners of war and reduced to slavery.'[73] The Karmatis held the Black Stone, so imbued with symbolism, for more than 20 years and only returned it to its place under pressure from the Fatimids, to whom these rebels had once given allegiance. Isma'ili diplomacy always made great efforts to blot out the memory of that incident during the pilgrimages, but any unusual deployment of Shi'ite caravans toward Mecca revived it. On that day in the oases between San'a and Mecca the splendour of 'Ali al-Sulayhi's caravan was reflected in the dazzled eyes of the children.

The royal caravan was moving slowly over the silent sands when suddenly an order was given to stop at a watering place named Bir Umm Ma'bad. Sa'id Ibn Najah was spying on the caravan from a distance with the clear view that is only possible in the great deserts. It seemed that 'Ali, the murderer of his father, was going to rest a while at this watering place. The strange thing is that it was 'Ali himself who had insisted on halting there, unknowingly choosing the place where, as fate would have it, day would never break for him again. Because of his studies with his Shi'ite teachers, he knew better than anyone the detailed history of the Prophet's travels in this region. Yet he was convinced (wrongly, as was later proved) that the Prophet had stopped at Umm Ma'bad five centuries earlier, and so he stopped there. It was an absurd conviction that dressed death in the enchanting robes of a memory that partook not of reality but of the fascination of dreams!

When the news of the tragedy reached San'a, the grief-stricken populace looked in vain for the woman whom 'Ali loved so much, but no trace of al-Hurra Asma was found. San'a searched long and hard for its queen, and its armies went on the offensive to find her and take revenge on those who had taken her captive. When Asma was finally freed and returned to San'a, it was from her that her son al-Mukarram took his orders. And when he fell ill, it was to his wife 'Arwa that the people turned in search of leadership in building the future.

8
The Little Queens of Sheba

———————

An Arab people ruled by a queen, happy to be so, and adoring their queen: is this not a surrealistic idea in a modern Arab world in which our men, somewhat overwrought by the electronic revolution, nervously advise us to put on the veil, as if such a move was going miraculously to stabilize our debt-ravaged economies? Covering up women and their power did not seem a major concern of the Yemenis of the eleventh century. The chroniclers describe them to us as men perfectly happy with having their women quite visible, active, and dynamic – women who thought, spoke out, and made decisions. And everyone seemed to profit by it, individuals as well as the whole nation. And in these ancient records we are happy to find assurance that a strong couple united by democratic inter-change, which once upon a time was declared evil for all of us, is not a betrayal of our ancestors nor a mechanical imitation of the West.

Asma Bint Shihab al-Sulayhiyya wore power and pearls with the same distinction. Alongside her husband and with him she directed all the important affairs of the realm until his death in 458/1066. In the beginning, as a young wife fascinated by the magnetic brilliance of her companion, she happily accepted the obscure, humble life that the Shi'ite commitment imposed on her husband, who had chosen to take the difficult path of preparing for the imamate. Asma shared the constraints of the clandestine life that Shi'ite secrecy demanded of them. She had the patience to support her husband during the 15-year waiting period, to believe in him, in his genius, and in his undertaking. Yes, patient she was, but never self-effacing.

The chroniclers report that she attended the councils of state 'with her face uncovered'. No veil for a woman who loved her husband and believed in him, and no false humility for an Arab woman who had something to say! When 'Ali was officially authorized to declare himself the sovereign, he presented her with the most royal gift that can be offered a woman – to associate her publicly with his life, to acknowledge her as an equal and a partner. The *khutba* would be said in her name. The mosques of Yemen would proclaim her name after the names of the Fatimid sovereign and her husband: 'May Allah prolong the days of al-Hurra the perfect, who manages the affairs of the faithful with care.'[1] Such moments in our history are never chosen as subjects for primary and secondary schools. Scholastic history is a sequence of conquests and captures of cities and territories, a series of battles strewn with thousands of dead in which it would be utterly shameful for the hero to dare to be thinking about his wife. However, Queen Asma created a veritable tradition of a couple sharing power, raising her son, al-Mukarram, in the idea that a wife is a force that it would be absurd to leave to stagnate in the shadow of the harem. And al-Mukarram made his wife, 'Arwa Bint Ahmad al-Sulayhiyya, an associate and partner. The only notable difference between the two queens is the length of their reign. While that of Asma was very short, that of 'Arwa lasted more than half a century.

The official title borne by Asma and 'Arwa was *al-hurra*, a sovereign woman who obeyed no superior authority. In addition to these two queens, this title was also borne by al-Malika al-Hurra Alam, who reigned in the principality of Zubayd, a city near San'a, which, as we have seen, was in a perpetual state of hostility with San'a. Al-Hurra Alam was the talk of the town in her time because at the beginning she was a mere *jarya*, a singer slave of the king of Zubayd, Mansur Ibn Najah, before she caught his attention as a politician of the first rank. Mansur was so 'impressed by her intelligence and learning . . . that he put the management of the realm into her hands and made no decisions concerning it without consulting her. And she discharged her task with distinction.' After the death of her husband, al-Hurra Alam continued to govern Zubayd. But, according to the sources, she never had the privilege of the *khutba* proclaimed in her name, as did Asma and 'Arwa. As prestigious as it was, the title *al-hurra* seems to have been often used by a good number of women active in the political domain in Yemen, as it was in the Muslim West in the Maghrib and Andalusia. But the Yemenis bestowed upon queens a title that was theirs alone

– *balqis al-sughra*, 'little queen of Sheba', or more precisely 'young queen of Sheba'.

Calling a Muslim queen 'queen of Sheba' is very paradoxical, since that queen belonged to the *jahiliyya*, the time of ignorance, the pagan time, before the arrival of the Prophet Muhammad and the revelation of the Koran.[2] Islamic time is ordered according to a two-part division that allows for no nuance: there is a before and an after. It does not allow for any gradations or relativizing of this binary division. There are only two times: the *jahiliyya*, the time before, intrinsically and fundamentally negative, for then human beings were ignorant of the distinction between good and evil; and the time after, that is, after the coming of the Prophet Muhammad, the time when human beings finally had in hand the Koran, the holy book that revealed the criteria for distinguishing good from evil. Since she belonged to the *jahiliyya*, the fate of the queen of Sheba is, so to speak, decided in advance, and to set her up as an object of pride is an act that is at the very least ambiguous. And yet, this was the name that Yemenis liked to give their queens: 'Some poets,' Muhammad al-Thawr tells us, 'carried away by their admiration of Asma, went so far as to declaim that if the throne of the queen of Sheba had been magnificent, that of Asma was still more so.'[3]

It was easy for the poets to embroider around the name of Asma, as it came from the same root as the word *sama* (sky). Asma is one of the oldest known women's names in Arabia. It has a connotation of elevation, loftiness.[4] Comparing the throne of Queen Asma to that of the queen of Sheba has the effect of making a direct allusion to the Koran. In the Koran, in sura 27, 'The Ant', where her meeting with King Solomon is related, the queen of Sheba is one of the few women recognized as playing an eminently political role.

She appears in the description that a bird gave to King Solomon, who had the rare privilege of understanding their language. Solomon, in passing the birds in review, noted that the hoopoe was absent. He promised to punish it if it did not justify its absence. And when the hoopoe reappeared and was questioned by the King, its knowledge was only equalled by its insolence:

22. But he was not long in coming, and he said: I have found out (a thing) that thou apprehendest not, and I come unto thee from Sheba with sure tidings.

23. Lo! I found a woman ruling over them, and she hath been given (abundance) of all things, and hers is a mighty throne.[5]

This is the way Balqis, the queen of Sheba, is presented in the Koran – in full exercise of royal power. But she and the people whom she leads are on the wrong path – that of the devil. The hoopoe is absolutely certain of that:

> 24. I found her and her people worshipping the sun instead of Allah; and Satan maketh their works fair-seeming unto them, and debarreth them from the way (of Truth), so that they go not aright.[6]

At the end of the narrative, the queen loses her throne. A jinn, working for Solomon, steals it from her; but although stripped of her material assets, Balqis would gain in spirituality. She ceases to worship the sun and makes a double surrender – first to Allah, and then to his prophet Solomon:

> 44. . . . She said: My Lord! Lo! I have wronged myself, and I surrender with Solomon unto Allah the Lord of the Worlds.[7]

The Koranic text has a limpid beauty due to its lack of adornment and the wondrous clarity of its message focused on the essential point, which was the throne and its transfer from the female to the male. What is most fascinating about the story of Balqis, however, is that it prompted the commentators to get involved in a long, tangled, oversubtle exegesis of the problems which seemed to torture them personally and which the Koran superbly ignored. One of the principal problems the writers stumbled over was the nature and importance of the queen's throne. It absolutely had to be reduced in importance, even if the unfortunate creature finally lost it. *'Adhim* (mighty) is the adjective used to describe the throne of Balqis. It is a word whose shades of meaning are very difficult to express. But Tabari found a means to diminish it: it is not the size of the throne nor its 'material importance' that the word *'adhim* describes, he tells us, 'but rather the danger that it represented'. Nevertheless he does mention that its material aspect was not negligible: the throne was of gold encrusted with pearls and precious stones.[8] The other problem that the Koran totally neglects (for it apparently considers it unimportant even though it disturbs the experts) is the marital status of the queen. Was she a virgin when she met King Solomon, or had she earlier contracted a marriage? One early historian, Tayfur, marries her, as was obligatory, to her cousin, Ibn Zara.[9] Kahhala, a modern biographer who is so fascinated by women that he has devoted a many-volume 'Who's Who' to them, felt the need to give a good-conduct report of the queen: 'Balqis was a woman of irreproachable conduct; she remained chaste. And as she was not the slightest bit interested in men, she remained a virgin until she met Solomon and married him.'[10]

Did she really marry Solomon? There is nothing in the Koranic text to lead us to such a conclusion. Nevertheless, the theologians and historians took it upon themselves to decide. Muhammad al-Qannuji promised hell to anyone who dared to think that Solomon married Balqis: 'Ibn al-Mundhir stated that Solomon later married Balqis . . .. This is an extremely reprehensible statement.'[11] For him Balqis and Solomon were two different entities. And since a woman at the height of power does not at all conform to the profile of a marriageable young woman of our day, Balqis poses a problem and has always posed a problem for historians. Some of them resorted to the irrational in their attempts to explain this strange woman. Mas'udi (died in 346/tenth century) sowed doubts about her origin by revealing that she had a human father and a mother who came from the jinns. With a throne and a whole people at her feet, Balqis could not be completely human:

> The birth of this queen is surrounded by supernatural circumstances that have been reported by the transmitters. They recount that her father was out hunting, found himself in the presence of two serpents, one black and the other white; that he killed the black one and then saw appear before him two jinns, of whom one was old and the other young; that the old [jinn] gave his daughter in marriage to the king with certain conditions; and that the fruit of that union was Balqis.

Mas'udi was a historian of unparalleled intelligence, and any Muslim of even the most modest intelligence knows that in order to be convincing one must be logical. Nevertheless, in the matter of Balqis, Mas'udi, usually so sure of himself, had twinges of conscience. He felt obliged to explain this story of the jinn: 'As for us, we only credit facts of this type if they conform to beliefs that religious law compels us to accept.'[12] In this case, religious law compelled nothing at all. The Koran did not consider it interesting or necessary to tell us about either the father or the mother of Balqis. It was Mas'udi's personal problem; he could not bear to see a woman depicted on a throne, even in the Koran, without feeling the need to attack her and put her humanity in doubt.

Despite everything, Balqis has held her own in the face of the historians' attempts to reduce or humiliate her. She continues to reign in the literary and poetic imagination. The danger now comes from scholars who are in the process of piling up proof that historically she never existed: 'To appreciate properly the much discussed story of the Queen of Sheba . . . who is said to have visited Solomon, it is decisive that all that we know of Saba' and Ma'in contradicts the supposition that there were queens there.' This is the verdict of scholars in the *Encyclopedia of Islam*. 'In any case,' they say, 'we are not to see in this story evidence of the existence of the rule of queens in Saba'.'[13] That being said, can scholarly explorations succeed in destroying the legendary power of Balqis? It is very unlikely, for the name of Balqis is not mentioned in the Koran – a fact that should not be ignored. The Koran speaks of 'a woman ruling over' the people of Sheba.[14] But she has no name in our holy book. It is historians like Mas'udi and the authors of commentaries like Tabari who have given the name of Balqis to the sovereign unnamed in the Koran. The essential point is that Balqis comes to us directly out of the *jahiliyya*, and despite scholarship and its dictates her life is as enduring as her legend. Scholarship or no, Balqis reigns supreme today in Arab poetry, and many contemporary poets use her to suggest a female presence that fascinates and enchants.[15]

Happily, the Yemenis of the eleventh century did not have to suffer the great displeasure of reading the insolent claims about our Balqis in the *Encyclopedia of Islam*. It was to her they compared the women who ruled them – Asma and 'Arwa – and whom they called *malika hazima*. Right up to the present the epithet *hazim* is the description that all politicians wish to have applied to themselves. It implies 'the ability in a person to control the course of his life and affairs, and of making decisions with firmness . . .. When one says of a man that he is *hazim* that means that of his people he is the most experienced, the one who makes knowledgeable decisions and relies on reason in doing so.'[16] A *hazim* person does not make decisions all alone. He listens to others, asks the opinion of experts, and takes it all into account before settling matters. Moreover, this explains the 'firmness' of a man who is *hazim*, for he never alters a decision once it has been made. Ibn Manzur didactically recalls that it is from this word that the word *hizam* (belt) comes, and that the act of buckling up expresses the idea of the word very well. The *hazim* is never caught unawares and so never has to make rash, hasty decisions, for he constantly thinks about everything, foresees events, and weighs the pros and cons of every possibility. *Al-hazm* is certainly one of the qualities most highly regarded among the Arabs in general, and in their leaders in particular, today as well as yesterday, and many poets have made a fortune by the prodigious attribution of this quality to the princes they flattered.

One finds the same admiration among the modern Yemeni historians. Muhammad al-Thawr cannot praise Asma enough:

> She was one of the most famous women of her time and one of the most powerful. She was munificent. She was a poetess who composed verses. Among the praises given her husband al-Sulayhi by the poets was the fact that he had her for a wife . . .. When he ascertained the perfection of her character, her husband entrusted the management of state business to her. He rarely made decisions that went against her advice.[17]

In conclusion, the author adds that her husband 'regarded her with very great respect and never gave any other opinion precedence over hers'.[18]

The people and the elites showed their true feelings about Queen Asma when tragedy struck the princely couple on the road to Mecca. Asma could not suspect that this pilgrimage of year 458/1066, begun in a festive mood, would end in disaster in the humid shadows of an ordinary watering place named Bir Umm Ma'bad. When the caravan stopped for the night and the royal tents had been pitched, Asma attended to her duties among her court and her *jawari*, and her husband to his among his own entourage, as protocol prescribed. In his tent 'Ali al-Sulayhi was having a discussion with his brother when death appeared at his threshold. It had the face of the Ethiopian enemy, Sa'id Ibn Najah, the prince of Zubayd, come to avenge his father. With his 70 men carefully placed at strategic points, Sa'id succeeded, once 'Ali was killed, in making himself master of the whole convoy in a few hours.

He put to the sword all those who counted, especially the Sulayhi princes, and ordered Asma to be brought to him alive. She was spared, and he only dealt with her fate after that of the army. In order to make an impression on the pilgrim groups from all the corners of the Muslim world, 'Ali was accompanied on this journey by 5,000 soldiers. Once the murder was carried out, Sa'id Ibn Najah had no trouble winning them over for the simple reason that they were all Ethiopians. He played on their feelings of ethnic solidarity and persuaded them to join the army of Zubayd. Once military victory was assured, Sa'id turned his attention to Asma. She was sequestered in a secret prison, and to remind her of her misfortunes, he ordered that the severed head of her husband be planted on a pole clearly visible from her cell.

Asma remained some time in her prison, trying in vain to contact her son al-Mukarram and his wife 'Arwa in San'a. Her jailers kept careful watch to ensure that they would get no news of her. It was a year before Asma succeeded in getting a message to her son. And when the news of her captivity spread around San'a, the notables of the city mobilized behind al-Mukarram 'to save the honour of their imprisoned queen'.[19] Three thousand furious horsemen rode out of the city behind al-Mukarram and in a few hours succeeded in routing the 20,000 Ethiopian soldiers defending the city of Zubayd. The city was stormed and captured, and al-Mukarram, leaving all the others behind, rushed into the dungeon of the prison where his mother was held, not knowing that when he came out he would never be the same.[20] A great emotional shock was going to change the course of his life. And it all unfolded as in a dream. His steps led him to the secret cell where his mother awaited his arrival. When he arrived at the door of Asma's cell, he recited the formula of greeting and asked her permission to enter. But his mother's reaction was cold and guarded in the face of this masked visitor who was trying to make contact with her. In his haste al-Mukarram had not removed the mail helmet that Arabs wore on military expeditions.[21]

'Who are you?' his mother asked him.
'I am Ahmad, the son of 'Ali,' replied al-Mukarram.
'There are many Ahmads the sons of 'Ali among the Arabs,' responded the still suspicious queen.[22]

At that moment, he raised the helmet and revealed his face to his mother, who greeted his action by paying homage to the new king that he had become: 'Welcome to our master, al-Mukarram.'[23] Al-Mukarram was overcome by the double shock of the emotion of finding his mother and the royal greeting she gave him even though she had not seen him enthroned, all of which reminded him of the tragic death of his father and his new responsibility. His body was shaken by a long shudder, which left him permanently disabled.[24] He emerged from the prison in a state of *falaj*, partial paralysis, and remained so for life.

Queen Asma, surrounded by horsemen, took the road back to the capital, bringing to San'a the partially inert body of the valiant al-Mukarram, known until then for his boldness on the battlefield. Al-Mukarram had a cousin, Saba Ibn Ahmad al-Sulayhi, who had all the qualities needed for taking power and who was in the prime of life, but no one thought of him when the cortege entered San'a. Queen Asma took over the management of the country until her death in 480/1087, and al-Mukarram officially delegated all his powers to his wife 'Arwa after his mother's death. 'Arwa had been recognized since childhood by 'Ali, al-Mukarram's father, 'as the only person capable of assuring the continuity of the dynasty in case something should happen to us.'[25]

'Arwa, who had lost her parents very young, had been brought to the palace in San'a to live with her uncle 'Ali. And it was Asma herself who had supervised her education.[26] 'Arwa had grown up side by side with her cousin al-Mukarram in a palace where power was the business of a couple and not the privilege of a man. In 461, at the age of 17, 'Arwa had married al-Mukarram; it was a princely union celebrated with magnificence and rejoicing. The bride received the principality of Aden as her dowry.[27] From then on she took charge of its management, named its governors, and collected its taxes. As in a fairy-tale, 'Arwa's happiness was made complete by the joys of motherhood. She gave two sons to al-Mukarram, but it was she, and no one else, whom San'a considered as the natural inheritor of power. The passing of power to 'Arwa was no surprise, but rather the continuation of a tradition.[28] The mosques of Yemen would ring once more with the *khutba* proclaimed in the name of a couple and not of an individual. However, there was one difference between the new queen and the former one: unlike Asma, who ruled with her face uncovered, 'Arwa veiled her face during working sessions. Why? She was young and beautiful – only 34 years old – and her husband was handicapped. This was the only concession she made to tradition. But even this was not really a concession, since she herself imposed it. It was a sensible decision for a woman who had decided to devote herself to a military objective: to gain the unique decisive victory that would show Yemen and the rest of the Muslim world that the Sulayhi dynasty, despite the misfortunes that had struck its men, was still powerful. And that victory, 'Arwa had decided, could only be the head of Sa'id Ibn Najah, the still living assassin of her father-in-law. After the taking of Zubayd by al-Mukarram, Sa'id had decided to flee by sea. Once the city was judged to be irremediably lost, he retreated to the escape boats that he had duly equipped and stationed in the harbour in order to get away by sea in case of a rout.[29]

In pursuit of her aims, 'Arwa first decided to transfer her capital from San'a to Jabala, a small fortress-city clinging to the mountainside. She installed her husband and the Sulayhi treasures there and began to tighten the noose around Sa'id Ibn Najah by negotiating new alliances. One year later, in 481/1088, her army crushed Sa'id in the vicinity of Jabala.[30] 'Arwa's success was due more to her use of the terrain and to the spreading of false rumours than to her military superiority. She persuaded Sa'id to attack her by making him believe that all her allies were in the process of abandoning her. In fact she had demanded that they go to Ibn Najah and hint to him that in case of attack on Jabala they would not come to her aid. Sa'id fell into the trap and attacked Jabala, completely confident that al-Hurra was isolated and weakened. Once Sa'id had been killed, his wife, Umm al-Mu'arik, was brought as a prisoner to 'Arwa. 'Arwa ordered that Sa'id be decapitated and his head planted on a pole in front of his wife's cell as had been done before with 'Ali.[31] The law of vengeance required a perfect symmetry in symbol and deed. And this act, which proved that al-Hurra was just as cruel a politician as Sa'id, the enemy of her dynasty, should remove all illusions of any possible feminine compassion.

The historians emphasize that 'Arwa gave her full attention to military conquests, needing to prove that the dynasty was still as strong as ever despite the loss of its great leader 'Ali and the disability of al-Mukarram. In politics, unlike in music, being a woman does not soften behaviour. Yasin al-Khatib al-'Amri, a nineteenth-century historian, describes 'Arwa as a sovereign who 'perfectly understood how to manage the affairs of state and of war';[32] and a modern author calls her 'an intellectually gifted and accomplished woman'.[33] For Zarkali, 'Arwa 'was an efficient queen and a matchless administrator'. She left some very beautiful architectural and engineering monuments, especially the famous San'a mosque and the road to Samarra. She also took great interest in the setting up of cultural and religious centres and seeing that scholars and teachers were well paid.[34] But above all she is remembered for her role as a spiritual leader and the service she rendered Shi'ism in propagating it throughout Asia.

For Zarkali, the author of the *A'lam*, the collection of biographies of celebrities, she was 'one of the leaders of Isma'ilism'.[35] Other more cautious writers make a distinction between the temporal power that 'Arwa received from al-Mukarram and the religious power that the latter transmitted to his cousin Saba. Al-Thawr specifies that 'Arwa was officially given the temporal power by her first husband al-Mukarram when he fell ill, but that he delegated his title of *da'i*, Shi'ite missionary, to his cousin Saba, with whom 'Arwa contracted a second marriage.[36] What is certain is that during 'Arwa's rule Isma'ilism began to spread into the Indian subcontinent under the influence of missionaries from Yemen.[37] Since the days of the Shebans, Yemen has always had close commercial ties with India because of its geographical location: 'Merchandise was brought by sea from India to Yemen at Hadhramaut, and then the Yemenis transported it to Ethiopia, Egypt, Phoenicia, etc.'[38] Muslims, as the propagators of new ideas and intellectual ferment, were inveterate travellers and made use of the traditional commercial routes, and Yemen was well placed for that. It was the Yemeni missionaries who were the originators of today's Indian Isma'ili Bohora community.[39]

Ultimately it is not of great moment whether 'Arwa was one of the champions of Shi'ism. What is indisputable is that her power came from the triumph of one of the most illustrious branches of Shi'ism and that in her era the balance of power had tipped to the side of that vision of Islam which until then had been condemned by the established Sunni regimes. The access to power of the Sulayhi dynasty would have been inconceivable if the Fatimids had not succeeded in orchestrating a Shi'ite offensive on the international level. Despite her abilities and military successes, 'Arwa none the less had to suffer from the fact of being a woman. A man more powerful than she was going to challenge her accomplishments. He was the supreme imam, Caliph al-Mustansir in Cairo, her superior in the Isma'ili Shi'ite hierarchy.

The first crisis that al-Mustansir faced her with took place at the death of her husband. It was a crisis that awaited anybody called to exercise power; that person had to beg for the benediction of the caliph, who conferred recognition and legitimacy. This time the caliph was Shi'ite, and as the Shi'ites always claimed to be revolutionaries and defenders of the poor and excluded, one could not imagine that with women they would take a different position, especially since the Fatimid caliphs asserted their authority as descendants of Fatima. Was the Fatimid caliph of Cairo going to behave differently from the Sunni caliph of Baghdad who, as we have seen, systematically opposed the access of women to power? The attitude of the Fatimids toward 'Arwa will clarify an essential question for us: does Shi'ite Islam distinguish itself from Sunni Islam when it comes to the political rights of women? Does Shi'ite Islam accept more readily than Sunni Islam that a woman govern a country? Since Shi'ism is above all the historical expression of challenge to established power, it should be *a priori* more egalitarian toward women. This question brings us back to our original point: did the queens of Yemen have the right to the *khutba* issued in their name because they were Shi'ites or because they were Yemenis? Is their exceptional case explained by religion (Shi'ism) or ethnicity, that is, by cultural specificity, by local tradition, especially the importance of women in the myths and legends of South Arabia?

After the death of al-Mukarram, 'Arwa discovered to her cost the attitude of the Shi'ite hierarchy. For Muslims the death of a head of state is a moment of rupture when the only thing that is certain is anxiety about the unforeseen. And it was the tradition of the Prophet that made this inevitable. By refusing to designate a successor from his own family despite pressure from it, the Prophet Muhammad gave a very strong signal that the will of God was against the Arabs' aristocratic tradition of power, which had been the rule during the *jahiliyya*.[40]

By his refusal to designate his successor, the Prophet expressed the essential point of the egalitarian principle of Islam. Since the seventh century this fundamental act has obliged every politician who aspires to the leadership of a community of Muslims to explain to the faithful the origin of his power and to justify his legitimacy. The death of a leader, whatever his title – caliph invested with a divine mission, or sultan drawing his power from a fiercely materialistic army – obliges his successor to settle the problem of legitimacy in one way or another by answering one simple question: where does his power come from? Who authorizes him to govern? It is absolutely inconceivable for a person to govern without justifying himself, since power in Islam is characterized by the fact that the world here below is inseparable from the Beyond, the material inseparable from the spiritual. 'Arwa publicly exercised material power during the lifetime of her husband, who had delegated it to her, but al-Mukarram remained the holder of spiritual power, the inheritor of the Isma'ili *da'wa* in Yemen, and as such he got his legitimacy from the eighth Fatimid caliph of Egypt, who was called al-Mustansir.

Far from being a minor sovereign, al-Mustansir asserted his power in the world as a dangerous caliph who had under his command a network of terrorists put at his service by Hasan al-Sabbah, the master of the order of *al-hashashin*, the Assassins. With al-Mustansir the Isma'ilis reached their apogee, since it was during his reign that the Shi'ite armies invaded Baghdad and had the *khutba* given in his name in the al-Mansur mosque, the seat and symbol of Abbasid authority and the high place of Sunnism.[41] The reign of al-Mustansir, which lasted 60 years, set a record. Born in 410, 34 years before 'Arwa, he took power in Cairo in 428, when he was 18 years old, and he lived until 487, to the age of 77.[42] He gained sorry fame for the waves of political terrorism orchestrated with his benediction by a *da'i*, the legendary Hasan al-Sabbah, who came to him for confirmation in 479. Hasan al-Sabbah operated from the fortress of Alamut situated on a lofty, almost inaccessible rock in the heart of the Elburz mountains north-north-west of Kazwin.[43] Even in his lifetime he was considered one of the most fascinating personalities of the century. Philosopher, astrologer, and mathematician, he dazzled his contemporaries, and many of them became his recruits and followed his orders to the letter. At his fortress of Alamut, he had developed a whole system of training and initiation that led converts to consider the political assassination of Sunni Muslims as something natural and even praiseworthy. Some historians attribute to him the assassination of two Abbasid caliphs, al-Mustarshid (512/1118 to 529/1136) and al-Rashid (529/1136 to 530/1136).

Alamut or not, as a Shi'ite queen, 'Arwa could only bow to the will of the Fatimid caliph, her hierarchical superior, her imam. For the Shi'ites the imam is *ma'sum*, infallible. (This is one of the points that irremediably divides Shi'ites and Sunnis, for to ascribe infallibility to a human being is shocking in the eyes of Sunnis, who attribute this quality to God alone.[44]) So Queen 'Arwa could not challenge the decisions of Caliph al-Mustansir, the sole person in a position to recognize her, as he had previously recognized her predecessors, 'Ali and al-Mukarram.

One might easily think that in Isma'ili Shi'ism there would be a sort of specific respect for women, considering their claim of descent from Fatima, the daughter of the Prophet, who occupies an eminent place in Isma'ili Shi'ism. This place is challenged by some Sunni caliphs, who consider that power cannot be inherited through a woman because she is excluded as a matter of principle from the greater imamate, that is, from the political and spiritual leadership of the community. We have two extremely important letters on this subject, exchanged between the Sunni caliph al-Mansur (136/754 to 158/775), the second caliph of the Abbasid dynasty, and his Shi'ite challenger, the famous al-Nafs al-Zakiyya, great-great-grandson of 'Ali, whose full name is Muhammad Ibn 'Abdallah Ibn al-Hasan Ibn al-Hasan Ibn 'Ali.

Al-Nafs al-Zakiyya was living quietly in Medina and until then had resisted the urging of those who offered him weapons and money to rise against the first Abbasid, al-Safah, the father of al-Mansur and the founder of the Abbasid dynasty. But upon the death of al-Safah and the accession of his son al-Mansur, al-Nafs al-Zakiyya succumbed to temptation. Following the classic model of Shi'ite challenge, al-Nafs al-Zakiyya, who in the beginning hid his pretensions to power, one day publicly declared himself the sole legitimate caliph. His partisans drove al-Mansur's governor out of the city. Then began an exchange of letters between the Abbasid caliph and his challenger that is a goldmine for those interested in the logic of legitimating power in the two major divisions of Islam, even though al-Nafs al-Zakiyya ended up beheaded like all his predecessors.[45]

Anybody who talks about legitimacy necessarily talks about birth, and anybody who talks about birth talks about maternity. One of the key axes of the debate between the Sunni caliph and his Shi'ite challenger was the clarification of their position regarding the role of women in the transmission of power: whether a woman can transmit political power. The debate now introduced into an essentially monotheistic political scene the otherwise carefully veiled phantom of maternity. Maternity is totally ignored in its physical aspect by the *shar'ia*, which recognizes only paternal law: children born of a Muslim marriage necessarily belong to the father. This principle is so fundamental that the status of an illegitimate child (that is, a child who has only its mother) is practically non-existent, making it impossible for Muslim parents to adopt a child legally. Adoption, which risks reproducing a fiction of paternity, is rejected by the *shar'ia*. Today this presents insoluble problems to the qadis, since in most Muslim countries all adoptions of children are more or less illegal.[46]

Returning to the epistolary joust, let me point out that al-Mansur's mother was a non-Arab *jarya*, a Berber slave named Sallama. Some say that Sallama was from the Nafzawa tribe; others maintain that she was of the Sanhaja.[47] The first insult that the Shi'ite pretender addressed to the Abbasid caliph was that he, al-Nafs al-Zakiyya, was a pure Arab on both paternal and maternal sides, while the Abbasid caliph could not say as much. According to al-Nafs al-Zakiyya, al-Mansur's descent was doubly stained, first because Sallama had *ajam* (non-Arab) blood in her veins, and secondly because she was an *umm walad*, a slave who is bought and sold in a *suq*.[48] He, al-Nafs al-Zakiyya, had on his side only women from a chain of illustrious aristocrats that led straight back to Khadija, the first wife of the Prophet, Khadija 'the pure, the one who was the first to pray before the *qibla*'.[49] It was to her that the Prophet confided the revelation of his mission, and it was she who accompanied him when he went to the sanctuary of the Ka'ba to reveal his new religion to the world. Khadija bore several daughters, and the one preferred by the Prophet was Fatima. She is considered the 'first lady' of Shi'ism, and al-Nafs al-Zakiyya in his letter to the caliph described her as 'the best of women and the first among the noble ladies of Paradise'.[50] How could the Abbasid caliph respond to such an illustrious female genealogy?

Caliph al-Mansur's reply, which based his legitimacy on his descent from the Prophet through a man, his uncle al-'Abbas, was simple, logical, and above all correct:

> I received your letter and read your remarks . . .. Actually your whole argument rests on your pride in your descent through women. And God did not put women on the same level as uncles and fathers . . .. Indeed you are the descendants of the Prophet through his daughter, but she had no right to inherit the *wilaya* [political succession], and she did not have the right to be imam. So how can you inherit from her something to which she had no right?[51]

According to the Abbasids, the claims to power of those descended from 'Ali are completely unfounded, because the transmission of the caliphate through women is impossible. Women, excluded by definition from the major leadership of the state (*al-imama al-kubra*), cannot transmit it.

It should be pointed out that, based on the principle of the primacy of Fatima, some Shi'ites developed different inheritance laws. In homage to the memory of Fatima, one of the extremist sects, known as the Ghurabiyya, went so far as to make the daughter the sole heir, thus violating the Sunni *shari'a*, which gives her only half the share that goes to the son.[52] The Ghurabiyya, which was based in the city of Qum, threatened to kill a brave qadi who insisted on the necessity of applying the *shar'ia* and ordered that the daughter be given only half of what went to her brother.[53] The qadi found out to his cost that a female's place in inheritance is not the same in all cases. For example, when a man dies leaving a daughter and a grandson (the son of his son), the *shi'a* excludes the grandson from inheriting and gives the whole remaining fortune to the daughter, which is an aberration for the Sunnis. According to the latter, in this case the fortune is divided into two equal parts, one going to the daughter and the other to the grandson.[54]

After the doctrine of the infallibility of the imam, inheritance laws are one of the major points of conflict between Sunnis and Shi'ites, although there are also others on which the two communities do not agree. In his very concise summary of the differences in personal status laws between Shi'ites and Sunnis, Ahmad Amin adds *mut'a* marriage to the list. *Nikah al-mut'a*, literally 'pleasure marriage', is a contract that links a man and a woman for a specified limited time, from a few days to a few months or more, at the end of which the husband must pay the woman a certain sum fixed in advance. The Sunnis consider this agreement nothing but *zina* (fornication) pure and simple, a form of prostitution. The principal reason for the Sunni condemnation of this practice is that *mut'a* marriage does not require witnesses and is thus deprived of the public character so essential to Sunni marriage. A second reason is that it does not give the partners the right to inherit from each other, and a third is that the fate of any children born of the union is more than uncertain. Obviously there is no possibility for repudiation in this form of marriage, since the marriage is self-annulling upon the fixed termination date.[55] After all these divergences in matters of marriage and inheritance, in which women seem to play a different role, one might expect a similar outlook in political matters, with the Shi'ite caliph of Cairo displaying a more conciliatory attitude and being better disposed toward a queen like 'Arwa, an attitude that would not be a homologue of Sunni law.

However, Caliph al-Mustansir reacted exactly like a Sunni caliph to the death of al-Mukarram: he opposed her assumption of power and dispatched messengers who sharply advised her to get married and remain in the background behind her spouse. All would be in order if 'Arwa would consent to marry Saba Ibn Ahmad, her husband's cousin, whom al-Mukarram had designated as his successor (*'ahd*) on his deathbed. But here the historical sources, until now in agreement, diverge on the details of this succession and the conditions of 'Arwa's second marriage.

Some historians specify that al-Mukarram had carefully divided responsibilities between 'Arwa and Saba, bequeathing to 'Arwa the *wasiya* and to Saba the *da'wa*. The *wasiya* confirmed 'Arwa in her position as holder of earthly political power, and the *da'wa* designated Saba as inheritor of the spiritual mission as leader of the Isma'ili community of Yemen.[56] Other historians simply say that al-Mukarram gave the *'ahd* to his cousin Saba without specifying what it covered.[57] The word *'ahd*, which has the meaning of 'obligation', 'engagement', 'pact', 'treaty', or 'convention', is the accepted word for the political decree by which a reigning sovereign designates a successor. The meaning of 'testament' is so obvious in the word *'ahd* that in Arabic it is used to designate the Old and New Testaments of the Bible (*al-'ahd al-'atiq* and *al-'ahd al-jadid*).[58]

In any case, according to al-'Amri, whatever al-Mukarram's *'ahd* had been, 'Arwa effectively exercised *mulk* (earthly power) without interruption from the time of the illness of al-Mukarram in 473 until her death in 530. This means that she ruled for practically half a century despite the opposition of the caliph.[59] But she had to come to terms with the caliph. Some say that al-Mustansir ordered 'Arwa to marry Saba, and she carried out the order and submissively married him. He is supposed to have confronted her with a *fait accompli* by sending her a letter saying: 'I give you in marriage to Amir of Amirs Saba.'[60] Others say that Saba took the initiative and proposed marriage to 'Arwa five months after the death of her husband.[61] She is supposed to have accepted this demand, although others say that she rejected it, and that the rejection was badly received by Saba; wounded in his *amour propre*, he is supposed to have besieged 'Arwa in her fortress at Jabala.[62] The proponents of this hypothesis say that, in order to make her relent, he used her brother, Ibn Amir, to reason with her and bring her to change her mind and accept Saba as her husband. 'Arwa's brother is supposed to have told her that it was Caliph al-Mustansir in person who desired her marriage with the *da'i*, and he, the caliph, would pay an astronomical dowry of 10,000 dinars (pieces of gold) and 50,000 other gifts in order to regularize this succession, which he was finding very annoying.[63]

Apparently these arguments and pressures induced 'Arwa to yield and accept Saba as her husband. The temptation to enrich herself was probably the least deciding factor. She was already very rich, being the guardian of the dynasty's treasures. One of the reasons she had decided to move her capital from San'a to Jabala was to put these treasures in a secure place. Some say that the marriage was never consummated; others assert the contrary: the marriage was consummated but without offspring.[64]

The proponents of the unconsummated marriage theory recount in detail the story of an eventful wedding night. According to them, after the signing of the marriage contract, Saba left the fort of Ashiakh were he was living to go to Jabala where his bride lived. He entered the Dar al-'Izz Palace that al-Mukarram had built for her and was shown to the room where his wife was to join him. 'Arwa came, but he did not recognize her, because she was dressed as a *jarya*. She waited on him the whole night, without his paying any attention to her because he believed that the woman bustling about was only a *jarya*. As Saba was very pious, he never raised his eyes to her, completely absorbed as he was in waiting for the queen. Dawn arrived, and the queen was still not there; there was only the *jarya* still serving him. He left the palace to return home without realizing that the slave who had been there with him was the queen in person.[65]

Consummated or not, the marriage lasted 11 years, from 484 to Saba's death in 495. 'Arwa continued to reign with the aid of viziers and without any husband/screen, apparently ignoring the orders of the caliph. In 495/1102 'Arwa was past 50, and the Fatimid caliphate, torn by the succession struggles that had followed the death of al-Mustansir in 487, was no longer as strong as before. The Isma'ilis were divided into two branches, each following one of the sons of al-Mustansir and thus creating a schism that was to bring on the end of their empire. Al-Mustansir had designated his elder son Nizar as heir apparent and had confided this to the legendary Hasan Ibn al-Sabbah, the master of Alamut, when the latter, disguised as a merchant, came to see him to conclude with him the entente that would guarantee success to the Shi'ite empire. According to this pact Alamut would mobilize its terrorists against the Abbasids, beginning in Persia. The name of the successor was a key issue for the *da'i* of Alamut, who had to know who his master was going to be after the death of al-Mustansir, given the importance of hierarchy in the Shi'ite universe.[66]

However, at the death of al-Mustansir in 487 Nizar was pushed aside and his brother, al-Musta'li, was declared caliph in Cairo despite the wish of his father. Al-Musta'li was considered an impostor outside Egypt, and 'to this day the Isma'ilis recognize only Nizar as the imam.'[67] This split greatly weakened the caliphate of Egypt. Whole regions of the empire refused to recognize al-Musta'li, who cruelly went so far as to immure Nizar, who had fled to Alexandria, where he was proclaimed caliph: 'When al-Musta'li had Nizar "brought back", he constructed a wall around him.'[68] The cycle of the martyred imam, the just imam, and the sacrificed innocent took on new life. This time, however, the geographical implications were immense, for after Nizar's death the most powerful *da'i*, the lord of Alamut, Hasan al-Sabbah, declared himself supreme chief and claimed the title of *huja* (sage). 'After his death the leadership continued with the rulers of Alamut. Beginning with the fourth ruler, Hasan *'ala dhikrihi al-salam* (557/1162), they came to be recognized as imams.'[69]

'Arwa remained loyal to Cairo. Thanks to her, al-Musta'li was recognized not only by the whole Isma'ili community in Yemen but also by that in India dependent on it.[70] Unfortunately, al-Musta'li was not grateful to her and in 512/1119 sent one of his men, Najib al-Dawla, who, believing al-Hurra to be too old and probably also too popular, tried to seize the realm from her. But he got a great surprise: Yemen still loved its queen and would not hear of being governed by anyone else. Army and people mobilized behind her to do battle with the caliph's envoy: 'When Najib al-Dawla declared war on al-Hurra, with the idea of taking power away from her, she received so much support from the majority of the amirs of the country that Najib al-Dawla had to renounce his mission.'[71] Despite the enmity of the caliph of Cairo, her hierarchical superior, she remained in power until her death in 532/1138. 'Arwa died of natural causes, something of a miracle for an Arab sovereign, after exercising full powers as head of state in Yemen for another 20 years.

If Asma and 'Arwa, especially the latter, were able not only to govern but also to have the *khutba* said in their name and to have the notables and the people of the country on their side, was it due to their being Shi'ites or to their being Yemenis? In view of the attitude of Shi'ism towards women and politics, it seems that the religious variable can be eliminated. This leaves only one possible explanatory variable: the local cultural dimension, the specifically Yemeni tradition which seems to accept women as partners in the political game. Although history shows that Shi'ites and Sunnis are in opposition about everything, they at least agree on the lot reserved to women in political affairs. Shi'ite caliphs, just like Sunni caliphs, find the idea of a woman governing a Muslim community repugnant. One might even hold that the conflict between Sunnis and Shi'ites about the role of Fatima is the best example one can find to illustrate how political opportunists use the woman question to suit their interests. The Islam of the politicians, the Islam of the palace, changes its colours according to the circumstances. The politicians who are caliphs and qadis can at will bend *Islam-risala*, the Islam of the Prophet's message in the holy book, the Koran, to suit the precise interests they wish to defend. If succession by women is the only way for the Shi'ites to gain themselves legitimacy and a palace, their religious authorities are going to set to work to prove it. If the Sunni palace in Baghdad needs to disavow women as transmitters of legitimacy, the religious authorities will find no difficulty in making the holy book say what they need it to say. The only difference is that the Fatimid caliph's interests caused him to take two contradictory positions concerning women and their place on the political scene. He said yes to their pre-eminence in an esoteric debate about the transmission of power, Fatima being claimed as an ancestor through whom legitimacy and political power were passed. But he said no to the presence of women as partners on the political scene, and 'Arwa was disavowed and declared incapable of governing a Shi'ite state.

The history of the Fatimids constitutes a unique field of investigation for those interested in women and politics. Other, extraordinary circumstances thrust a Fatimid princess into occupying the caliph's place and fulfilling his imperial duties for four long months. She was Sitt al-Mulk, who took power in 411/1020 after the mysterious disappearance of her brother, the imam al-Hakim Ibn 'Amri Allah, who one fine morning declared to his people in a delirium that he was God in person and that they should worship him as such.

The story of Sitt al-Mulk is as fascinating as it is exemplary. It is the story of a woman forced by circumstances to take on the unimaginable: to assume the place of a caliph in order to save millions of the faithful from the madness of the imam. This was not, as in the case of 'Arwa, just a matter of exercising *mulk*, purely earthly power, but of occupying the empty place of a caliph become unfit to carry out his responsibilities. Sitt al-Mulk took the place of an infallible imam whom madness had transformed into a hallucinating killer whose acts no longer had any logic or legitimacy in the eyes of the faithful. The case of Sitt al-Mulk is without doubt an extreme case, in which the female presence, on principle relegated to the harem, invaded the caliphal throne. In order to protect itself, the system completely denied the existence of Sitt al-Mulk; the *khutba* was never said in her name in the mosques. After four months of direct rule she herself, a woman of great capability, on whom the historians readily bestowed the adjective *hazima*, sought to set up a screen, to hide herself.

9
The Lady of Cairo

Sitt al-Mulk, born in a Fatimid palace, did not need to add a title
to her name, which means 'lady of power'. Nor did she have to
struggle to gain first place in the eyes of the caliphs. They were
always pressing around her, fascinated by that mixture, so irresistible
to Arabs, of great beauty allied to great intelligence. But – curse
or destiny – none of the caliphs who adulated her was her husband,
and she remained a hostage of the clan, its powers, and its ambiguous passions. The caliph al-'Aziz, her father, idolized her, and her
brother al-Hakim tormented her like a lover with his jealousy.
Finally it was in the name of a third caliph, her nephew al-Dhahir,
that she exercised power for four years.[1] She administered the
empire between 411/1020 and 415/1024 in the name of a child on
whom she bestowed the title of *al-dhahir*, 'the eminently visible',
because her power, as the holy law demanded, was circumscribed
by invisibility.[2] The *khutba* was never preached in her name. It was
in the name of the child-imam that the faithful chanted the ritual
Friday prayers. And yet it was certainly she who administered the
empire and she who 'showed exceptional ability, especially in legal
matters, and she who made herself loved by the people'.[3] And to
make yourself loved by the Egyptian people has never been an easy
matter. Her father al-'Aziz and her brother al-Hakim regularly
received insulting letters from their subjects, and this despite the
very great difference between the two; the first being a man of
gentleness and tolerance, and the second a man of irrational,
unjustified violence.

Sitt al-Mulk was one of the most beautiful Fatimid princesses.

With hands covered with the dynasty's most precious jewels and skin perfumed with rare fragrances, she was adorned by hundreds of *jawari* who had the task of making her even more beautiful. They draped her in tunics of the finest silk, linen and royal brocade, specially designed by an industry that served only the dynasty.[4] The strange thing is that the Fatimids, who took power in Egypt promising simplicity and asceticism as an alternative to Abbasid pomp, which according to their propaganda was a sign of decadence, rapidly became engulfed in a life of luxury unequalled up to then in the Muslim Empire. And Sitt al-Mulk, like the rest of the princely family, patronized the government costume supply house founded by her grandfather al-Mu'izz, where master artisans were assigned the task of creating clothes of dazzling brilliance, in accordance with the official Fatimid imagery of luminous splendour and divine light. The Fatimids dressed in white to show their difference from the Abbasids, whose ceremonial robes were black, but the white was enhanced by gold and silver embroidery spangled with precious stones to reflect the luminosity of the divine.[5] Born in 359/970, at the height of their success, and just one year after the conquest of Egypt by her grandfather, Sitt al-Mulk reflected their luxurious life and their influence. From the first she was caught up in the power that encircled her.

The first to succumb to the charm of Sitt al-Mulk was her father, Caliph al-'Aziz, the fifth Fatimid caliph (365/975–411/1020). He added two of its most beautiful palaces, Qasr al-Bahr (the river palace) and Qasr al-Dhahab (the golden palace), to the Cairo created in 359/970 by his predecessor, his father al-Mu'izz. Sitt al-Mulk spent her happy childhood years in the extraordinary Qasr al-Bahr, the river palace designed by the royal astrologers to be in alignment with the stars, which had no equal in the East or the West.

Her father was so in love with her mother that the character of their relationship influenced the political practices of his reign.[6] In fact, this love was considered pernicious by some dignitaries, for Sitt al-Mulk's mother was a Christian *jarya* of Byzantine origin, proud of it and determined to remain Christian. Many looked with a jaundiced eye on the amorous frolicking of a Shi'ite imam-caliph, in principle still involved in a holy war against the Byzantines, and on an enemy *jarya* laying down the law in his palace.[7] The xenophobia of the court fanatics was exacerbated by the fact that al-'Aziz, who 'loved pardon and used it often',[8] extended his political tolerance to Christians. Under his rule non-Muslims – Christians and Jews – had the right to privileges they had never had before. They had access to the highest offices of the empire; they participated in all political activities, making decisions and acquiring a pre-eminence that aroused jealousy and made the caliph the target of criticism and insults from those who did not share his ideas of ecumenism and openness.[9] The naming of two high officials – the first a Christian, 'Issa Ibn Nasturas, to the post of vizier, and the second a Jew named Mancha, to be his representative in Syria – brought down on al-'Aziz's head the thunder of the most fanatical of the believers he ruled.[10] He was assailed with criticism for giving so much influence to non-Muslims.[11] But al-'Aziz held out against the pressure and made his political tolerance the ideal of the education that he transmitted to his daughter, Sitt al-Mulk. She inherited his personal qualities, especially his openness and tolerance, and stood by him to encourage him to keep Nasturas in office when al-'Aziz faltered under attack and dismissed him.[12]

Born of a mixed marriage between an imam and a Christian, Sitt al-Mulk was proud of her double identity and defended it as an ideal. Instead of being torn between two rival communities, she sought to open them to each other. Her respect for Christians and Jews was one of the issues that put her in opposition to the following caliph and endangered her life. She insisted that her two Christian uncles, Arsenius and Aristes, keep their influential posts when opposition to them was growing. In evaluating a caliph, Muslim historians never fail to take into consideration his degree of tolerance and his ability to avoid bloodshed. A great caliph is first of all a tolerant caliph; a disastrous reign is one in which blood is spilled. And everyone recognises the reign of al-'Aziz, which lasted 21 years, as successful, and he is considered an exceptional prince. Ibn Khallikan describes him as 'generous, courageous, with a propensity for clemency, since he gave pardons freely'.[13]

Al-'Aziz was an exceptional sovereign from every point of view. A very handsome dark-haired man with large clear eyes and wide shoulders, he was passionately fond of horses and hunting, especially lion-hunting. He was also cultivated and virtuous.[14] Sitt al-Mulk inherited two of her father's characteristics – the beauty that was close to perfection and the courage that equalled that of heroes.[15] Very early her father made her a party to power by asking her opinion and encouraging her to express it. While still an adolescent Sitt al-Mulk was used to seeing her opinion taken into consideration, and this did not change after the death of her father.

Al-Hakim was Sitt al-Mulk's younger brother. It was he who

pushed Egypt into the tragic abyss of fanatical madness and irrational murder, transforming the promises of openness into implacable hatreds. Al-Hakim grew up like any other child, alongside his sister, 16 years his elder, in a palace open to the broad reaches of the river. Al-Hakim was at play when his tutor, al-Ustadh Burjwan, a eunuch slave, ordered him to stop immediately and prostrated himself before him, kissing the earth under his feet and murmuring, '*Al-salaam 'ala amir al-mu'minin*' (peace be unto the commander of the faithful).[16] The military chiefs and the dignitaries clothed him in the robes of power less than an hour after the death of his father; this took place in a bathhouse in the city of Bilbays as a result of poorly understood instructions concerning a dangerous medication that he was to take in the bath. There was no way to foresee that destruction would worm itself into the city with the smile of a child.

At the time of his death Al-'Aziz was only 42 years old, but he was brought down by a freak accident while on an expedition against the Byzantines. It was Ramadan of year 386 (14 October 996).[17] The burial was carried out with such haste that the eunuch in charge of protocol in the palace did not have time to find, much less to have built, a coffin large enough to hold the great sportsman with wide shoulders. With dumbfounded astonishment, the city watched the royal funeral, which would have been a solemn occasion but for one unusual detail: the feet of the dead caliph hanging out of the coffin.

Cairo, which had watched the departure of al-'Aziz in the midst of his impressive military force, at sunset watched the arrival of an 11-year-old child dressed in a monochrome robe, wearing a turban ornamented with precious stones, walking beneath the royal canopy with a lance in his hand and a sword at his waist, with flags flying, and preceded by the corpse of al-'Aziz.[18] The town-criers crisscrossed the city with the announcement of the death of the father and the enthronement of the son, accompanied by the classic phrase that reflects the deep anxiety that a succession engenders: '*Amanakum Allah ta'ala 'ala amwalikum wa arwahikum*' (Allah, the most high, is the guarantor of the security of your goods and your lives).[19] It was an enthronement that Cairo would never forget. No one ever suspected that with this child, with his look of surprise and his brow bound with precious stones, madness and horror would enter the city.

Al-Hakim terrorized Cairo with his public excesses, and Sitt al-

Mulk with his private jealousy. He was obsessed with the idea of her many lovers. He saw them everywhere, especially among the great generals of his army. His suspicions and jealousy would drive Sitt al-Mulk into fratricide and a chain of murders. The death of al-'Aziz came too suddenly and unleashed violent mental agitation that the child-king himself did not understand. And from that, everything that followed unfolded with the hallucinating rhythm of fate.

More and more out of control, more and more morbid and bloody, one event followed another in a veritable nightmare, leading to that spring night of 411 when news spread in Cairo that Caliph al-Hakim had disappeared. A caliph does not disappear. You have your choice between a quiet death in bed (a rare case, it is true), a courageous death on the battlefield, a pious death on the road to Mecca, or a premeditated assassination by palace plotters. But a disappearance – that the Muslim community was not prepared to expect. The mob in Cairo, troubled by such an unusual event, divided into two factions: a majority which accepted the disappearance of al-Hakim, and a minority which still waits for him today. They are the Druze, who now live in the mountains of Lebanon. Persecuted by the Egyptians, they were obliged to migrate north and hide out in an isolated mountain area in order to guard their cult, which was considered heretical.

In 411 the majority of the inhabitants of Cairo already had that no-nonsense character that makes the Egyptians one of the most fractious of the Arab people – they immediately began to believe in the hypothesis of an assassination. Many Cairenes had already thought about regicide when the nocturnal ramblings of Caliph al-Hakim, punctuated with violence and summary executions, began to terrify the city. And it was this terror that explains the extraordinary event that followed: the assumption of power by Sitt al-Mulk, who occupied the position of caliph and fulfilled his duties for several months – an absolutely unthinkable situation in normal conditions. The *fuqaha* (religious experts) had considered all situations except this one. It was their task to foresee everything and describe everything that might happen if the caliph's throne fell vacant, in order to avoid disorder in the community of the faithful. Madness is one of the reasons that release the faithful from their *bay'a*, their commitment of obedience to the imam. When such a calamity fell on a Muslim community, no one knew how to cope with it. And the most bizarre thing was that the apocalyptic transfer of power from a brother to a sister took place with the greatest calm – a calm that clashes with the classic agitation and inevitable *fitna* (disorder) that usually accompanies an interregnum.

Upon the death of al-Hakim only his under-age son could officially claim power. But everything was so unforeseen and unexpected that all thought of ritual and protocol was forgotten, and Sitt al-Mulk appeared as an acceptable and normal alternative. However, nothing was normal in the course of events that the Fatimid dynasty considered to be dictated by the stars – neither the disappearance of al-Hakim nor the expectation that followed it.

Concerning the disappearance, there are several versions that agree on one point: al-Hakim had the habit of going out too much.

> He had overdone [his eccentricities]. One Saturday he made no fewer than six appearances. One on horseback, one riding a donkey, a third in a litter hoisted on to the head of porters. At the fourth appearance he was seen on the Nile in a boat. And on this occasion it was noticed that the caliph was not wearing a turban.[20]

But it was his frequent nightly wanderings that sowed the first seeds of anxiety in people's minds.

Al-Hakim's fascination with the stars was well known. But this was not out of the ordinary, since all the Isma'ili imams were well versed in astrology. For them it was an initiation into mysteries, a science, and a diversion. In al-Hakim's day the greatest astrologers of the Muslim world were invited to Cairo to keep the sovereign company. Observation of the stars and calculation of their movements were important for Isma'ili Shi'ism, which was based on the idea of 'cyclical time', in which earthly events are only explained by their esoteric reality, that is, in relation to the 'drama of the heavens', whose dénouement they were in fact preparing.[21] From the beginning, *'ilm al-nujum* (science of the stars) held a central place in Isma'ilism, and its forecasts served various interests. In his discussion of the sources of Isma'ilism, Ibn al-Nadim recalls, for example, that the astronomer-philosopher Muhammad Ibn al-Hasan, whose surname was Zaydan, won great success in al-Kurkh when he announced that according to 'astral laws' the Arabs were going to regain power from the Persians, thanks to the transfer of a certain triangular constellation from Scorpio to Sagittarius.[22] Calculation of the moment when the providential imam, the expected mahdi (*al-mahdi al-muntazar*), would appear and of the exact time for a *da'i* to reveal his true identity were among the astrological forecasts that required wide knowledge of the firmament and its laws.

The Isma'ilis made profuse use of astrological speculations for foreseeing events and, more prosaically, for deciding the number of days in a month, since they did not have a lunar month like the Sunnis. For them, it was necessary 'to allow the imam to fix the beginning of the month without being obliged to await the appearance of the moon. In practice, the beginning of the month was fixed according to astronomical calculations in such a way that it often fell one or two days before that of the other Muslims.'[23] So it is understandable that the study of the stars and mathematics were taught to al-Hakim as an integral part of the education of a Fatimid heir apparent.

But al-Hakim's fascination with the stars was not enough to explain his excessive desire to prowl around at night. Many of the faithful began to think that he was an insomniac. And his insomnia became an obsession with the Cairenes and led to a series of bizarre incidents that culminated in murder. It was also to his insomnia that they attributed the order to merchants and artisans to work at night and sleep in the day so that al-Hakim's retinue could saunter around a Cairo lit up and teeming with activity. At first fascinated by the gaudy spectacle of the retinue that accompanied the caliph on his nightly rounds, the people were soon disappointed, for after a short time al-Hakim turned to a life of the greatest asceticism. Race horses with harnesses of gold and silver encrusted with enamel and precious stones were no longer seen. Some of them used to wear around the neck 'chains of gold and collars of amber. Sometimes the horses that had been trained for ceremonial dressage paraded with anklets of gold. The leather of the saddles was replaced by a piece of red or yellow brocade or simply by embroidered silk of many colours.'[24]

One fine day the ostentatious display that the caliph had accustomed the crowds to disappeared. He, whose costumes had formerly glittered so brilliantly, was seen walking alone, as if abandoned, neglected, dressed in a humble wool tunic. He let his hair grow and neglected to wear his turban, that most distinctive sign of the dynasty that was the first to decorate a turban with jewels and devise a way of winding it to create a headpiece truly fit for a prince.[25] The crowd recalled those times of magnificence as the figure of the caliph, stripped of ornament and wandering alone through the Cairo nights, became a nightmarish vision. The anxiety grew in intensity that mysterious spring night in 411 when al-Hakim left his palace never to return. For several days before there had been rumours of a bitter jealous scene between the caliph and his sister. He had threatened her – and the lovers he accused her of – with death. The city was beset with rumours, and the news of the caliph's disappearance could only increase them. Various versions circulated about the causes of his disappearance, and the historians faithfully reported them but never succeeded in arriving at the truth of the situation.

The most commonly accepted version is that of Ibn al-Athir:

> On Monday night, when there were still three nights left in the month of Shuwal 411 [13 February 1021], al-Hakim Ibn 'Amri Allah Abu 'Ali al-Mansur Ibn al-'Aziz bi Allah Ibn Al-Mu'izz, the Alawite, the master of Egypt, disappeared, and no one had any information about him. His disappearance occurred when he went out for a walk at night as he was accustomed to do . . . . He walked to the east of Hilwan, and he was accompanied by two equerries . . .. People went out searching for some trace of him up until the end of Shuwal. On the third of the following month a team of people from the palace went out, led by al-Mudhaffar al-Saqlabi, who was the keeper of the *madalla* [the canopy, one of the symbols of power]. They arrived at Hilwan and climbed the hill . . .. They saw al-Hakim's donkey, which had sword wounds on its front legs, but still carried its saddle . . .. They followed the hoofprints, which led them to his clothes . . . which had been hacked to pieces . . . . The team returned, and there was no longer any doubt about who had killed him.[26]

Al-Hakim had set the city against him so that there was an infinite number of potential killers: 'The inhabitants of Cairo hated him because of all the misfortune he had brought upon them,' explains Ibn al-Athir. 'He used to send them letters in which he insulted their ancestors . . .. And then he ordered that Cairo be burned.'[27]

In 410/1020 al-Hakim had in fact given an order to burn down *al-fustat* (which today is called *Masr al-'atiq*, old Cairo) when the Egyptians had inundated him with insulting lampoons after the riots following the proclamation of his divinity. He had ordered his black troops to pillage and burn *al-fustat*. A fight to the death ensued between the caliph's army and the people.[28] Other foreign troops stationed in Cairo, particularly Turks and Berbers, were let loose on the people, and many Egyptians had to ransom their wives and children who had been taken hostage by the soldiers and literally reduced to slavery.[29] The people of Cairo had been outraged by al-Hakim's declaration of his divinity, not just because of the absurdity of the idea itself, but because it 'obliged them to prostrate themselves every time his name was pronounced in a meeting or a mosque or in the street. All those who heard his name had to prostrate themselves and kiss the ground to glorify his greatness.'[30] So the disappearance of al-Hakim surprised no one. It did, however, create much anxiety, for everything connected with al-Hakim had something of the irrational, the unforeseen about it, something that baffled simple people. Al-Hakim might have decided to just disappear for a few days, to retire to the desert to meditate 'wearing bedouin sandals on his feet and a kerchief on his head'.[31]

This is the reason why, after the caliph's disappearance, the Egyptians not only made no difficulty for Sitt al-Mulk, but became her accomplices and allies, remaining calm and avoiding the disorder that usually accompanies the death of a caliph. This peacefulness and calm were all the more surprising considering that many people thought that she had masterminded the disappearance. During the five following days she sent equerries and soldiers to comb Cairo and its hills, especially those that al-Hakim used to frequent regularly. Normally a clear succession is required, in which only those close to the sphere of power are involved, those who have the privilege of choice. Succession takes place as rapidly as possible, given the dangers of *fitna*, that is, any possibility for the people to intervene and disturb the order maintained by the elite. Either the death of the caliph is kept secret until the heir arrives, if he is far away, or it is announced only while the enthronement ritual of the successor is being arranged.

Strangely, in this springtime of 411 no one thought of disturbing the palace and the intrigues of the power brokers. Cairo held its breath. The military, like the people, retreated into silence. For once a power void had an inhibiting effect. Scorned by the official historians, the people, who never had a chance to express themselves except in street battles on the rare occasion of an interregnum when the walls of the political theatre were showing cracks, acted with surprising lethargy.[32] A lethargic Cairo is even more surprising than a Cairo in open revolt. It is a city that since its birth has been fascinated by its own state of disorder to the point of becoming identified with it. Cairo has always been

the meeting-place of comer and goer, the stopping-place of feeble and strong. Therein is what you will of learned and simple, grave and gay, prudent and foolish, base and noble, of high estate and low estate, unknown and famous; she surges as the waves of the sea with her throngs of folk.[33]

While Sitt al-Mulk conducted the search for her brother, the people of Cairo, watching and waiting, with eyes fixed on the palace, could not believe in the death of al-Hakim. He had accustomed them to his inexplicable behaviour; he was capable of absolutely anything; his pathological vagaries had no limit. Had he not declared war on dogs?

In 395 al-Hakim had indeed ordered the systematic hunting down and killing of all the dogs in Cairo and had sent orders to his governors throughout Egypt to do the same.[34] Maqrizi says that the killing was so thorough that the breed was decimated. Ibn Khallikan adds a detail that gives an idea of the psychological atmosphere of a city in which killing, even of animals, became official business: 'When al-Hakim ordered the killing of dogs, as soon as one appeared in the suq, the alleys, or the great avenues, it was immediately put to death.'[35] Why dogs? What crime had they committed against the caliph? The most plausible argument is the one advanced by Maqrizi: 'It is useless to search for reasons for the actions of al-Hakim. The dreams that haunted him defy interpretation.'[36] Some historians explain his decision to kill off the canine species by the suggestion that their barking disturbed his sleep.

As a matter of fact, the whole city gradually became engulfed in the problem of insomnia. It began first in 389 with the convoking of nightly sessions of the *majlis* (governing council). At that time he was 14 years old: 'Al-Hakim decided that the *majlis* would sit at night, and all the top state officials were obliged to carry out his order.'[37] But after a few sessions he gave up the idea and began his nightly wanderings. In the beginning these took the form of an official procession that encouraged people to go out and amuse themselves very late at night: 'The people spent enormous sums to light and decorate the streets . . .. This nocturnal activity encouraged the people to eat and drink out of doors; singing, entertainments, and spectacles increased beyond all limits.'[38] This provoked al-Hakim to harsh action against 'debauchery' and against women, who were held responsible for disorders to come.

Forgetting that his nocturnal perambulations were what started the whole thing, al-Hakim tried to re-establish order in a Muslim city that was beginning to enjoy the pleasures of the night a bit too much. 'He forebade women to go out at night and men to sit down in shops.' A few years later he put an end to his nightly outings and forbade the people to go around at night and amuse themselves. 'But the prohibitions escalated. In 410 he forbade singing in public and walking along the banks of the Nile. He also forbade the sale of wine, and an order was given that no one should go into the streets between sunset and dawn.'[39] Taking pleasure boats became a forbidden act because it was enjoyable and especially because it allowed men and women to share the same space. Al-Hakim ordered all houses that looked on to the river to close their doors and windows, because the view gave pleasure.[40] But above all, it was women, their bodies, and their moving about that became a veritable obsession with al-Hakim.

Women and everything related to pleasure haunted the caliph. All his prohibitions were aimed at the same objective: to eliminate them from daily life, to make them invisible, to hide them, to obliterate their existence as if their presence was in some way or other the cause of the inflation, drought, and epidemics that were scourging the city. As with the dogs, the decisions about women were accompanied by violence. The ban on going out was at first limited to the night. Then it was extended to the point of making their life a prison-like existence both physically and mentally. Paradoxically, weeping as well as laughing and amusing themselves were forbidden to them: that is, weeping and lamenting at burials. 'And then they were banned from attending burials and soon they were even prohibited from visiting cemeteries. As a result one saw no women at the cemeteries during the holy days.'[41] The prohibitions continued to escalate. Soon al-Hakim forbade women to walk in the streets with their faces uncovered. Then it was adornments that became the object of particular attention. Al-Hakim no longer wanted women to go about the streets adorned and bejewelled.[42] The definition of adornment continually changed depending on who had the power to define it. Stopping women in the street and questioning them increased until it resulted in what seemed like the logical next step: keeping them locked up. 'Women were forbidden to go into the streets. And soon women were no longer seen. Shoemakers were ordered to no longer make shoes for them, and their bathhouses were closed.'[43] And, Hanbali reminds us, 'women remained prisoners and did not set foot in the street for seven years and seven months, until the death of al-Hakim.'[44]

Egyptian women could be counted on not to accept in silence the fate that the caliph had allotted them. Like the Cairenes of today, their grandmothers refused to obey the caliph and his crazy orders: 'Some went out despite the ban, and they were killed.'[45] Delegations of women pleaded their case to al-Hakim, explaining that 'not all women have a man to take care of them, and they take care of themselves.'[46] Then al-Hakim, in response to their complaints, had a brilliant idea that the historians repeat with a seriousness not lacking in irony:

> He ordered the merchants to bring to women everything sold in the suq and the streets so that women could make their purchases. He gave precise instructions to the vendors. They should equip themselves with an instrument similar to a soup ladle with a very long handle. With this instrument they were supposed to push the merchandise in to the woman hiding behind the door, and she could ask the price if she wanted to buy it. In this way the vendor could avoid seeing his client.[47]

Contrary to what one might suppose, the majority of Muslim men did not appreciate this kind of absurdity, and Ibn al-Athir concludes that 'people were very put off by this sort of measure.' Many women who tried to resist 'were killed, one group being put to death by drowning. Al-Hakim got rid of many old women.'[48]

Who were the women who preferred death to being locked up? Aristocrats and wives of notables proud of their privileges, or poor women who had to go about the streets in order to earn their living? Who were these Egyptian women who braved the unjust prohibitions of a caliph 1,960 years ago and decided to transgress his orders, to walk in the streets that he had declared belonged to men alone? Were they educated women or illiterates? Were they peasants driven to Cairo by drought, or the coddled daughters and wives of the bourgeoisie? Were they mothers of families or barren women, women with all the advantages or marginal creatures whom no one cared about? These are the questions that young women at Cairo's universities will one day choose as dissertation topics. And on that day we shall see unfold before our eyes a history of the people of Cairo very different from the one that the misogynistic tradition wants us to believe in – a history of a fractious, combative people whose rage against injustice has no sex. We will see a rage that inflames women with the same fierceness that it does men and sends them side by side, probably hand in hand, into the streets where sometimes death and sometimes freedom await them. The historians emphasize one fact that explains the dynamics of the Cairo of that day: the men were deeply affected by the prohibitions that fell on their wives, and the humiliation they felt was in no way different from that of their wives, daughters, or lovers. In those days the people of Egypt already knew and understood that any violence in the city, even against dogs, was violence against them. And they knew that with the imprisonment of women it was the freedom of all that was in jeopardy. And they were right.

Soon the list of prohibitions grew still longer. This time it concerned foods so ordinary, so innocent that no one could imagine their being proscribed. The first one was – O delicacy of delicacies – *mulukhiyya*. Al-Hakim banned the sale of *mulukhiyya* (a vegetable much loved by Egyptians even today) because 'A'isha and Mu'awiya, enemies of the Shi'ites, had liked it.[49] But the food bans did not stop there. The sale of beans, certain shellfish, and fish without scales was forbidden.[50] Raisins and grapes for winemaking were banned, and stocks of them destroyed.[51] Tons of them were dumped into the Nile, great quantities were burned, and transport of them was forbidden. Violations of these orders were punished by death, which resulted in public executions. All these prohibitions increased the opportunities for violence by those in charge of applying the law and preserving public order. Other very grave problems were rife, especially a galloping inflation that produced a severe shortage of bread and draconian control measures. A punishing drought lowered the waters of the Nile so dramatically that provisioning of the city became almost impossible. All the while he was multiplying the bans on moving about, eating, and finding amusement, al-Hakim was constantly changing the tax rates in the hope of curbing inflation, but in vain. Bread riots increased.[52] In order to see that the new laws were respected, al-Hakim unleashed on the country an army of spies, instructed to inform him about everything, particularly about his relatives and the people of the court.[53] Not that the use of spies was unknown before him, but in his case the rumours that were reported to him enraged him, 'and when he was enraged, he could not control himself, and so scores of men were executed and whole generations decimated'.[54]

The use of spies by a caliph was considered absolutely normal, according to al-Jahiz, who dates the practice back to the caliph 'Umar:

'Umar knew his remote governors and subjects so well that it was as if he had spent the night in the same bed with them, lying on the same pillow. In no country, in no region was there a governor or a general who was not accompanied and constantly followed by one of the caliph's spies. The words of the inhabitants of the east and the west were reported to him every night and every morning.[55]

In his manual on good government, al-Jahiz advises the leader of a community to make use of spies. He says that the good king should 'know the secret thoughts of his entourage and his family and keep spies around them in particular and around the people in general'.[56] To those of his readers who still doubt the legitimacy of such a practice, he recommends that they read the letters that 'Umar 'addressed to his governors and their agents, whose lives were so well documented that each of them was suspicious of his closest relatives and his most intimate friends'.[57] Al-Jahiz gives a list of caliphs who practised espionage with great success – caliphs such as Mu'awiya, the first Umayyad; and Harun al-Rashid, with whom espionage reached the limits of refinement and became an art.[58] But although the Umayyad and Abbasid caliphs made use of information, both in time of war and in time of peace, never did it result in the systematic physical liquidations that the Egyptians knew under al-Hakim. The possibility of finding oneself at fault increased sharply with the augmentation of prohibitions that no longer concerned exceptional acts, but ordinary acts like eating, dressing up, and going out for a drink or a stroll.

After the dogs, the women, and the physical restrictions, al-Hakim sought a new magical solution to the very grave economic problems that were shaking the country. He targeted the *dhimmi*, the 'protected ones', that is, the Jews and Christians. Breaking with a tradition of tolerance, al-Hakim forbade them the purchase and consumption of wine, even for religious ceremonial. He destroyed their places of worship and ordered their cemeteries profaned. And this despite the fact that the non-Muslim population was institutionally under the protection of the Muslim caliph. The Christians and Jews, who are called *ahl al-kitab*, people of the book (of Scripture), had certain privileges, especially the right to practise their religion and to live according to their own laws.

Under the reign of al-Hakim they were the object of innumerable public persecutions and humiliations. As with women, the prohibitions against the non-Muslims had to do with the body, clothing, and space. He forced the Christians and Jews when in the bath to wear a badge that distinguished them from Muslims. He compelled the Christians to wear a cross and the Jews a small bell hung around the neck. Then he imposed on them the wearing of black belts and black turbans and head veils. Christians were compelled to wear a large wooden cross around the neck; they were also forbidden to ride horses, leaving them to use more lowly mounts such as donkeys. All the high Jewish and Christian officials were dismissed and some were executed. In order to escape these persecutions, Christians and Jews asked to become Muslims, and there were mass conversions.[59] But neither the banishing of women from public space and their seclusion in their houses, nor the persecution of Jews and Christians and their subsequent desire to become Muslims seemed to stem the inflation nor make the waters of the Nile rise. The economic crisis continued unabated and the search for bread became the major problem.

The caliph resumed his nightly and daily ramblings. As they increased in number, incidents of violence along his route became almost inevitable:

> One day as he passed a butcher's shop he seized the butcher's chopper and with it struck and killed one of his attendants, passing on without paying any more attention to the body; the terrified crowd did not dare to do anything and the body remained there until al-Hakim sent a shroud in which to bury him.[60]

People walked with wary eyes through the shadowy streets on the lookout for the shameful phantom whose solitary wandering reflected the loneliness of each of his subjects. They had lost all contact with who was supposed to lead them to Paradise. Entangled in a vicious circle that chained an unloved caliph to his frightened and disillusioned subjects, they no longer knew the way to Paradise.

In this state of affairs the presence of Sitt al-Mulk in the palace was all the more reassuring. The people of Cairo were kept informed by the rumours spread by the thousands of artisans, slaves, and servants employed at the palace. They knew her character and had heard about her vain attempts to reason with her brother and to counteract the effects of his caprices and the influence of the extremist Shi'ite *da'i*s who crowded around him. One man in particular had appeared in his entourage and had come between al-Hakim and his sister, pushing him over the brink into madness by telling him that he was God in person, not just a mere imam.[61]

There were all sorts of extremist *da'i*s in Fatimid Cairo. They were hangers-on at the court just as were the astrologers, mathematicians, and ideologues. But Hamza Ibn 'Ali was like no one else, and no one else could weave such megalomaniac dreams as that of *al-ta'aluh*, the dream, so tempting for all mortals, of escaping death. Was death not the only mystery that could turn a caliph into an insomniac? We will never know what it was that tormented al-Hakim, what drove the commander of the faithful into night-shrouded streets and forests to gaze at the stars, which seemed to defy death by their fixity. We will never know what fears impelled the prince to desert the precincts of the palace with its luxury and comfort. What is certain is that the *da'i* Hamza was in a position to propose a remedy for those fears and that the decision of the prince to declare himself *Ilah*, God in person, and thus immortal, made sense for him in some way or other. Not only did al-Hakim let himself be convinced by Hamza, but he yielded to the latter's pressure to make a public announcement and compel the Muslims to worship him.[62]

Although the majority of Muslims chose disobedience to a prince who had gone beyond the limits, to this day a small minority in the mountains of Lebanon keeps the memory of al-Hakim and Hamza alive. For the Druzes the disappearance of al-Hakim is only a *ghayba*, an absence that is part of the cosmological order of the imamate and its mysteries, which surpass common understanding.[63] Hamza Ibn 'Ali, the founder of the Druze sect, declared to his adherents that 'al-Hakim is veiled [*ihtajaba*] and will return to earth after his absence [*ghayba*] to assure the rule of the faith.'[64] Today the Druzes play a very modest role; few people are acquainted with their vision of the world and the key figures of their cult. The two most famous Druzes of the modern world (at least for people of my generation) were Farid al-Atrash and his sister Asmahane, two of the greatest modern singers. Of princely descent, handsome and gifted, Farid al-Atrash and Asmahane led a life stamped with the fascinating quality of extremist Shi'ism – the mysterious power to unleash the imagination. And it is the savour of the unreal and escape into the unusual that is found in the sad songs and hybrid melodies of Farid and Asmahane, melodies that are not exactly oriental nor exactly occidental, not intrinsically Arab nor totally Asian. For me, a North African, they were my first contact with the Druzes and the opportunity to discover that there existed another Islam different from Sunnism.[65] But although one group of adherents always kept alive the memory of al-Hakim with respect and devotion, the same cannot be said of the Egyptians of that time.

Upon the declaration in the mosques of the caliph's divinity, with all the necessary pomp and with strong backing from the qadis and the *'ulama*, the people of Cairo reacted with anger. The Egyptians made use of two means of expression that would become among the most powerful in the modern world: individual writings such as are found in the published press, and handwritten messages scribbled on public walls. Al-Hakim's palace was inundated with insulting letters, and the authorities had their hands full cleaning the walls of the messages ridiculing the Fatimid's claim to divine status. Mad with rage that the Egyptians dared to cover the walls of the medina with messages of insubordination and disobedience, al-Hakim gave the order to set the city on fire,[66] and some chroniclers say that he found a cynical pleasure in watching its destruction.[67] With the city in flames, the decision of Sitt al-Mulk to take action is scarcely surprising. But although virtually all the historians agree in making her the murderer of al-Hakim and thus a fratricide, only one suggests that the murderer was someone else. According to the distinguished historian Maqrizi, who produced the most vivid pictures of Fatimid Cairo in his *Khitat*, a book that is still one of the most respected sources on the Fatimid regime, the assassin of al-Hakim was a man of the Bani Husayn, who publicly declared in 415 that it was he who had killed the caliph with the complicity of three other men. When he was asked to explain how he did it, 'the man drew out a knife and plunged it into his heart saying, "That's how I killed him," and he committed suicide before the people.'[68] Why did he kill him? He answered that he acted to defend the honour of Islam and Allah.[69]

But Maqrizi's anonymous assassin carries little weight compared to the unanimity of all the other historians, who point to Sitt al-Mulk as the instigator of the murder. She had good reason to do away with him: he had wounded her pride by sending her humiliating letters accusing her of *zina* (fornication) and threatening her with death.[70] She then wrote to Ibn Daws, a great general in al-Hakim's retinue, whom the latter had imagined to be her lover, and she arranged a meeting with him: 'In the course of this meeting she concluded a bargain with this military man and promised to share power with him in exchange for his doing away with the caliph.' When Ibn Daws's mission had been carried out and al-Hakim killed, Sitt al-Mulk discovered to her great surprise that once you embark on the course of political murder, you cannot put an end to it. What was she to do with Ibn Daws, who knew everything, and with the servants who had helped him? But there was something more pressing to be done: the enthronement of al-Hakim's son, who was still a child, something banned by the *shar'ia*, since to be caliph it was required that one be an adult. And who better than Ibn Daws, the strong man of the empire, to reason with the qadis and persuade the religious authorities to collaborate?

Once the son of al-Hakim was crowned with the royal turban and ritual and order was re-established in the palace and the city, Sitt al-Mulk could undertake a task that was becoming ever more urgent: getting rid of Ibn Daws, who knew her secret and had the power to blackmail her. She thought up a strategem that would produce a death in public. She sent some guards to a meeting of viziers and notables, and they pointed to Ibn Daws and accused him of having killed 'our master the caliph' and then killed him right there in the meeting. Once the palace was cleaned out and the regency officially organized, Sitt al-Mulk chose some competent ministers and settled down for four years to putting the economy in order and calming the population. She succeeded on both counts.

This was a unique case. Exceptional circumstances had brought on a power vacancy during the first months of unrest following the disappearance of the caliph. During this time a woman had carried out virtually all the functions of caliph and had directed the affairs of the empire as regent. Nevertheless, the important lesson to be learned is that this Fatimid queen never dared to ask that the *khutba* be said in her name. Although she must certainly have dreamed of it, Sitt al-Mulk, practised observer of the caliphal scene that she was, knew better than anyone the law of the harem that marked its inhabitants forever – the law of the veil. Her story also confirms to us that, on the question of women, Shi'ites and Sunnis are in agreement: the access of women to the greater imamate, to the leadership of the state, is an event that is accompanied by disorder and is the expression of it. Women do not have the same political rights as men. Because of their very essence, they must be strangers to politics.

This is further confirmation that the case of the Yemeni queens was due not to the Shi'ite variable but to regional cultural factors. The logic of belonging to the harem imposes the mask, the veil, for all those who violate the *hudud*, who go beyond the limits and find themselves on the other side, on the caliphal scene. The veil relates to theatre and ritual, and in that way it is more troubling than absence and death. Whatever you may say about absence or death, it is existence that is important. The dead and the absent do not exist – although in varying degrees, it is true. But what is involved in the ritual of the veil is the annihilation of the free will of beings who are physically present, of women who are here and who look at you with wide-open, alert eyes. It was not the presence of Sitt al-Mulk on the throne of Egypt that was disturbing. It was rather

her sovereign will, which the *khutba* is designed to magnify. This is the reason why the Arab man is not upset by intelligence in a woman. A very intelligent woman is always something to be admired, and the huge infiltration of women into universities in the Arab world in less than 30 years of educational opportunity corroborates this. The access of women to knowledge, to the universities and academies is not upsetting, provided that this phenomenon does not spill over into politics. What is disturbing is the decision of a woman to exist as an independent will. And there is a great difference between intelligence and will. A woman's intelligence can always be put at the service of the one who owns her, but a sovereign will can never be. A will is or is not. And if it is, it can only be in competition with another, above all with that of the man to whom she owes obedience.

This is the reason Arabic has a word, *al-nashiz*, to define a woman who rebels against the will of her husband. The concept of *nushuz* is only applied to women. It is a declaration by a woman of her decision not to follow the will of her husband. A *nashiz* is a woman who declares herself to be an individual, and no longer just a being who aligns herself with the will of someone else. And *nushuz* is obviously synonymous with *fitna*, disorder. The definition of citizenship in the Universal Declaration of Human Rights is a synonym for *nushuz*, because it involves the emergence of the will of the individual, whatever the sex, as sovereign on the political scene. The individual will and its place on the political chessboard of modern Islam is the key problem around which all debates revolve, whether those of imams or of secular men of the left, whether speeches of heads of state or writings by political prisoners. So in the Arab world all discussion about women is a discussion about the development of the individual and his or her place in society. As long as our will is veiled, that of the men who do not live in the entourage of the prince and who do not participate in its privileges will also remain so. In the realms of the women who took power in Islam, only the women close to the prince, whether he was father, brother, husband, or son, succeeded in infiltrating the political scene. The women who did not live within the privacy of the palace had no more chance of access than did ordinary men. And it is this aristocratic essence of the political process that is called into question by the right to vote and universal suffrage. That is why, as the fundamentalists well understand, the election of Benazir Bhutto constituted a total break with caliphal Islam. It represented the dual emergence on the political scene of that which is veiled and that which is obscene: the will of women and that of the people.

Universal suffrage tears away two veils, two veils that give substance to the two thresholds of political Islam in its cosmic architecture: the *hijab* (veil) of women and that of the caliph. For, paradoxical as it may seem, women are not the only ones to hide themselves behind a *hijab*. The Muslim caliph, the ultimate concentration of all the wills of the faithful, of those who choose submission, who choose negation of the will for the benefit of the group, needs more than anyone else to protect himself. The *hijab* of the caliph, his veil, is an institution just as fundamental to political Islam as is the veil of women, and if it is never directly invoked in the desperate cry for the return to the veil, it is because it hides the unmentionable: the will of the people, the will of the *'amma*, the mass, which is just as dangerous as that of women.

Conclusion
The Medina Democracy

———•••◦◉◉◉◉◉◉•••◦———

Veils hide only what is obscene. And even more obscene than the sovereign will of women is that of the *'amma*, the mass of people, defined from the beginning as lacking in reason. If the caliph is the highest point of the political architecture, the *'amma* constitutes the lowest point, the most earthly. As all the historians will tell you, the *'amma* cannot think, for in order to think one must have criteria for ordering, distinguishing, judging, and evaluating. And the *'amma* lacks understanding and discernment. This makes it resistant to order and its representative, the caliph, whose natural enemy it is and whose life it constantly puts in danger.

This is what creates the necessity to protect the caliph, to hide him behind a *hijab*, a veil-barrier. This *hijab al-khalifa*, caliph's veil, is not a minor detail. It is a key institution which has its rituals and its agents to watch over it. The caliph's *hijab* made its appearance with the series of assassinations, in the mosque itself, of the first Muslim rulers, with 'Umar at the head of the list.

'Umar Ibn al-Khattab, an irreproachable leader of exemplary rectitude, humble before God and just with men, was cut down in the heart of the mosque as he performed his duties as the imam. He was preparing to lead the prayers when a malcontent stabbed him. 'Umar was the second caliph after the Prophet, and his death was a traumatic event. However, although he was the first, he was scarcely the last. His death unleashed a murderous hatred between the leader and his subjects. Every time a caliph appeared, a murderer lurked in the crowd. Caught between the duty to pray and the lack of dialogue with the imam, his subjects transformed the mosque into a place of sacrifice and the imam into the victim. The corpses of caliphs piled up in the courtyards of the mosques. To stop the massacre, the Muslim political system was obliged to create another threshold and to set up another *hijab*: the *hijab* of the caliph, this time eminently and intrinsically political, the aim of which was to remove the representative of God on earth from the violence of the people whom he was duty-bound to lead. The caliphal palace was thus caught between the *hijab* of women and that of the *'amma*, the earthly masses, conditioned to an almost animal hatred towards the sacred and its representatives. The murder of Caliph 'Umar can be considered the key event that brought on the division of political space and the exiling of the obscene populace behind a threshold barrier.

Let us unreel the action again, since Muslim history does not live by historical chronology, but endlessly reverts to primordial scenes. One day in year 13 of the Hejira (634), 'Umar was walking in the street as he did each day. He was accosted by Abu Lu'lu'a, a dissatisfied non-Arab slave. Known for his love of justice, but also for his *ghilda*, strictness, 'Umar, for reasons of security, had forbidden non-Arabs to stay in Medina. One of the Prophet's Companions, al-Mughira Ibn Shu'ba, had asked permission for Abu Lu'lu'a, a Persian Mazdakite from Nihawand and a blacksmith in his employ, to stay in the city. The slave went to the caliph to complain about his master, whom he accused of extorting too high a payment for the residence permit that the latter had obtained for him. The caliph defended the master. The slave went to the caliph a second time to complain, and this time he threatened him. 'Umar merely remarked, 'This slave has just threatened me!' But he took no action, and one day

> Abu Lu'lu'a hid a dagger in his clothing and near dawn went to the mosque where he crouched down in a corner, awaiting the arrival of the caliph, who would come to call the faithful to prayer. As the caliph passed close to him, the slave sprang upon him and stabbed him three times, wounding him mortally below the navel. Of the twelve people that he subsequently attacked, six died of their wounds. Then he killed himself with his dagger.[1]

It was with this scene of horror, at dawn in the mosque of Medina, with the caliph stabbed and the bodies of the faithful and that of the assassin laid out side by side, that the war between the caliph and the people began.

This assassination was followed by many others, notably that of 'Ali Ibn Abi Talib, also in the mosque. It was that assassination, provoking the first split in Islam, which was to harden the caliph's distrust of the crowd of the faithful assembled in a mosque that might be sheltering a murderer. In his unequalled *Al-Muqaddima*, Ibn Khaldun laments:

> Look at the caliphs who have been assassinated in the mosque at the time of the call to prayer and how their assassins lay in wait for them at precisely that time. This proves that they personally presided over the prayer service and had no others substitute for them in that duty.[2]

With the series of assassinations of caliphs, the *umma*, the ideal community of the faithful, gave way to an *'amma* full of hatred for the caliph and the desire to kill him.

The *hijab*, the veil that blocks off the exterior and filters it in order to protect the caliph, henceforth cut the caliph off from his subjects, who had become the *'amma*. From then on, the fiction of the just caliph was the prisoner of earthly space and its violent reality, a violence that fractured the political scene in two: the space of caliphal decision-making, and the space of the *'amma*, excluded from that decision-making and forever exiled outside the walls of the palace. According to Ibn Khaldun, the institution of the caliphal *hijab* appeared simultaneously with the transformation of the caliphal ideal into earthly despotism:

> When the caliphate was transformed into theocratic royalty and when there appeared the institutions of the sultanate with their titles [that is, when the caliph began to delegate the powers of the imam – prayer, justice, and financial management], the first thing done was to close the door to the public, because of the princes' fear of attacks by the Kharijites and other dissidents . . .. Leaving that door open had another disadvantage: it permitted the crowd to besiege the princes and prevent them from attending to their important business. The dignitary chosen for that office was called the *hajib*.[3]

The word *hajib* has the same root as the word *hijab* – *hajaba*, to hide, to veil, to put up a barrier, to divide space in two by a *sitr*, a veil. The only difference between *hajib* and *hijab* is that the first is a man, the second an object, a veil or barrier of some sort. But the two have the same function: to divide space in two, the inside and the outside, with the aim of protecting the inside from the outside. The *hajib* 'interposes himself between the sultan and the public [*al-'amma*] and closes the door to the latter or opens it depending on the rank of the visitor, and does this at hours fixed by the prince.'[4]

There are some very beautiful passages in Arab history about the lonely situation of pious caliphs – caliphs like 'Umar Ibn 'Abd al-'Aziz, who wanted at all costs to stop the violence and have a dialogue with the rebels. He spent his time receiving them and writing them long letters to explain himself and try to understand them. 'Umar Ibn 'Abd al-'Aziz died – alas! – too soon. Too soon to institutionalize dialogue with an opponent instead of cutting off his head. The pious caliph suffered from being separated from the people by the *hijab*. He was conscious that it was impossible for him to fulfil his duties, which, according to the ideal, required him to be head of state and head of government, minister of justice, minister of finance, and commander of the army.[5] The job of qadi was one of the functions included in the caliphate. It was the qadi's duty to decide between litigants in order to put an end to disputes and cut short court cases, but only by applying the prescriptions of divine law drawn from the Koran and the Sunna. This is the reason why this office was part of the duties of the caliph.[6] However, very quickly it became impossible for the caliph to carry out every duty that required face-to-face contact with the people: 'In the first years of Islam the caliphs exercised it [the function of qadi] themselves and did not delegate it to someone else. The first to delegate it to another person, to whom he gave complete powers, was 'Umar (may God agree to it).'[7] So much for justice.

'Umar, the second orthodox caliph, died in year 13 of the Hejira (634), and since then Muslim justice has not been administered by the one who is responsible for it according to the divine plan – namely, the caliph himself. As we have seen, Harun al-Rashid was the first to delegate the function of imam, sending someone to lead the prayer service in his place. From that time on, the caliph and the people, who no longer had any opportunity to engage in dialogue, were locked into a cycle of violence and sedition followed by execution. The caliph barricaded himself in his palace, to which the people were denied entry. He only saw the world through the *hijab*. An elitist court, made up of viziers, high officials, *'ulama* (religious authorities), and army generals, surrounded him and obstructed his view.

The *'amma* followed whoever made himself their leader, without differentiating between talent and incompetence, without distinguishing truth from error. If the reader really wants to reflect on what we are talking about, let him cast his eyes on the assemblages of scholars; he will find them replete with men of the elite in whom shine forth discernment, virtue, and intelligence. On the other hand, let him examine the *'amma* in the places where they repair and congregate. He will only find them gathered around a bear trainer or a buffoon who makes monkeys dance to the sound of his drum. He will notice that they go where pleasure and frivolity are found; there they make frequent visits to a juggler, a conjurer, a charlatan; there they lend their ears to the lying tales of a popular preacher.[8]

This contemptuous harangue by the historian Mas'udi against the people, the like of which is found in the speeches of many Muslim leaders, is deeply rooted in the mentality of today's officials. The definitive statement of it, since become proverbial, came from Caliph 'Ali Ibn Abi Talib, who also fell to the dagger blows of a rebel. He was asked what he thought of the *'amma*. 'It is a herd of beasts following any loudmouth,' he replied, 'never seeking the light of knowledge. Thus it is with reason that the epithet "cloud of grasshoppers" is applied to the crowd.'[9] All the crusades that certain reactionary Muslim politicians wage today against the West and its parliamentary democracies, considered alien to the spirit of Islam, stem from the fact that parliamentary democracy totally destroys their idea of political power, which, as we have seen, has nothing to do with the ideal of the caliph at the beginning of the Hejira. This was a conception of an imam enlightened by the *shari'a* and attentive to his people, who were close to him in a mosque without barriers. And it is in this ideal of a political Islam which 15 centuries of despotism failed to shake that the miracle, the enigma, and the challenge of modern times is to be found.

One may speak of a *miracle* because the dream of the ideal defies history and shows itself to be completely impervious to its lessons. One may also speak of an *enigma* because for 15 centuries the people have been constantly rising up against the despotism of their leaders without their anger and sorrow finding any way out of the circle of violence. Finally, one may speak of a *challenge* because since national independence, universal suffrage – borrowed from the secular West, it is true – has become institutionalized, however limited it may be. It is interesting to note that in today's Muslim world there is no longer any debate about the legitimacy of universal suffrage. Nowadays it is about the degree of falsification of election results. This is a big step forward toward the acceptance of the people as the source of sovereignty. And yet, there is nothing more foreign to political power in Islam than the recognition that sovereignty resides in the people – a bizarre idea that would never have crossed the mind of the most pious caliph.

Islam has known many pious caliphs who have suffered from being unable to put into practice what the holy book laid out as the *shari'a* and the way to justice on earth and paradise in Heaven:

> It is recounted that one day a violent hurricane unleashed over Baghdad was about to send all the buildings crashing to earth, burying their inhabitants in the ruins. Then Mahdi [husband of Khayzuran and father of Harun al-Rashid] was seen prostrating himself in the palace and praying: 'Lord, you have entrusted to my care the nation of Your apostle. Do not punish it for the numerous sins that I have committed. Out of regard for the ever living image of Muhammad, save this nation!' Thus he fervently prayed until the storm ceased.[10]

Who can ever know the solitude of a caliph tortured by the longing for an impossible reign of justice? This is the other side of Muslim history, which must be written one day. Who can know the sleepless nights of an imam? Often, like Mahdi, they prayed like a lonely child by the light of the moon:

> Rabia, his chamberlain, told me the following: 'I was informed one night that Mahdi had risen and was alone in his room praying. I went into that room, which was simply whitewashed and without any decoration. The white light of the moon, which fell on the walls and the divan, brought out the red in the carpet on which Mahdi, dressed in white,[11] stood, with his face turned toward the divan. He was reciting the Koran in a soft voice and did not notice my presence. I stood in admiration before that room, the moonlight that illuminated it, the caliph imploring God, and his melodious voice.'[12]

Many Muslim caliphs sank into prayer in the hope of finding a way to counteract the violence, rebellion, and sedition that the *hijab* hid from them.

Contrasting the very negative idea of the *'amma* to the very positive, eminently Western, idea of a citizen people shows us why in Islam all debate on human rights is in fact an obscene debate that can only be formulated in terms of veils, of the *hijab*, that is, of thresholds that prohibit and boundaries that protect. The obscenity is double: it comes from the fact that the sovereignty of a citizen people wrenches political legitimacy from the vault of Heaven and brings it down to earth, and that it raises the standard of Western individualism against the law of the group, which rules the East and legitimates its despotisms. This double obscenity is all the more difficult to deal with because since acquiring independence the Muslim states have stamped their fragile existence with the paradox of ambiguity: Islam will be the state religion; and the state, by installing parliaments elected by universal suffrage, will recognize that sovereignty has come down from Heaven to the low place where dwell the shaky free wills of the undernourished people of the urban shanty-towns. From now on, the Muslim state can only sustain itself by enacting its drama on two fundamentally contradictory stages – caliphal and parliamentary. And from this comes the increase in veils and the unrestrained multiplication of barriers.

Since the end of colonization and the coming of independence, a second stage has been set up alongside the traditional caliphal arena, where the people are marked with the negative stamp of *'amma*, bearer of disorder. This is the parliamentary stage, where the people are endowed with reason and enjoy all rights, including the right to designate the supreme head of state – all of which can end up in so-called aberrations like the election of a Muslim woman.

Article 1 of the Universal Declaration of Human Rights constitutes an out-and-out violation of the *hijab* and its logic: 'All human beings are born free and equal in dignity and rights. They are endowed with reason and conscience.' Article 19 constitutes a total break with the conception of a bloodthirsty, unruly *'amma*: 'Everyone has the right to freedom of opinion and expression; this right includes freedom to hold opinions without interference and to seek, receive and impart information and ideas through any media and regardless of frontiers.' This is the definition of *fitna* – disorder on the caliphal stage, which is based on the obedience of the *'amma* and the silence/masking of women. *Fitna* is the election of Benazir Bhutto to the position of head of government; *fitna* is the victory of a woman elected by the vote of the Pakistani *'amma* in 1410 of the Hejira (1988) to the post of supreme political leader, an act which closes that huge parenthesis of 15 centuries of despotism, of *mulk*, to borrow a term from Ibn Khaldun, who trembled for his life yesterday as they all do today.

The Universal Declaration of Human Rights, which was ratified by almost all the Muslim states after World War II, thus destroyed the unity of the political field and split it between two scenes, perhaps contradictory but both necessary. Necessary because the Muslims no longer control the march of empires, the rhythm of the stars, and the measure of time as they did in the time of Harun al-

Rashid. Alongside their calendar which still counts the months of the year 1414 by the moon, they have hung another calendar, strange and foreign, high-speed and disquieting, which strips off the months of a parallel year numbered 1992. Two scenes, two calendars, creating a feeling of vertigo about time. Time no longer signifies what it used to signify; it has to be split in two, to be tattooed with another time that belongs to others, in order to be maintained, to make sense. We have two calendars, each serving masters with conflicting demands. One calendar for prayer and the other for paying the foreign debt; one calendar that tells the holy hour in Mecca and another that details the caprices of the stock market and reflects the ups and downs of the dollar.

Two scenes, two calendars, two identities – sovereign citizens there; submissive, faithful Muslims here. In order to survive, we are forced to learn to dance to the disjointed rhythm of what one might call the 'medina democracy'.

It is this coming and going, this demented dance between two not only opposed, but irreconcilable scenes that is exhausting us, the inhabitants of the medina democracy. In one scene, the caliphal scene, sovereignty is singular, that of a group/*umma* concentrated in a divine will that is of necessity unique and unified. In the other scene, the parliamentary scene, sovereignty is atomized among millions of individuals each as important as the other. We must constantly be on the alert, adjust our masks and posture, and above all know how to hold our tongue, depending on whom we are facing. Speaking freely, a sacred right of the citizen in the parliamentary scene, is decried and condemned as *bid'a*, a crime, in the caliphal scene. The tongue of the believers is monofunctional: to recite the knowledge of the ancestors is its duty and *raison d'être*. In contrast, the tongue of citizens is multifunctional; it can certainly repeat the learning of the ancestors, but everyone is encouraged to say new things, to imagine not only new knowledge but a new world. Believers do not have the right to say or write whatever they want, and especially what comes into their head, which should contain no thoughts that tradition has not sanctioned. This is why the inhabitants of the medina democracy who forget that they belong simultaneously to two ideologically contradictory scenes take their pen in hand to write books that bear no resemblance to those of the Sunna and then find themselves from time to time challenged by the imams. The latter, logical despite appearances, can only point out the obvious to us. One cannot be Muslim, submissive by definition, and speak out at the same time.

In December 1988, at the constituent assembly of the Moroccan Human Rights Organization, an eminent *'alim* from southern Morocco, the guest of honour whose speech was awaited by everyone, astonished the audience of mainly teachers and lawyers by saying: 'I have the impression, brothers and sisters in Islam, that many of you who have spoken and have dealt with freedom of expression forget that a good *mu'min* [believer] cannot say just anything. There are many things that he does not have the right to say.' No one in the auditorium rose to challenge him and claim the right of free speech. Why? Because in a medina democracy free speech can lead you straight to prison, unless you master to perfection the dance of masks and the games of *volte-face*. Look at those poor 'prisoners of conscience', who are numbered in the thousands in the Muslim countries according to the latest report from Amnesty International. What is their problem, and why have they ended up there? They forgot one thing that the imams remind us of every morning: in the caliphal scene there is room for only one opinion, that of the caliph, laid down as sacred truth.

The problem that we, the inhabitants of the medina democracy, have is that we are our own partner. We act the play by ourselves and waltz between two irreconcilable scenes. And this is what complicates things for our poor psyche, which, like a motor trying to run on empty, has to put out an incredible effort just to maintain equilibrium.

There is no problem for the people who live in the straight-out democracies, where the right to freedom of expression borders on licence, nor for those who live in the straight-out theocracies, where no one except the leader has the right to speak out. All know their place and the code which rules the movement of the tongue. A Moroccan proverb summarizes the situation to perfection: '*Al-lisan ma fih 'adhm*', the tongue contains no bony elements, so it can *tazliq*, slide easily; and slips of the tongue, alas, do not have the same import in all languages. In France a slip of the tongue is just a minor matter that delights the psychoanalysts, the great gurus of the parliamentary scene. But let your tongue slip in the presence of the caliph and in his scene, and you will witness the apocalypse. Paradoxically, in that scene, where the opinion of an individual carries no weight, a slip of the tongue is like a thunderbolt that shakes Heaven and earth and makes the offender guilty of a blasphemous obscenity.

One day when I was little and came home from the Koranic school with feet swollen by the *falaqa* (a device that holds the feet in place so that the soles can be beaten), my grandmother, who always tried to teach me how to be happy, asked me, 'But, little one, what exactly did you do?' I held back my tears of humiliation and started to formulate my answer: 'I wanted to say to the *faqiha* [teacher] . . .' And my grandmother, who had 50 years of the harem behind her, interrupted me before I could even finish my first sentence: 'Child, don't bother to go further. You committed a very grave fault. You wanted, you, to say something to your *faqiha*. You don't say something at your age, especially to someone older. You keep silent. You say nothing. And you will see, you won't get any more beatings.' My grandmother died when I was 13 years old, on a beautiful summer afternoon. I grew up, developed broad shoulders, left the Koranic school, and went out into the world with a sure step in search of dignity. But my progress has always been interrupted by the dismayed advice of those who love me and wish me happiness. They always say the same thing: you must keep quiet if you don't want to be beaten.

In a medina democracy, individuals focus all their efforts on one basic body organ – the tongue. And its acrobatics make them forget the essential – the brain and the act of thinking. While Westerners concentrate on thinking, we, the inhabitants of the medina democracy, invest our efforts in the art of talking. But to express what? Most of the time we do not even know. That is why our meetings go on until midnight and our conferences are interminable. This also explains the flood of words of our planners, politicians, technicians, and intellectuals, whatever their political colour. A flood of words which, when subjected to a rigorous analysis of content, turn out to be just talk without any new ideas – or very few – at the level of real thinking. Perhaps this is because the ability of human beings to develop their minds depends on the degree of responsibility they take for what happens on *their* earth. If the earth belongs to someone else, the need to think becomes superfluous.

A citizen and a believer do not behave the same way in space, for the good and simple reason that Heaven and earth are governed by different laws but exist together in a cosmic scheme. In the caliphal scene one is in the midst of the immense vastness and omnipresence of Heaven, which crushes earth with its divine power and sacred sovereignty; here earth, as populated as it is, has little importance. It is minuscule compared to the overwhelming majesty of Heaven. Above all it is degraded in comparison to the luminous spirituality that sets Heaven aflame. The earth of the believers is low, physical, and heavy with sensuality. Degraded and degrading is this caliphal earth, because it is peopled by lilliputian beings compared to the immensity of divine eternity. When measured against this immensity and its space and time, the earth and its inhabitants are minuscule.

On the other hand, in the parliamentary context there is no Heaven, or, if there is, it is offstage in the political drama. The earth occupies the whole space, and the citizens are giants, each as sovereign as the other, treading with their mortal feet an earth whose grandeur lies in its tragic finitude. This finitude is calculated by a superpowerful human intelligence, which has developed instruments for measuring everything, including how many years are left before the earth and its galaxy fall into the black hole.

We, the inhabitants of medina democracies, are whirling around between Heaven and earth, astronauts despite ourselves, without space suits or oxygen masks, launched into that planetary dance with bare faces and open palms. And there is one far from negligible difference: we women have to do all that whirling around wearing the veil.

Heavens!

When I think about our power! But shh! We mustn't talk about it. We might attract the evil eye!

11
Notes

————◄◄◉◉◉◉◉◉◉●●◄◄◄———

INTRODUCTION

1 Nawaz Sharif rose to be Prime Minister of Pakistan after the fall of Benazir Bhutto.
2 The first year of the Muslim calendar, corresponding to AD 622, is the year of the Hejira, when the Prophet left Mecca, his native city, to migrate to Medina. This symbolic year was chosen because it was then that the Prophet became the leader of the first Muslim community. The year 1992 corresponds with Muslim year 1413–14, months of the Muslim calendar being lunar and thus shorter than in the Christian calendar. Every year the Muslim calendar gains a few days on the Christian calendar. Generally speaking, throughout this book I will write dates listing the year according to the Muslim calendar first, followed by the year according to the Christian calendar.
3 Nawaz Sharif's IDA won only 55 seats. Benazir Bhutto's People's Party won 92 of the 207 seats that are elected by direct vote. There are 237 seats, of which 30 are reserved for special categories: 10 for minorities (especially the Christian minority) and 20 for women.

CHAPTER 1   HOW DOES ONE SAY *QUEEN* IN ISLAM?

1 Ibn Khaldun, *Al-Muqaddima* (Beirut: Dar al-Kitab al-'Arabi, n.d.). There is also the French translation by G. Sourdon and L. Bercher: *Recueils de textes de sociologie et de droit public musulman contenus*

dans les Prolégomènes *d'Ibn Khaldun* (Algiers: Bibliothèque de l'Institut d'Etudes Supérieures Islamiques d'Alger, 1951). This translation poses a problem because the authors translate *mulk* as *royauté théocratique*. I consider this translation incorrect and in addition misleading for the person who wants to understand Islam, because *mulk* has nothing of the theocratic about it. It is precisely a power that claims no God and no law except the passions and ravings of the leader. Ibn Khaldun compares *mulk*, essentially and intrinsically human, to the caliphate, which is a government of divine inspiration. So translating *mulk* as *royauté théocratique* adds a spiritual dimension Ibn Khaldun precisely wants to deny. So I have used this translation, but I have simply replaced *royauté théocratique* by *mulk*. However, when it seems to me that the translation does not render the Arabic text well, I have translated that passage myself. And in such cases, I have given the Arabic reference.

2 Ibn Khaldun, *Muqaddima*, pp. 190–1.

3 Ibid.

4 Ibid.

5 See *Lisan al-'Arab*, the most entertaining dictionary currently available. It is a work of history, linguistics, literature, etc., even including anecdotes. In six volumes, it is a fabulous look into the depths of the mind. Its author, Ibn Manzur, was born in Cairo in 630/1232 and died in 711/1311.

6 All that I say in this paragraph concerning the imam and the caliph, the sultan and the king, can be found in the following: *Lisan al-'Arab*, sections on 'sultan', 'malik', 'caliph'; Ibn Khaldun, *Muqaddima*, ch. 26; Ibn Khaldun, *Recueils de textes*, p. 76.

7 For a clear, concise summary of the caliphate, see Louis Millot, 'Théorie orthodoxe ou sunnite du khalifate', in *Introduction à l'étude du droit musulman* (Paris: Recueil Sirey, 1970), pp. 48ff.

8 We will see in ch. 9, 'The Lady of Cairo', how the Fatimid queen Sitt al-Mulk took the reins during a power gap created by the bizarre disappearance of Caliph al-Hakim, and how she then administered the empire — from her harem, of course. She was never officially recognized as the ruler, and did not even claim the title of malika or sultana. She was content to bear her own name, Sitt al-Mulk, Lady of Power.

9 Since one of the objectives of this book is to demystify history and to make it easily accessible, I will make a point of revealing my sources, to evaluate them, and especially to indicate how the lazy or the very busy can get information quickly. But I also want to dispel the inhibitions of intimidated readers and encourage them to go 'directly' to those books of Muslim history which reactionary forces threaten us with and use against us to block our rights. To do this, alongside the 'orthodox references' I will cite texts that explain the various phenomena in a few paragraphs, and especially those which are easily avail-

able, whether in French, Arabic, or English. Since our ignorance of the past is being used against us, we must act. Read the past!

Let us begin with dates. I presume that the reader, like me, always feels lost when trying to understand history as a series of dates. And the juxtaposition of two calendars – the Muslim and the Western – makes things no easier. As to the dates of dynasties and the Muslim sovereigns and their genealogical trees, I will constantly refer to two works that I recommend: *Encyclopedia of Islam*, 2nd edn (Leiden: E. J. Brill, 1960), and Stanley Lane-Poole, *The Mohammadan Dynasties: Chronological and Genealogical Tables with Historical Introductions* (London: Constable, 1894), translated and published in Arabic with the title *Tabaqat salatin al-Islam* in 1982 by Al-Dar al-'Alamiyya li al-Nashr (place not indicated). Lane-Poole's book is so practical and well done that earlier an Egyptian, Dr Ahmad al-Sa'id Sulayman, published under his own name a book with the title *Tarikh al-duwal al-Islamiyya ma' mu'jam al-usar al-hakima* (Cairo: Dar al-Ma'arif, 1972). This is so like Lane's book (with some additions) that I am quite confused about who is the author of what.

10   Ibn Battuta, *Rihla* (Beirut: Dar Beirut, 1985). [Translator's note: The following English translations of Ibn Battuta have been used in this book: *The Travels of Ibn Battuta AD 1325–1354*, translated by H. A. R. Gibb from the French translation of the Arabic text by C. Defrémery and B. B. Sanguinetti (Cambridge: Cambridge University Press, vol. 1, 1958; vol. 2, 1962); and *The Rehla of Ibn Battuta (India, Maldive Islands and Ceylon)*, translation and commentary by Mahdi Husain (Baroda, India: Oriental Institute, 1976). The particular translation used will be cited in each instance. (The references to Radiyya are in the latter work on pp. 34 and 35.) In the rare instances where the material quoted is not included in the English translations, reference is made to the French translation by Defrémery and Sanguinetti (Paris: Maspero, 1982).]

11   Sultana Shajarat al-Durr is mentioned in all the books of 'official' Arab history that are concerned with this era. For those who like short, entertaining accounts, see ch. 13 in Amin Ma'luf, *Les Croisades vues par les Arabes* (Paris: Lattès, 1983, pp. 253ff).

12   The other empire was that of the Muwahhidin, who followed them and ruled 1130–1269. For information about Zainab, see Abi Zar' al-Fasi, *Al-anis al-mutrib bi rawd al-qirtas fi akhbar mulk al-Maghrib wa tarikh madina Fas* (Rabat: Dar al-Mansur, 1972), p. 132.

13   *Lisan al-'Arab*, see the root *shin ra fa* (*sharafa*).

14   Ibid., see the root *ha ra ra* (*harara*).

15   Ibid.

16   Ibid.

17   Ibid.

18 'Abdallah Inan, *Nihayat al-Andalus* (Cairo: Maktaba al-Madani, 1987), pp. 198ff.
19 Ibid., p. 196.
20 Ibid., p. 197.
21 Ibid., pp. 198ff.
22 Ibid., p. 202.
23 This is the case, for example, with some Spanish documents of 1540, which relate the negotiations between the Spaniards and Sayyida al-Hurra after a raid by pirates on Gibraltar in which 'they took much booty and many prisoners' (Colonel de Castries, [R. G. M. E. de la Croix, duc de Castries] *Sources inédites de l'histoire du Maroc*, vol. 1), pp. 89, 107.
24 'Abd al-Qadir al-'Afiya, *Imra'at al-jabal, al-Hurra Bint 'Ali Ibn Rashid* (Tétouan: Maktaba al-Nur, 1989), p. 18.
    Sayyida al-Hurra has, in fact, been given a new lease of life with the interest shown in her by historians from northern Morocco, who today mostly speak Spanish. They are rehabilitating her by writing articles and studies about her, often based on European sources. The following are some examples: 'Abd al-Qadir al-'Afiya devotes a chapter to her in *Al-hayat al-siyasiyya wa al-ijtima'iyya wa al-fikriyya bi Shafshawan* (Political, social, and cultural life of Shafshawan) (Rabat: Ministry of Islamic Affairs, 1982), pp. 121ff; Muhammad Ibn 'Azuz Hakim, *Sida al-Horra, exceptionelle souveraine*, Mémorial du Maroc, 3 (Rabat: Nord Organization, 1982), pp. 128ff; Muhammad Dawud, *Tarikh Tatwan* (Tetouán: Institut Moulay Hassan, 1959), vol. 1, pp. 117ff; Muhammad Ibn 'Azuz Hakim, *Al-Sitt al-Hurra hakima Tatwan* (Tetouán: Mu'assasa 'Abd al-Khaliq al-Torres, 1983). One other source that throws light on her reign is: Chantal de la Véronne, *Sida el-Horra, la noble dame* (Paris: Hespérides, 1956), pp. 222–5.
25 See n. 24 above.
26 A. Joly, *Tétouan*, Archives Marocaines 5 (Rabat, 1905), p. 188.
27 'Afiya, *Imra'at al-jabal*, p. 10.
28 Ibid.
29 Ibid.
30 Muhammad Dawud, *Tarikh Tatwan*, vol. 1, p. 117; Muhammad Ibn 'Azuz Hakim, *Al-Sitt al-Hurra hakima Tatwan*; Ahmad al-Nasiri, *Al-istiqsa fi akhbar al-maghrib al-aqsa* (Casablanca: Dar al-Kitab, 1956), vol. 4, p. 154.
31 Al-Maqrizi, *Al-Khitat* (Cairo: Maktaba al-Thaqafa al-Diniyya, 1987), vol. 2, p. 285; Abi al-Falah 'Abd al-Hayy Ibn al-'Imad al-Hanbali, *Shazarat al-dahab fi akhbar man dahab* (Beirut: Manshurat Dar al-Afaq al-Jadida, n.d.), vol. 3, pp. 192ff (the author died in year 1089 of the Hejira); Ibn al-Athir, *Al-kamil fi al-tarikh* (Beirut: Dar al-Fikr, n.d.), vol. 7, pp. 304ff.

32 Khayr al-Din al-Zarkali, *Al-a'lam, qamus ash'ar al-rijal wa al-nisa'
   min al-'arab wa al-musta'rabin wa al-mustashraqin* (Beirut: Dar al-'Ilm
   li al-Malayin, 1983), 8 vols. See section on 'Sitt'.
33 Al-Damdi, *'Aqa'iq al-Yaman*, quoted in Zarkali, *A'lam*, in the section
   on 'Sharifa'.
34 *Encyclopedia of Islam.*
35 Mahmud Fahmi al-Muhandis, *Kitab al-bahr al-sakhir*, quoted in Zarkali, *A'lam*, in the section on 'al-Ghaliyya al-Wahhabiyya'.
36 *Encyclopedia of Islam*, article on 'Ilkhans'.
37 Bernard Lewis, *Islam from the Prophet Muhammad to the Capture of
   Constantinople* (Oxford: Oxford University Press, 1987), vol. 1, pp.
   89–96.
38 Ibn Battuta, *Travels of Ibn Battuta*, vol. 2, p. 340.
39 On the Kharijites see: Muhammad Abu Zahra, 'Al-Khawarij', in
   Al-madahib al-Islamiyya (Cairo: Maktaba al-Adab, 1924), pp. 96ff;
   Ahmad Amin, 'Al-Khawarij', in *Fajr al-Islam* (Beirut: Dar al-Kitab
   al-'Arabi, 1975).
40 Ibn Hazm al-Andalusi, 'Niqat al-'arus fi tawarikh al-khulafa', in *Al-
   Rasa'il* (Collection of letters and short essays), ed. Hasan 'Abbas
   (Beirut: Al-Mu'assasa al-'Arabiyya li Dirasat wa Nashr, 1981), vol. 2,
   pp. 119–22. Ibn Hazm (384–456) is one of the great experts on the
   Quraysh and the author of the standard book on the subject: *Jamhara
   ansab al-'Arab* (Cairo: Dar al-Ma'arif, n.d.).
41 Jurji Zaydan, *Tarikh al-tamaddun al-Islami* (History of Muslim
   civilization) (n.p., n.d.), vol. 1, p. 138; Lane-Poole, *Mohammadan
   Dynasties.*
42 Ma'luf, *Les Croisades vues par les Arabes*, pp. 253ff; Lewis, *Islam*,
   pp. 77–96.

CHAPTER 2   THE CALIPH AND THE QUEEN

1 *Encyclopedia of Islam*, 2nd edn (Leiden: E. J. Brill, 1960) article on
   'Lakab'.
2 Ibn al-Jawzi, 'Al-muntazim', manuscript in Berlin, cited by Adam
   Metz in his *Al-hadara al-Islamiyya* (Muslim civilization), the original
   of which is in German. My references all come from the Arabic
   translation in two volumes (Cairo: Maktaba al-Khanji, 1968).
3 She is not to be confused with another khatun of the same name,
   whom we will encounter later after the Mongol seizure of power. The
   Seljuk sultana mentioned here never succeeded in becoming the
   official head of state, while the other one did succeed in that with the
   help of the Mongols.
4 Ibn al-Athir, *Al-kamil fi al-tarikh* (Beirut: Dar al-Fikr, n.d.), vol. 8,
   p. 482.
5 Ibid., p. 484.

6 'Umar Kahhala, *A'lam al-nisa'* fi *'alamay al-'Arabi wa al-Islami* (Famous women in the Muslim and Arab worlds) (Beirut: Mu'assasa al-Risala, 1982), vol. 2, p. 288.

7 See *Encyclopedia of Islam*, article on 'Lakab', for original wording in Arabic.

8 Hanbali, *Shazarat* (see ch. 1 n. 31 above), vol. 5, p. 288.

9 Ibid., pp. 268ff; al-Maqrizi, *Al-Khitat* (Cairo: Maktaba al-Thaqafa al-Diniyya, 1987), vol. 2, pp. 237ff.

10 Kahhala, *A'lam al-nisa'*, vol. 1, p. 448; *Encyclopedia of Islam*, article on 'Iltutmish'.

11 *Encyclopedia of Islam*, article on 'Atjeh'.

12 Ibid. For details of their reign see Badriye Uçok Un, *Al-nisa' al-hakimat* fi *tarikh*, tr. from Turkish by Ibrahim Daquqi (Baghdad: Matba'a al-Sa'dun, 1973), pp. 152ff.

13 Ibn Khaldun, *Al-Muqaddima* (Beirut: Dar al-Kitab al 'Arabi, n.d.), p. 191.

14 Ibn Khaldun, *Recueils de textes* (see ch. 1 n. 1 above), p. 76.

15 Ibn Rushd, *Bidaya al-mujtahid wa nihaya al-muqtasid* (Beirut: Dar al-Fikr, n.d.), vol. 1, p. 105. Ibn Rushd died in year 595 of the Hejira.

16 Ibn Khaldun, *Muqaddima*, p. 191.

17 Ibid., p. 193.

18 Ibid., p. 196.

19 Ibid., p. 209; *Recueils de textes*, p. 74.

20 Mas'udi, *Les Prairies d'or*, translation of *Muruj al-dahab* by A. C. Barbier de Meynard and A. J.-B. Pavet de Courteille (Paris: Société Asiatique, 1971), vol. 3, p. 821. The Arabic text of this work, which I sometimes cite, was published in 1982 (Beirut: Dar al-Ma'rifa).

CHAPTER 3   THE *JAWARI* OR REVOLUTION IN THE HAREM

1 *Jarya* is the singular form of the plural noun *jawari*.

2 Tabari, *Tarikh al-umam wa al-muluk* (Beirut: Dar al-Fikr, 1979), vol. 8, p. 189.

3 This is the game plan used without exception by all the Islamic fundamentalist movements today.

4 Tabari, *Tarikh*, vol. 2, p. 174.

5 Ibid., p. 177.

6 Ibid., pp. 174ff.

7 Ibn al-Athir, *Al-kamil* fi *al tarikh* (Beirut: Dar al-Fikr, n.d.), vol. 5, pp. 246ff.

8 Mas'udi, *Maruj al-dahab* (Beirut: Dar al-Ma'rifa, 1982), vol. 3, p. 210.

9 Abu al-Faraj al-Isbahani, *Kitab al-aghani* (Book of songs) (Beirut: Dar Ihya al-Turath al-'Arabi, 1963). The biography of Hababa is in vol. 15, p. 122.

10 Over and over Muhammad asserted that women occupied an important place in his life, and that 'A'isha, who often accompanied him on military expeditions, was the person he loved most in the world. The Prophet's sexual prowess with his numerous wives was part of his image as a leader, which went well beyond that of ordinary mortals in all areas, including the emotional and sexual. His caring treatment of his wives was certainly something the Prophet seemed very proud of. For a lengthy exposition of this subject see the second part of my book *Women and Islam: An Historical and Theological Enquiry* (Oxford: Basil Blackwell, 1991) or the US edition, *The Veil and the Male Elite: A Feminist Interpretation of Women's Rights in Islam* (Reading, Mass.: Addison-Wesley, 1991).

11 Hanbali, *Shazarat* (see ch. 1. n. 31 above), vol. 3, p. 78; Miskawiya, *Kitab tajarib al-umama* (Cairo: Sharika al-Tamaddun al-Sina'iyya, 1915), vol. 7, p. 39.

12 Miskawiya, *Kitab*, p. 42.

13 See the following chapter for the sources on this subject.

14 Tabari, *Tarikh*, vol. 12, p. 16.

15 Ibid., p. 37.

16 Ibid., p. 38.

17 Ibn Hazm, 'Niqat al-'arus' (see ch. 1. n. 40 above), p. 98.

18 'Ali Ibrahim Hasan, *Nisa' lahunna fi al-tarikh al-Islami nasib* (Cairo: Maktaba al-Nahda al-Misriyya, 1970), p. 96.

19 Ibid., p.9.

20 Ibid., p. 96. The word *rumi* for a man and *rumiyya* for a woman had just about the same meaning that they have today; they designate the European Christians of the Mediterranean peoples who are our neighbours. In the medinas today, tourists who have a Western look are called *rum*. And if in Baghdad the *rum* were the Byzantines, and in Andalusia they were Spaniards or French, it just shows that the term designated others who were different, who were Christians and European, but were neighbours, geographically close.

21 Ibn Hazm, 'Risala fi fadl al-Andalus wa dhikr rijaliha', in *Rasa'il* (see ch. 1. n. 40 above), vol. 2, pp. 191ff.

22 Ibid., p. 194.

23 Ibid.

24 Al-Maqarri, *Nafh al-tib min ghusn al-Andalus al-ratib* (Beirut: Dar Sadir, 1967), vol. 1, p. 386. The author was born in 986 at the beginning of the seventeenth century AD.

25 There is no doubt about the rivalry that existed between the eastern Muslim empire, ruled by the Abbasids, who expelled the Umayyads and then took their place, and the western Muslim empire (that is, Andalusia), created by the descendants of that very Umayyad dynasty that had been evicted by the Abbasids. The purchase of al-Aghani's book is mentioned in Maqarri, *Nafh al-tib*, vol. 1, p. 386.

26 Ibn Hazm, 'Risala', p. 194.
27 Maqarri, *Nafh al-tib*, vol. 1, p. 383.
28 'Abd al-Wahid al-Murakushi, *Al-mu'jib fi talkhis akhbar al-maghrib*, 7th edn (Casablanca: Dar al-Kitab, 1978), pp. 46ff.
29 Maqarri, *Nafh al-tib*, vol. 3, p. 88.
30 Ibid., vol. 1, p. 602.
31 Ibid.
32 'Abdallah Inan, *Tarajim Islamiyya, sharkiyya wa andalusiyya* (Cairo: Dar al-Ma'arif, 1947), p. 172.
33 Ibid.
34 Ahmad Amin, *Fajr al-Islam*, 11th edn (Beirut: Dar al-Kitab al-'Arabi, 1975): this first part of the trilogy discusses the attitudes and intellectual life in Islam from its beginning to the end of the Umayyad dynasty; Ahmad Amin, *Duha al-Islam*, 6th edn (Cairo: Maktaba al-Nahda al-Misriyya, 1961): three volumes devoted to the social and cultural life, scientific movements, religious sects during the first Abbasid epoch; Ahmad Amin, *Zuhr al-Islam*, 4th edn (Cairo: Maktaba al-Nahda al-Misriyya, 1966): four volumes on the cultural, scientific, and literary life and the religious movements during the second Abbasid epoch.
35 Ahmad Amin, *Zuhr al-Islam*, vol. 3, p. 126.
36 Murakushi, *Mu'jib*, p. 48.

CHAPTER 4   KHAYZURAN: COURTESAN OR HEAD OF STATE?

1 Tabari, *Tarikh al-uman wa al-muluk* (Beirut: Dar al-Fikr, 1979), vol. 10, p. 56.
2 Nabia Abbott, *Two Queens of Baghdad: Mother and Wife of Harun al-Rashid* (Chicago: University of Chicago Press, 1946).
3 Ibn Hazm suggests that she was of mixed origin, with an Arab father and a non-Arab mother. Ibn Hazm, 'Risala fi ummahat al-khulafa'', in *Risa'il* (see ch. 1 no. 40 above), vol. 11, p. 120.
4 A very clear exposition of the regulation of slavery in Islam is given by Ahmad Amin in *Duha al-Islam*, 6th edn (Cairo: Maktaba al-Nahda al-Misriyya, 1961), vol. 1, pp. 79ff.
5 Abbott, *Two Queens*, p. 22.
6 Ibid., p. 26.
7 Ibid., pp. 38–9.
8 Marmaduke Pickthall, *The Meaning of the Glorious Koran* (New York: Dorset Press, n.d.).
9 Tabari, *Tafsir, jami' al-bayan 'an ta'wil ayi al-qur'an*, ed. Mahmud Muhammad Shakir (Cairo: Dar al-Ma'arif, n.d.), vol. 7, p. 541.
10 Abu al-Faraj al-Isbahani, *Kitab al-aghani* (Beirut: Dar Ihya al-Turath al-'Arabi, 1963), vol. 15, p. 28.
11 Ibid.

12	Ibid., vol. 18, p. 170.
13	Ibid., p. 164.
14	Ibid.
15	Ibid., vol. 16, p. 5.
16	Ibn 'Abd Rabbih al-Andalusi, *Al-'iqd al-farid* (Beirut: Dar al-Kutub al-'Ilmiyya, 1983). Vol. 7 is devoted to women. The author died in year 368 of the Hejira.
17	Ibid., p. 139.
18	Ibid., p. 138. Islam recognizes all the Jewish and Christian prophets as the predecessors of the Muslim Prophet. The Prophet was building self-confidence in Safiyya by advising her to remind the attackers that the Jewish religion was a prestigious religion that included prestigious prophets whom the Muslims recognized as their own and respected as such.
19	Ibid., pp. 139–40.
20	On this subject see 'The Prophet as military leader' and 'The *Hijab* descends on Medina', the last two chapters of my book *Women and Islam* (US title: *The Veil and the Male Elite*); see ch. 3 n. 11 above.
21	Ibn 'Abd Rabbih, *Al-'iqd al-farid*, vol. 7, p. 139.
22	Ibid.
23	Ibn Hazm, 'Niqat al-'arus', p. 104.
24	Ibn Hazm, 'Risala fi ummahat al-khulafa'', p. 121.
25	Tabari, *Tarikh*, vol. 10, p. 21.
26	Ibid., vol. 9, p. 165.
27	Mas'udi, *Muruj al-dahab* (Beirut: Dar al-Ma'rifa, 1982), vol. 3, p. 122. See also Ahmad Amin, *Duha al-Islam*, 6th edn (Cairo: Maktaba al-Nahda al-Misriyya, 1961), vol. 1, p. 9.
28	For specific information on slavery and the *jawari* under the first Abbasids, see Ahmad Amin, *Duha al-Islam*, esp. vol. 4, pp. 79ff. On the *jawari*, and esp. the deterioration in the situation of free aristocratic women under the effects of slavery, see Jurji Zaydan, *Tarikh al-tamaddun al-Islami* (n.p., n.d.), vols 4 and 5. Zaydan's analysis is very pertinent, but unfortunately the way he scatters his material here and there in these two volumes prevents the reader from arriving at a general synthesis on either women or slavery. However, there is in fact an incredible amount of material here on these two subjects. Unfortunately, Ahmad Amin also organizes his nine volumes on Muslim civilization chronologically, so one must leaf through the volumes to find the subject one is researching.

	Those who like a synthetical approach can fall back on the excellent chapter on slavery by the German orientalist, Adam Metz, in vol. 1 (pp. 295ff) of his *Al-hadara al-Islamiyya* (Cairo: Maktaba al-Khanji, 1968). In a few pages he gives an exposition of the phenomenon by comparing the Arab slavery practices to those of the Jews and Christians. In his presentation, the Church looks very bad, and the Jews

had the right to reduce their own children to slavery. In short, one is
happy to be living in 1992.

29 Ibn Batalan, *Risala fi shari al-raqiq* (Cairo: Maktaba al-Janna, 1954),
    p. 352. The author died in 444.
30 Ibid., pp. 378ff.
31 Ibid., pp. 365ff.
32 Ibid., pp. 370ff.
33 Lutfalla al-Ghazali, *Hidaya al-murid fi taqlib al-'abid* (Cairo: Maktaba
    al-Janna, 1954).
34 Ibn al-Athir, *Al-kamil fi al-tarikh* (Beirut: Dar al-Fikr, n.d.), vol. 5,
    pp. 84ff. There are numerous sources on Khayzuran. She has been
    the subject of some whole books, and she is mentioned in all the
    works on women and biographies of famous people. I will, however,
    use only some of the great classical historical works: Tabari, *Tarikh*
    (Khayzuran is mentioned in vol. 10, pp. 33, 34, and 52); Mas'udi,
    Muruj (the information on Khayzuran is in vol. 3, pp. 319ff); Ibn al-
    Athir, *Kamil*, vol. 5, pp. 81ff; Hanbali, *Shazarat* (see ch. 1 n. 31
    above), vol. 1, p. 245.
35 Ibn al-Athir, *Kamil*, vol. 5, p. 84.
36 Ibid., p. 79.
37 Ibid., vol. 5, p. 88.
38 Tabari, *Tarikh*, vol. 10, p. 33.
39 Ibn al-Athir, *Kamil*.
40 Tabari, *Tarikh*, vol. 10, p. 33.
41 Ibid., p. 33; Ibn al-Athir, *Kamil*, vol. 5, p. 79.
42 Tabari, *Tarikh*, vol. 10, p. 34.
43 Ibid., p. 33.
44 Al-Baghdadi, *Kitab al-muhabbar* (Beirut: Al-Maktab al-Tijari, n.d.),
    pp. 309ff. The author died in year 245 of the Hejira.
45 *Lisan al-'Arab*, section on 'Haram'.
46 Tabari, *Tarikh*, vol. 10, p. 34.
47 Ibid.
48 Imam al-Nasa'i, *Al-Sunan*, with commentary by al-Suyuti and notes
    by Imam al-Sindi (Cairo: Al-Matba'a al-Misriyya, n.d.), vol. 2, p. 56.
49 Tabari, *Tarikh*, vol. 10. p. 34.
50 Ibid., p. 38.
51 Ibn al-Athir, *Kamil*, vol. 5, p. 80.
52 *Lisan al-'Arab*, section on 'Hirm'.
53 Ibn Hajar al-'Asqalani, *Al-isaba fi tamyiz al-sahaba* (Cairo: Maktaba
    al-Dirasa al-Islamiyya, n.d.), vol. 8, p. 18.
54 One of the most gripping accounts of the Battle of the Camel is found
    in Tabari, *Tarikh*, vol. 5, pp. 161ff.
55 Ibid.
56 Mas'udi, *Muruj*, vol. 2, p. 376.

CHAPTER 5 THE CRITERIA OF SOVEREIGNTY
IN ISLAM

1 *Encyclopedia of Islam*, 2nd edn (Leiden: E. J. Brill, 1960); article on 'Lakab'; for details on the historical event see Ibn al-Athir, *Al-kamil fi al-tarikh* (Beirut: Dar al-Fikr, n.d.), vol. 8, p. 226.
2 Ibn al-Athir, *Kamil*, vol. 8, pp. 226–7.
3 Ibid., p. 450.
4 Hanbali, *Shazarat* (see ch. 1 n. 31 above), vol. 7, p. 153.
5 The *shahada* is one of the four pillars of Islam. It consists of the fundamental declaration: 'There is no God but Allah, and Muhammad is His Prophet.' The four other pillars are prayer, the *zakat* (giving of alms), the Ramadan fast, and the pilgrimage to Mecca. The reference to the first Muslim coins is in Jurji Zaydan, *Tarikh al-tamaddun al-Islami* (n.p., n.d.), vol. 1, pp. 142ff.
6 Ibid., vol. 1, p. 142.
7 Ibid.
8 This word is commonly transliterated as *muezzin*.
9 *Encyclopedia of Islam*, article on 'Khutba'.
10 All the treatises on *fiqh* have a *Kitab al-jum'a* (Friday book), which normally comes after the *Kitab al-salat* (Book of prayer). For a short exposition of the subject, one can consult the 20-page chapter on the Friday service in al-Bukhari, *Salih* (Beirut: Dar al-Ma'rifa, 1978), vol. 1, pp. 157–78. If, in addition, one wants to learn the details of each concept, word, and component of the Friday ritual, one should read the commentary of Ibn Hajar al-'Asqalani in his work known as *Fath al-bari* (Cairo: Maktaba Mustafa al-Halabi, 1959), vol. 3, pp. 3–74.
11 Tabari, *Tarikh al-umam wa al-muluk* (Beirut: Dar al-Fikr, 1979), vol. 1, p. 256.
12 Ibn Sa'd, *Al-tabaqat al-kubra* (Beirut: Dar al-Fikr, 1980), vol. 1, pp. 230, 239. Ibn Sa'd lived in the ninth century; he died in year 230 of the Hejira.
13 Ibid., p. 240.
14 Ibid., p. 247.
15 The *taslim* is the invocation of peace which consists of the following formula: *Al-salam 'alaykum* (Peace be upon you); while the *takbir* is: *Allahu akhbar* (God is great).
16 *Encyclopedia of Islam*, article on 'Khutba'.
17 Ibn Sa'd, *Tabaqat*, vol. 1, p. 238.
18 One of the most fascinating descriptions of the Prophet's mosque is in Imam al-Nasa'i, *Sunan* (see ch. 4 n. 48 above), vol. 2, pp. 31–59.
19 Ibn Sa'd, *Tabaqat*, vol. 1, p. 250.
20 Mas'udi, *Muruj al-dahab* (Beirut: Dar al-Ma'rifa, 1982), vol. 1, p. 287.
21 Ibn Sa'd, *Tabaqat*, vol. 1, p. 250.

22 Mas'udi, *Muruj*, vol. 3, p. 30; *Prairies d'or* (see ch. 2 n. 20 above), vol. 3, p. 725.

23 Al-Tannukhi, 'Al-faraj ba'd al-shidda', quoted by Metz, *Al-hadara al-Islamiyya* (Cairo: Maktaba al-Khanji, 1968), vol. 2, p. 98.

24 Metz, *Al-hadara al-Islamiyya*, vol. 2, p. 97.

25 Mas'udi, *Muruj*, vol. 2, p. 299; *Prairies d'or*, vol. 3, p. 584.

26 Mas'udi, *Muruj*, vol. 2, p. 309.

27 On the question of the *hijab*, one must distinguish between two different veils:
(a) On the veil that the sovereign installs between himself and his subjects in public life, see al-Jahiz, 'Kitab al-hijab', in *Rasa'il al-Jahiz* (Cairo: Maktaba al-Khanji, 1968), vol. 2, p. 25 (the author died in 255 of the Hejira).
(b) On the veil that the sovereign installs between himself and his courtiers in private life, see ch. 3 of the French translation of *Kitab al-taj fi akhlaq al-muluk*, attributed to al-Jahiz, translated by Charles Pellat (Paris: Les Belles Lettres, 1954), p. 49.

28 Al-Jahiz, 'Kitab al-hijab', pp. 25ff.

29 'Asqalani, *Fath al-bari*, vol. 3, p. 34.

30 Imam Nasa'i, *Sunan*, vol. 2, p. 32.

31 Ibid.

32 Ibid.

33 Ibid., p. 33.

34 Ibn al-Jawzi, *Kitab ahkam al-nisa'* (Beirut: Al-Maktaba al-'Asriyya, 1980), p. 201.

35 Ibid., p. 202.

36 Ibid., p. 205.

37 Ibid., p. 209.

38 Ibn Battuta, *Travels of Ibn Battuta* (see ch. 1 n. 10 above), vol. 2, p. 300.

39 Muhammad Siddiq Hasan Khan al-Qannuji, *Husn al-uswa bima tabata minha allahi fi al-niswa* (Beirut: Mu'assasa al-Risala, 1981), p. 345.

40 This caliph was known as Al-Walid (II), and should not be confused with Al-Walid Ibn Al-Malik (I), the sixth Umayyad caliph.

41 Ibn Hazm, 'Niqat al-'arus' (see ch. 1 n. 40 above), pp. 72, 75 and 134. I recommend this essay for all those pressed for time who wish to have information on the Umayyad and Abbasid dynasties. Ibn Hazm is a master of concision and pertinence, as is shown in the telegraphic style in which he presents the details needed to understand the psychology of a prince, details such as physical defects, character faults, etc. On the 'monstrosities' of al-Walid, see also Mas'udi, *Muruj*, vol. 3, p. 223; and Tabari, *Tarikh*, vol. 14, pp. 288ff, and vol. 5, pp. 5ff.

42 Ibn 'Asakir, *Tarikh madinat Dimashq* (Damascus: n.p., 1982), pp. 411ff. The author died in year 571 of the Hejira (twelfth century).

43 Abi al-Hasan al-Maliqi, *Al-hada'iq al-ghanna' fi akhbar al-nisa': tara-*

jim shihirat al-nisa'. This book first appeared in 1978 in Libya and Tunisia. Dr Tayyibi found the manuscript in the Chester Beatty Library in Dublin and edited and published it.

44 'Umar Kahhala, *A'lam al-nisa' fi 'almay al-'Arabi wa al-Islami* (Beirut: Mu'assasa al-Risala, 1982).

45 Jacques Le Goff, 'Les mentalités: une histoire ambiguë', in *Faire de l'histoire: Les nouveaux objets* (Paris: Gallimard, 1974), vol. 3, p. 125.

46 Badriye Uçok Un, *Al-nisa' al-hakimat fi tarikh*, tr. I. Daquqi (Baghdad: Matba'a al-Sa'dun, 1973).

47 Ibid., p. 25.

CHAPTER 6   FIFTEEN QUEENS

1 Badriye Uçok Un, *Al-nisa' al-hakimat fi tarikh*, tr. I. Daquqi (Baghdad: Matba'a al-Sa'dun, 1973), p. 33.

2 Ibid.

3 See an illustration of this coin in Nelson Wright, *Catalogue of the Coins in the Indian Museum* (Calcutta: Oxford University Press, 1907), vol. 2, p. 26. Quoted by Uçok Un, *Al-nisa' al-hakimat*, p. 4.

4 This formulaic prayer is found in various sources with slight differences in wording. For instance: Al-Suyuti, *Al-mustazraf min akhbar al-jawari*, annotated by Salah al-Din al-Munajid (Beirut: Dar al-Kitab al-Jadid, 1976), p. 23; Ashur, *Misr wa al-Sham fi qasr al-Ayyubiyin wa al-mamalik* (Beirut: Dar al-Nahda al-'Arabiyya, 1972), p. 158; Yasin al-Khatib al-'Amri, *Al-rawda al-fayha fi tawarikh al-nisa'*, ed. 'Imad 'Ali Amra (n.p.: Dar al-'Alamiyya, 1987), p. 382; and al-Maqrizi, *Al-Khitat* (Cairo: Maktaba al-Thaqafa al-Diniyya, 1987), vol. 2, p. 237.

5 Al-Mansuri *Kitab al-tuhfa al-mulukiyya fi al-dawla al-Turqiyya* (Beirut and Cairo: Dar al-Misriyya al-Lubnaniyya, 1987). The author died in year 725 of the Hejira (fourteenth century). See also Hanbali, *Shazarat* (see ch. 1 n. 31 above), vol. 5, pp. 267ff.

6 On the Mamluks see: *Encyclopedia of Islam*, 2nd edn (Leiden: E. J. Brill, 1960), article on 'Mamluks'; S. Lane-Poole, *The Mohammadan Dynasties: Chronological and Genealogical Tables with Historical Introductions* (London: Constable, 1894), p. 80 for the Mamluks of Egypt, and p. 299 for the Mamluks of Delhi; Ahmad al-Sa'id Sulayman, *Tarikh al-duwal al-Islamiyya wa mu'jam al-usar al-hakima* (Cairo: Dar al-Ma'arif, 1969), p. 161 for the Mamluks of Egypt.

7 Shajarat al-Durr is one of the best-known sultanas; she is never ignored by the historians. See also biographies of her in the following: 'Umar Kahhala, *A'lam al-nisa' fi 'almay al-'Arabi wa al-Islami* (Beirut: Mu'assasa al-Risala, 1982); Zarkali, *A'lam* (see ch. 1 n. 32 above); Zaynab

Fawwaz al-'Amili, *Al-durr al-manthur fi tabaqat rabbat al-khudur* (Bulaq: Al-Matba'a al-Kubra, 1985); 'Abdallah Inan, *Tarajim, Islamiyya sharkiyya wa andalusiyya* (Cairo: Dar al-Ma'arif, 1947), p. 61; 'Ali Ibrahim Hasan, *Nisa' lahunna fi al-tarikh al-Islami nasib* (Cairo: Maktaba al-Nahda al-Misriyya, 1970), p. 115; 'Amri, *Rawda*; Uçok Un, *Al-nisa' al-hakimat*, p. 46.

8 Mansuri, *Kitab al-tuhfa*, p. 28.
9 Ibid.
10 *Encyclopedia of Islam*, article on 'Mamluks'; see also Maqrizi, *Khitat*, vol. 2.
11 *Encyclopedia of Islam*, article on 'Mamluks'.
12 Ibid.
13 Ibid.
14 Muhammad Yusuf al-Najrami, *Al-'alaqa al-siyasiyya wa thaqafiyya bayna al-Hind wa al-khilafa al-'Abbasiyya* (Beirut: Dar al-Fikr, 1979), pp. 122ff; see also *Encyclopedia of Islam*, article on 'Iltutmish'.
15 We have seen that among the Mamluks of Egypt, who were organized into a military caste with its schools, rituals, and symbols, emancipation took place automatically upon completion. Apparently the Mamluks had different rules for emancipation than did others.
16 *The Rehla of Ibn Battuta* (see ch. 1. no. 10 above), p. 33.
17 Ibid.
18 Ishwary Prashad, *Medieval History of India*, 88, quoted in Najrami, *Al-'alaqa al-siyasiyya*, p. 125.
19 *Rehla of Ibn Battuta*, p. 33.
20 Ibid.
21 Ibid., p. 34.
22 Ibid.
23 Uçok Un, *Al-nisa' al-hakimat*, p. 36.
24 Najrami, *Al-'alaqa al-siyasiyya*, p. 125.
25 Kahhala, *A'lam al-nisa'*, vol. 1, p. 448; Najrami, *Al-'alaqa al-siyasiyya*, p. 125.
26 Kahhala, *A'lam al-nisa'*, vol. 1, p. 450.
27 *Rehla of Ibn Battuta*, p. 34.
28 Ibn Battuta, *Rihla* (Beirut: Dar Beirut, 1985), p. 423; French translation (see ch. 1 n. 10 above), p. 371.
29 *Rehla of Ibn Battuta*, p. 35.
30 Ibid.
31 Zarkali, *A'lam*, vol. 4, p. 142.
32 All the biographies used here outdo themselves in praising her beauty and intellectual gifts. The quotation is from Zarkali, *A'lam*.
33 Ibid.
34 'Amri, *Rawda*, p. 387.
35 Maqrizi, quoted in Inan, *Tarajim Islamiyya*, p. 92.
36 Ibid.

37 Maqrizi, *Khitat*, p. 238.
38 As one finds many women on the political scene of that time with the name of Turkan Khatun, in order to avoid confusion I will refer to this one as Kutlugh Khatun.
39 *Encyclopedia of Islam*, article on 'Kirman'.
40 Ibid., article on 'Kutlugh Khanids'.
41 Ibid.
42 *Encyclopedia of Islam*, article on 'Ilkhans'.
43 Uçok Un, *Al-nisa' al-hakimat*, p. 83; *Encyclopedia of Islam*, article on 'Kutlugh Khanids'.
44 *Encyclopedia of Islam*, article on 'Kirman'.
45 Ibid.; on the Mongol dynasty see also Lane-Poole, *Mohammadan Dynasties*.
46 Erman, *Zeitschrift für Numismatik* (1880), quoted in Uçok Un, *Al-nisa' al-hakimat*, p. 98.
47 Almost all the sources on these two queens in particular and the Khutlugh Khanids in general, whether it be Uçok Un or the *Encyclopedia of Islam*, refer to the same book, *Simt al-ula*, written in 716/1316 by Nasir al-Din, son of Khawaja Muntajab al-Din Yazdi, confidant of Kutb al-Din (manuscript in Paris, BN Persan 1377, fol. 125).
48 Ibn Battuta, *Travels of Ibn Battuta* (see ch. 1 n. 10 above), vol. 2, p. 340.
49 Ibid., p. 342.
50 Ibid., pp. 485–6.
51 Ibid., pp. 343–4.
52 Ibid., pp. 482–3.
53 Ibid., p. 483.
54 Ibid. I have to say that, for an Arab woman like me, having my hand kissed by a Western man creates both troubling emotions and a shiver of pleasure. Why? Because I was always trained to kiss the hand of men, beginning with my father and my uncles. Even now, my older cousins, in a teasing gesture, never fail to offer me the back of their hand to put me in my traditional place.
55 Ibn Battuta, *Travels of Ibn Battuta*, vol. 2, pp. 485–9.
56 After Ahmad, there were Arghun (683/1284–690/1291), Gaykhatu (690/1291–694/1284), and Baydu (in power during 694–5/1295); finally Ghazan, the seventh Ilkhan, who took power in 694/1295, declared himself a Muslim.
57 *Encyclopedia of Islam*, article on 'Ilkhans'.
58 According to Uçok Un, Absh Khatun was the daughter of Bibi Khatun, one of the daughters of Turkan Khatun, the sovereign of Kirman, who then would have been her grandmother.
59 Uçok Un, *Al-nisa' al-hakimat*, pp. 101ff.
60 Uçok Un gives as reference the *Shiraz Nameh* of Zarkoub, p. 107.

61 Uçok Un, *Al-nisa' al-hakimat*, pp. 115ff. On Luristan see *Encyclopedia of Islam*.
62 Uçok Un, *Al-nisa' al-hakimat*, p. 117.
63 Ibid., p. 128. For details on the dynasty, see Lane-Poole, *Mohammadan Dynasties*, pp. 217–21.
64 Hanbali, *Shazarat*, vol. 7, p. 155. See also, 'Tindu, queen of Iraq', in Ahmad Sawayd, *Nisa' shihirat min tarikhina* (Beirut: Mu'assasa al-Ma'arif, 1985), p. 188.
65 Hanbali, *Shazarat*, vol. 7, p. 155.
66 Uçok Un, *Al-nisa' al-hakimat*, pp. 146ff.
67 *Encyclopedia of Islam*, article on 'Batuids'.
68 Ibid.
69 *Rehla of Ibn Battuta*, p. 204.
70 Ibid., p. 205.
71 Ibid.
72 Ibid., p. 211.
73 Ibid., pp. 202–3.
74 Ibid., p. 203.
75 Ibid., p. 202.
76 Ibid.
77 *Encyclopedia of Islam*, article on 'Atjeh'.
78 Ibid. See also Uçok Un, *Al-nisa' al-hakimat*, pp. 152ff.
79 Uçok Un, *Al-nisa' al-hakimat*, p. 166.
80 Ibid., p. 167.
81 Ibid.

CHAPTER 7   THE SHI'ITE DYNASTY OF
YEMEN

1 Zarkali, *A'lam* (see ch. 1 n. 35 above), vol. 1, p. 299.
2 Mahmud al-Kamil, *Al-Yaman* (Beirut: Dar Bayrut li al-Tiba'a wa al-Nashr, 1968), p. 171; Zarkali, *A'lam*, vol. 1, p. 279; 'Amri, *Rawda* (see ch. 6 n. 4 above), p. 358.
3 Zarkali, *A'lam*, vol. 1, p. 279. This author gives a list of the principal references on 'Arwa, especially a biography of her in al-Dahbi, *Siyar a'lam al-nubala'* (Cairo: Dar al-Ma'arif, 1958).
4 In fact in the eleventh century, at almost the same time as Asma's reign, Morocco was ruled by a Berber queen who shared power with her husband, but she did not have the right to have the *khutba* said in her name. She was Zainab al-Nafzawiyya, the wife of Yusuf Ibn Tashfin (453/1061–500/1108), the famous Almoravid sovereign who created an empire that took in North Africa and Spain and who founded the city of Marrakesh. The fact that Zainab shared power with him is well known.

5   Bernard Lewis, *The Political Language of Islam* (Chicago: University
    of Chicago Press, 1988), p. 66.
6   'Abdallah Ahmad Muhammad al-Thawr, *Hadhihi hiyya al-Yaman*
    (Beirut: Dar al-'Awda, 1979), p. 331. On the reigns of the imams of
    San'a to which reference is made, see: Sulayman, *Tarikh al-duwal* (see
    ch. 1 n. 9 above), p. 216; S. Lane-Poole, *Mohammadan Dynasties*
    (London: Constable, 1894).
7   Thawr, *Hadhihi*, p. 275.
8   Tabari, *Tarikh al-umam wa al-muluk* (Beirut: Dar al-Fikr, 1979), vol.
    5, p. 98; Mohammad Abu Zahra, 'Furuq al madhab al-shi'i', in *Al-
    madahib al-Islamiyya* (Cairo: Maktaba al-Adab, 1924), pp. 63, 64.
9   Tabari, *Tarikh*, vol. 5, p, 98.
10 Ibid.
11 Ibid.
12 Ibid. See also: Ahmad Amin, *Fajr al-Islam*, 11th edn (Beirut: Dar al-
    Kitab al-'Arabi, 1975), p. 268.
13 Ahmad Amin, *Duha al-Islam*, 6th edn (Cairo: Maktaba al-Nahda al-
    Misriyya, 1961), vol. 3, pp. 237, 278; Zahra, *Al-madahib al-Islamiyya*,
    p. 63.
14 Ahmad Amin, *Duha al-Islam*, pp. 209, 210.
15 This leads me to a pragmatic question: What works can one read to
    try to acquire an understanding of the *shi'a* phenomenon? The answer
    depends on what languages one reads. Those who read French or
    English should consult first of all the sections on 'Shi'a' and 'Isma'iliya'
    in the *Encyclopédie d'Islam* or the *Encyclopedia of Islam*, 2nd edn
    (Leiden: E. J. Brill, 1960). This will immediately make you feel
    superbly well informed. But if your curiosity is further awakened,
    which will surely happen, you should read the chapter 'Shi'isme et
    philosophie prophétique' by Henry Corbin in his book *Histoire de la
    philosophie islamique*, published by Gallimard in paperback (1964).
    After reading these sources, it would be very difficult to find yourself
    lost in a conversation on the subject. You will shine at dinner parties
    and be invited to speak on television. For those who also read Arabic,
    there are three extremely instructive texts, obviously my favourites:
    • Muhammad Abu Zahra, 'Furuq al-madhab al-shi'i' (n. 8 above), a
    concise exposition of unequalled precision in about fifty pages
    (pp. 51–104).
    • Ahmad Amin, ch. 2 of Part VII, 'Shi'a' in *Fajr al-Islam*, pp. 266–78.
    • Ahmad Amin, *Duha al-Islam*, vol. 3, ch. 2, 'Al-shi'a' (pp. 208–315),
    traces in about 100 pages not only the origins of Shi'ism but its points
    of disagreement with Sunnism in matters of dogma and jurisprudence.
    He also gives a brief historical-political summary of the key elements
    of the Shi'ites' conflict with the Abbasids – that is, the period that
    concerns us here.
16 *Lisan al-'Arab*, section on 'Shi'a'.

17 Ibid., section on 'Hizb'.

18 Almost all the old editions of books of the Muslim heritage are printed on poor-quality yellowing paper, but they are cheap, and that is not an unimportant detail. This explains the incredibly wide circulation of this literature and why at all the Arab book fairs these books outsell by far all the 'modern' books printed on good-quality paper.

19 Adam Metz, *Al-hadara al-Islamiyya* (Cairo: Maktaba al-Khanji, 1968), vol. 1, p. 120.

20 Ibid.

21 As one might imagine, the origin of the Fatimids is a subject of dispute. Ibn al-Athir, as a third-century historian, in his approach to this subject gives us a lesson in how to write objective history. One by one he details the arguments that the Fatimids were impostors, that they had nothing to do with 'Ali and Fatima, and then he applies logic to destroy these arguments, using the information available to him at that time: Ibn al-Athir, *Al-kamil fi al-tarikh* (Beirut: Dar al-Fikr, n.d.), vol. 6, p. 446.

22 Irene Frain, 'Rita Hayworth, la passion et la fatalité', in the 'Les grands amours' series in the 'Actualités' section of *Paris-Match*, 31 August 1989. Karim Khan, the current Aga Khan, succeeded his grandfather, Sultan Muhammad Shah, in 1957. The permanent seat of the imamate is Bombay. This branch of Isma'ilism is called the Nizariyya and is strongly tied to the 'lords of Alamut', the stronghold of extremist Shi'ism. They terrorized the region by sending out waves ;roups against the Abbasid caliphate of Baghdad. The Ala-ss was reduced only with the arrival of the Mongols, that is ⲁⲟ, ⲟⲉ grandson of Genghis Khan, who captured the fortress in 654/1256. For centuries the imams of this branch of Isma'ilism lived a clandestine existence. After trying to establish an independent state in Kirman, the branch of the Aga Khans finally settled in India in 1259/1843, Bombay becoming their permanent seat. On this subject see *Encyclopedia of Islam*, article on 'Isma'iliyya'.

23 See the genealogical tree showing 'Ali's descent and that of the Shi'ite imams, including the Fatimid dynasty, in Sulayman, *Tarikh al-duwal*, p. 133.

24 Tabari, *Tarikh*, vol. 6, p. 88.

25 Only one child from these marriages, Ibn al-Hanafiyya, literally 'the son of Hanafiyya', played a political-religious role.

26 The cult of 'Ali as the only one to bring about a reign of justice began under the third caliph, 'Uthman, who was of the Umayyad branch and who had displayed a flagrant disregard of justice by naming many members of his family to responsible positions. This nepotism was considered intolerable, and the protestors turned to 'Ali as the saviour, the one who could put the political machine back on the right road, that is, the road of justice. See Zahra, 'Furuq al-madhab', and Ahmad

Amin, *Duha al-Islam*, pp. 209, 120.

When did 'Ali Ibn Abi Talib become the symbol of the oppressed, the leader capable of bringing about the reign of justice? Historians point to the very troubled reign of the third caliph, 'Uthman, as the beginning of the downhill slide of Muslim justice and with it the identification of 'Ali, the relative of the prophet, as an alternative. They especially emphasize two points: 'Uthman's nepotism and the huge fortunes accumulated by him and his family. See: Mas'udi, *Muruj*, vol. 2, pp. 341ff; and *Les Prairies d'or* (see ch. 2 n.20 above), vol. 3, pp. 617ff; Tabari, *Tarikh*, vol. 5, pp. 43ff.

27 Ibn al-Athir, *Kamil*, vol. 6, p. 450.

28 Ibid.

29 Ibid., vol. 6, p. 452.

30 Ibid., p. 455.

31 Ibid., p. 447.

32 It is pertinent to remind those who listen to the radio that during the Iran–Iraq war the front-line reports from the national radio stations took on the tone of veritable Sunni/Shi'ite religious 'crusades', in which each side denigrated the legitimacy of the other. It was virtually a 'rerun' of the eleventh-century battle between Baghdad and Cairo, but with one significant difference – nine centuries ago the two sides were both Arab, and in the twentieth century one side was Arab and the other Iranian.

33 Ibn al-Athir, *Kamil*, vol. 8, p. 114.

34 What can one read to find a quick, concise exposition of this subject? I can suggest the summary by Ahmad Amin about the origin of Shi'ite ideas in *Fajr al-Islam*, pp. 276, 278, 279. In the same book, this author has an important chapter in which he analyses the Persian contribution to Muslim civilization, especially in the domain of religious ideas (pp. 98ff). See also Bernard Lewis's chapter, 'La signification de l'hérésie dans l'histoire de l'Islam', in *Le retour de l'Islam* (Paris: Gallimard, 1985), pp. 14ff.

35 On this first group of terrorists, the Kharijites, who were upset by the turn taken by the civil war between the caliph 'Ali (whom they had supported in the beginning) and Mu'awiya, his opponent, who would become the first caliph of the Umayyad dynasty, one should reread Mas'udi: 'In year 40 of the Hejira, a band of Kharijites gathered at Mecca were discussing the dissensions and wars that were overwhelming them when three of them agreed to kill 'Ali, Mu'awiya, and 'Amr Ibn al-As . . . .. They made a compact among themselves that each would pursue his chosen victim until he had killed him or perished in the attempt . . . .. The night of the seventeenth or, according to others, the twenty-first of Ramadan [28 January AD 661] was chosen for carrying out the crime'; Mas'udi, *Muruj al-dahab* (Beirut: Dar al-Ma'rifa, 1982), vol. 3, p. 683). See also Tabari, *Tarikh*, vol. 7, p. 83.

36 Metz, *Al-hadara al-Islamiyya*; Ibn al-Athir, *Kamil*, vol. 6, p. 449; Ibn al-Nadim, *Al-fihrist* (Beirut: Dar al-Ma'rifa, 1978), p. 264.

37 Metz, *Al-hadara al-Islamiyya*.
38 On Abu 'Abdallah the Shi'ite, see his biography (no. 199) in Ibn Khallikan, *Wafayat al-a'yan* (Beirut: Dar al-Thaqafa, n.d.), vol. 2, p. 192. On his connection to Ibn al-Fadl Ibn Hawshab, see Ibn al-Athir, *Kamil*, vol. 6, p. 449; and Ibn al-Nadim, *Fihrist*, pp. 264ff.
39 The biography of 'Ali is in vol. 3 of Ibn Khallikan's *Wafayat*, which is a biographical dictionary of famous people. Ibn Khallikan did not wait for the Anglo-Saxons to invent the form for describing the leading figures on the historical scene. The biography of *a'lam* (celebrities) is a classical genre in Arab history, and it included both men and women. Ibn Khallikan is one of the most brilliant writers in this form. His short, concise sketches crammed with information have won him great fame, and he is a source constantly used by other writers. He died in year 681 of the Hejira (thirteenth century).
40 Ibid.
41 According to Ibn Khallikan, the *da'i* of 'Ali was called al-Zawahi, while all the other biographers and historians give his name as al-Rawahi. So I conclude that the edition of Ibn Khallikan had a typographical error.
42 See also other biographies of 'Ali al-Sulayhi in Zarkali, *A'lam*, vol. 4, p. 328; Hanbali, *Shazarat* (see ch. 1 n. 31 above), vol. 3, p. 346; Thawr, *Hadhihi*, p. 27; Kamil, *Yaman*, p. 167; Salah Ibn Hamid al-'Alawi, *Tarikh Hadramawt* (n.p.: Maktaba al-Irshad, n.d.), pp. 340ff. The career of Ibn Hawshab, who was a native of Kufa, takes us straight back to the source of Shi'ite propaganda, 'Abdallah al-Qaddah. Ibn Hawshab was the companion, friend, and disciple of the son of al-Qaddah, the brains of the Shi'ite movement at the end of the third century. Ibn al-Athir names Ibn Hawshab among the central figures in the Shi'ite propaganda effort at that time (*Kamil*, vol. 6, p. 449).
43 *Lisan al-'Arab*, section on 'da'i'.
44 Ibid.
45 Ibn al-Nadim, *Fihrist*. Ibn al-Nadim died in year 385 of the Hejira. His book was published in 388.
46 Confusion, ambiguity, and contradictions reign regarding the details of the initiation process. But everyone agrees on one point: we know little about the initiation, and this is because of the secrecy that surrounded it and was an integral part of the doctrine. See Metz, *Al-hadara al-Islamiyya*, vol. 2, p. 76; *Encyclopedia of Islam*, article on 'Isma'iliyya'; Henry Corbin, *Histoire de la philosophie islamique* (Paris: Gallimard, 1964), pp. 66ff.
47 Corbin, *Histoire de la philosophie islamique*, pp. 67, 68.
48 Ibn Khallikan, *Wafayat*, vol. 3, p. 411. Some others also affirm that he was Sunni: Zarkali, *A'lam*, vol. 4, p. 328; 'Alawi, *Tarikh Hadramawt*, p. 340.
49 Ibn Khallikan, *Wafayat*, vol. 3, p. 411; Hanbali, *Shazarat*, vol. 3, p. 346.

50 Ibid.

51 Today the books on Shi'ism, those treasures of the ancients, are scattered and many are inaccessible. When one thinks about all the scholarly libraries on Islam still to be built, about the research on Muslim learning which hardly exists, about all the scholarly infrastructure that no one takes the trouble to set up and support, one realizes to what an extent the Muslim heritage is hostage to political opportunism. All the politicians speak in the name of this heritage and try to usurp the role of the intellectuals in its name. However, none of them dream of investing a part of their oil fortunes in saving it and systematizing it for coming generations in comfortable libraries with the latest technology or in cultural centres where film-makers, theatre men and women, teachers, and writers of books for children and adults could come for inspiration and archival research at little cost and without spending hours waiting at the few existing libraries, which are neglected and deserted by the experts, but which are all we have at the moment.

52 Ibn Khallikan, *Wafayat*, vol. 3, p. 411; Hanbali, *Shazarat*, vol. 3, p. 346.

53 Ibid.

54 Hanbali, *Shazarat*, vol. 3, p. 346. While Hanbali speaks of *Isma'iliyya*, Ibn Khallikan speaks of *Imamiyya*, which is another name for the Shi'ite doctrine centred on the idea of the imam.

55 Hanbali, *Shazarat*, vol. 3, p. 347; Zarkali, *A'lam*, vol. 4, p. 328; 'Alawi, *Tarikh Hadramawt*, p. 340.

56 Hanbali, *Shazarat*, vol. 3, p. 347.

57 Muhammad Ibn Habib al-Baghdadi, *Kitab al-mukhabbar* (Beirut: Al-Maktab al-Tijari, n.d.), p. 307.

58 Ibn Sa'd, *Al-tabaqat al-kubra* (Beirut: Dar al-Fikr, 1980), vol. 1, pp. 216ff. See also Tabari, *Tarikh*, vol. 2, pp. 230ff.

59 Hanbali, *Shazarat*, vol. 3, p. 347.

60 Ibid.

61 Ibid.

62 Ibn al-Athir, *Kamil*, vol. 8, p. 363.

63 Ibid.

64 Kamil, *Yaman*, p. 168.

65 Ibn Khallikan, *Wafayat*, vol. 3, pp. 412, 413; Hanbali, *Shazarat*, vol. 3, pp. 347, 348.

66 S. Lane-Poole, *The Mohammadan Dynasties: Chronological and Genealogical Tables with Historical Introductions* (London: Constable, 1894), pp. 89ff.

67 Ibn Khallikan, *Wafayat*, vol. 3, p. 413; Hanbali, *Shazarat*, vol. 3, p. 347.

68 Kamil, *Yaman*, p. 169.

69 Ibid.

70 Zarkali, *A'lam*, vol. 1, p. 305.
71 Ibn Khallikan, *Wafayat*, vol. 3, p. 413; Hanbali, *Shazarat*, vol. 3, p. 347.
72 On the attack by the Karmatis on Mecca, see Ibn al-Athir, *Kamil*, vol. 7, pp. 53ff; Hanbali, *Shazarat*, vol. 2, p. 274. On the Karmatis, see *Encyclopedia of Islam*, article on 'Karmati'.
73 Hanbali, *Shazarat*, vol. 2, p. 274.

CHAPTER 8 THE LITTLE QUEENS OF SHEBA

1 Zarkali, *A'lam* (see ch. 1 n. 35 above), vol. 1, p. 279. At the end of this biography the reader can find a list of the principal sources on Queen 'Arwa, especially a biography of her in the famous *Siyar al-'alam al-nubala'* by al-Dahbi (Cairo: Dar al-Ma'arif, 1958); vol. 2 contains biographies of women.

2 On the *jahiliyya* I would suggest the following: on the Islamic vision of time, see Tabari's fascinating introduction to his *Tarikh al-umam wa al-muluk* (Beirut: Dar al-Fikr, 1979). On the word *jahiliyya* itself, see how Tabari explains it in his *Tafsir* (Commentary on the Koran) (Beirut: Dar al-Fikr, 1984), vol. 22, pp. 4, 5, when he comments on verse 33 of sura 33 of the Koran, which reads: 'And stay in your houses. Bedizen not yourselves with the bedizenment of the Time of Ignorance' (Pickthall translation, see ch. 4 n. 8 above). This verse says that for a woman to 'bedizen' herself before going out into the street is definitely behaviour of the *jahiliyya*. The distinctive behaviour of a Muslim woman is characterized by modesty. And modest the queen of Sheba was not. For a short exposition of the subject see Ignaz Goldiziher, 'What is meant by al-Jahiliyya?', in *Muslim Studies* (Chicago: Aldine, 1966), pp. 208–19.

3 'Abdallah Ahmad Muhammad al-Thawr, *Hadihi hiyya al-Yaman* (Beirut: Dar al-'Adwa, 1979), p. 281.

4 The *Lisan al-'Arab* of Ibn Manzur, which I am mad about because he looks for the root of the word and in the process undertakes a veritable archaeological search into Islamic and pre-Islamic memory, often bringing out meanings hidden for centuries, is particularly afflicted with amnesia when it comes to the woman's name *Asma*. He deals with it first in vol. 1 with the first letter, the *alif*, when he speaks of the word *ism*, name. On this occasion he evokes two names of persons. The first is a masculine name, *Usama*, which, he tells us, is one of the words for 'lion'. Then he takes up the second, which is *Asma*, and tells us very briefly the obvious – that it is a woman's name – without adding anything more. Without adding, for example, something that was obvious to the Yemeni poets – that the word has a connotation of elevation and thus comes from the same root as *sama*. The word *sama* (sky) is taken up by Ibn Manzur in vol. 3, devoted largely to

the letter *S*. He tells us that it designates the sky, but that it also designates 'everything that is elevated, everything that is high', like *al-sumuw*, Royal Highness. *Sama* also designates high things like the ceiling, and high things that are connected to the sky, 'like clouds and rain'. *Sama* has the same root as *ism*, which means *sign*, that is, a sign designating a thing. There is a 'sense of superiority in the sign'. *Ism*, he tells us, 'is a design, a mark which is superimposed on an object to signify it'. And guess what is one of the plurals of *ism*! *Asma*! How did it happen that Ibn Manzur, the archaeologist of our Arab memory, did not see the link between the woman's name *Asma* and the word *ism* (name, sign), which, he tells us, come from the same root, *sama*? Is it because such a suggestion would have brought on the return of the repressed – namely, the fact that pre-Islamic Arabia worshipped goddesses and that the Prophet's battle against the *mushriqin* was very often a struggle against those goddesses? In any case, the eleventh-century Yemeni poets had no difficulty in seeing the link between the name of their queen and the heavens.

5 Pickthall, *The Meaning of the Glorious Koran* (New York: Dorset Press, n.d.), sura 27.

6 Ibid.

7 Ibid.

8 Tabari, *Tarikh*, vol. 19, p. 48.

9 Imam Ibn Tahir Tayfur, *Kitab balaghat al-nisa'* (Beirut: Dar al-Nahda al-Haditha, 1972), p. 129. The author died in year 280 of the Hejira.

10 Umar Kahhala, *A'lam al-nisa' fi 'almay al-'Arabi wa al-Islami* (Beirut: Mu'assasa al-Risala, 1982), vol. 1, p. 144.

11 Qannuji, *Husn al-uswa* (see ch. 5 n. 39 above), p. 179.

12 Mas'udi, *Muruj al-dahab* (Beirut: Dar al-Ma'rifa, 1982), vol. 2, p. 384.

13 *Encyclopedia of Islam*, 2nd edn (Leiden: E. J. Brill, 1960) article on 'Saba'.

14 Sura 27, verse 23.

15 One need only read the prolific poet Nizar Qabbani, for example. How could he express the pleasure he finds in women if he was forbidden to evoke Balqis? I believe he would go on strike against writing! And who would be the losers? Obviously it would be Arab women, who are the greatest consumers of his poetry, with me at the head of the list. One feels wonderful and serenely at peace with the world after reading a poem by Nizar.

16 *Lisan al-'Arab*, section on 'Hazm'.

17 Thawr, *Hadhihi*, p. 281.

18 Ibid.

19 Mahmud al-Kamil, *Al-Yaman* (Beirut: Dar Bayrut li al-Tiba'a wa al-Nashr, 1968), p. 169.

20 Salah Ibn Hamid al-'Alawi, *Tarikh Hadramawt* (n.p.: Maktaba al-Irshad, n.d.), vol. 1, p. 342.

21 Ibid.
22 Ibid.
23 Ibid.
24 Ibid.
25 Kamil, *Yaman*, p. 169.
26 Zarkali, *A'lam*, vol. 1, p. 279.
27 Thawr, *Hadhihi*, vol. 1, p. 169.
28 'Amri, *Rawda* (see ch. 6 n. 4 above), p. 358; Zarkali, *A'lam*, vol. 1, p. 279.
29 'Alawi, *Tarikh Hadramawt*, p. 342.
30 Ibn Khallikan, *Wafayat al-a'yan* (Beirut: Dar al-Thaqafa, n.d.), vol. 3, p. 414; 'Alawi, *Tarikh Hadramawt*, p. 343; Kamil, *Yaman*, p. 180.
31 Ibid.
32 'Amri, *Rawda*, p. 358.
33 'Alawi, *Tarikh Hadramawt*, p. 344.
34 Thawr, *Hadhihi*, p. 284.
35 Zarkali, *A'lam*, vol. 1, p. 279.
36 Thawr, *Hadhihi*, p. 282.
37 *Encyclopedia of Islam*, article on 'Isma'iliyya'.
38 Jurji Zaydan, *Tarikh al-tamaddun al-Islami* (n.p., n.d.), vol. 1, p. 23.
39 *Encyclopedia of Islam*, article on 'Isma'iliyya'.
40 There is a detailed account of the last days and hours of the Prophet in the *Sira* (biography of the Prophet) by Ibn Hisham. He recounts that 'Abbas, the Prophet's uncle, confided to 'Ali Ibn Abi Talib that he was convinced that the Prophet had not much longer to live and that it was absolutely necessary to go to him and find out if 'power should remain among us'. And Ibn Hisham adds that 'Ali emphatically refused to follow his uncle's advice and importune the Prophet on his deathbed. See Ibn Hisham, *Al-sira al-nabawiyya* (Beirut: Ihya' al-Thawra al-'Arabi, n.d.), vol. 4, p. 304.
41 Ibn al-Athir, *Al-kamil fi al-tarikh* (Beirut: Dar al-Fikr, n.d.), vol. 8, p. 342.
42 Ibid., p. 498.
43 What can I suggest to read about Hasan al-Sabbah? It all depends on how curious one is and how much time one has to spend. Those who are pressed for time should devour the article on al-Sabbah in the *Encyclopedia of Islam* and also the section on Alamut. For those who love novels there is the brilliant *Samarkand* by Amin Ma'luf, which describes the intellectual terrorism of the epoch through the thrilling life of Omar Khayyam, who was a classmate of al-Sabbah (Paris: Lattès, 1988). For those who wish to probe the subject more deeply, I can suggest the following in French and English: Silvestre de Sacy, 'Mémoire sur la dynastie des Assassins', *Mémoire de l'Académie des Inscriptions et Belles-Lettres* (Paris), 4: 2 (1818); C. Defrémery, 'Nouvelles recherches sur les Ismaïliens ou bathiniens de Syrie', *JA*, 2

(1854). pp. 353–87, and 1 (1854), pp. 130–210; Bernard Lewis, *The Assassins: A Radical Sect in Islam* (London: Weidenfeld & Nicolson, 1967); Marshall G. Hodgson, *The Order of Assassins: The Struggle of the Early Nizari Isma'ilis against the Islamic World* (The Hague: Mouton, 1955). For material in Arabic see: Athir, *Kamil*, vol. 9, pp. 36ff; Zarkali, *A'lam*, vol. 2, p. 193; 'Abdallah Inan, *Tarajim Islamiyya sharkiyya wa andalusiyya* (Cairo: Dar al-Ma'arif, 1947), p. 42.

44 For us Sunnis only Allah is infallible, and our primary-school teachers have no trouble presenting the Catholic Pope to us as an impostor because of his claims of infallibility.

45 For the details of the events of the year 145 of the Hejira, when al-Nafs al-Zakiyya officially declared himself 'Commander of the Faithful', see Tabari, *Tarikh*, vol. 10, pp. 201ff. A very concise summary of this affair and the contents of the exchange of letters can be found in Ahmad Amin, *Duha al-Islam*, 6th edn (Cairo: Maktaba al-Nahda al-Misriyya, 1961), vol. 3, pp. 277ff.

46 The latest statistics from the Arab world reveal that today there is a demographic revolution taking place. The most salient aspect of it is the later age for marriage of both men and women. And later age for marriage means an increase in the number of births of illegitimate children, for the traditional barriers to premarital sexual activity no longer exist. Those barriers consisted of separation of the sexes and parental control of the movement of their daughters. However, the increasingly advanced education of girls and their access to paid work reduce to nothing all the control systems based on the immobility of women. We know nothing about the illegitimate children because the doctors and judges carefully guard this secret, which is so highly explosive for the community's self-image.

47 Ibn Hazm, *Rasa'il* (see ch. 1 n. 40 above), vol. 2, p. 120.

48 Tabari, *Tarikh*, vol. 10, p. 211.

49 Ibid., p. 210.

50 Ibid.

51 Ibid., vol. 10, p. 212.

52 The reference is in the 'Tabaqat' of al-Sabki, quoted in Adam Metz, *Al-hadara al-Islamiyya* (Cairo: Maktaba al Khanji, 1968), vol. 8, p. 123. On the Shi'ite Ghurabiyya sect, see Zahra, 'Furuq al-madhab al-shi'i', in *Al-madahib al-Islamiyya* (Cairo: Maktaba al-Adab, 1924), p. 65.

53 Al-Sabki, 'Tabaqat', quoted in Metz, *Al-hadara al-Islamiyya*, p. 123.

54 Ahmad Amin, *Duha al-Islam*, vol. 3, p. 260.

55 Ibid., pp. 254ff.

56 'Alawi, *Hadhihi*, p. 282.

57 Among them are Zarkali, *A'lam*, vol. 1, p. 289; and 'Alawi, *Tarikh Hadramawt*, p. 342.

58 See *Encyclopedia of Islam*, article on ''Ahd'.

59 'Amri, *Rawda*, p. 358.
60 Zarkali, *A'lam*, vol. 1, p. 289.
61 Thawr, *Hadhihi*, p. 284.
62 'Alawi, *Tarikh Hadramawt*, p. 342.
63 Ibid.
64 Thawr, *Hadhihi*, p. 284.
65 'Alawi, *Tarikh Hadramawt*, p. 343.
66 Ibn al-Athir, *Kamil*, vol. 8, p. 294.
67 Ibid.
68 Ibid., p. 398.
69 W. Madelung in the article on 'Isma'iliyya', *Encyclopedia of Islam*.
70 Ibid.
71 Kamil, *Yaman*, p. 17.

CHAPTER 9   THE LADY OF CAIRO

1 There are many biographies of Sitt al-Mulk in Arabic. The early sources most often referred to are: 'Amri, *Rawda* (see ch. 6 n. 4 above), pp. 462–6; 'Abdallah Inan, *Tarajim Islamiyya sharkiyya wa andalusiyya* (Cairo: Dar al-Ma'arif, 1947), pp. 34–41; 'Amili, *Al-durr al-manthur* (see ch. 6 n. 7 above), pp. 240–1; 'Ali Ibrahim Hasan, *Nisa' lahunna fi al-tarikh al-Islami nasib* (Cairo: Maktaba al-Nahda al-Misriyya, 1970), pp. 108–14.

2 The complete title was *al-dhahir li i'zaz dim Allah*. See a biography of him in Ibn Khallikan, *Wafayat al-a'yan* (Beirut: Dar al-Thaqafa, n.d.), vol. 3, pp. 406ff, and an account of his enthronement in Ibn al-Athir, *Al-kamil fi al-tarikh* (Beirut: Dar al-Fikr, n.d.), vol. 8, p. 131.

3 Zarkali, *A'lam* (see ch. 1 n. 35 above), vol. 3, p. 78. See also Ibn Khallikan, *Wafayat*, vol. 8, p. 130.

4 *Encyclopedia of Islam*, 2nd edn (Leiden: E. J. Brill, 1960), article on 'Libas'.

5 Colour has always played a primordial role in the ritual and symbols of power in the Arab dynasties, and challenge to the established power was accompanied by the adoption of a different colour. See *Encyclopedia of Islam*, article on 'Libas'.

6 Ibn Khallikan, *Wafayat*, vol. 5, p. 372.
7 Some say she was a Copt. Inan, *Tarajim*, p. 34.
8 Ibn al-Athir, *Kamil*, vol. 7, p. 477.
9 See the biography of al-'Aziz under the name of Nizar al-'Ubaidi in Ibn Khallikan, *Wafayat*, vol. 5, p. 372.
10 Ibn al-Athir, *Kamil*, vol. 7. p. 477.
11 Ibid.
12 Inan, *Tarajim*, pp. 35, 36.
13 Ibn Khallikan, *Wafayat*, vol. 5, p. 371.
14 Ibid., p. 372.

15   'Amri, *Rawda*, p. 463.
16   Ibn Khallikan, *Wafayat*, vol. 5, p. 375.
17   Ibid.; al-Maqrizi, *Al-Khitat* (Cairo: Maktaba al-Thaqafa al-Diniyya, 1987), vol. 2, p. 285; Ibn al-Athir, *Kamil*, vol. 7, p. 477; 'Abdallah Inan, *Al-hakim bi'amri Allah* (Cairo: Dar al-Ma'arif, 1947).
18   Ibn Khallikan, *Wafayat*, vol. 5, p. 375.
19   Ibid.
20   Maqrizi, *Khitat*, vol. 2, p. 288.
21   Henry Corbin, *Histoire de la philosophie islamique* (Paris: Gallimard, 1964), pp. 128ff.
22   Ibn al-Nadim, *Al-fihris* (Beirut: Dar al-Ma'rifa, 1978), p. 267.
23   *Encyclopedia of Islam*, article on 'Isma'iliyya'. One can imagine the friction that this manner of calculating could create between Isma'ilis and Sunnis, especially when it came to fixing the month of Ramadan.
24   M. Canard, 'La procession du Nouvel An chez les Fatimides', *Annales de l'Institut d'Etudes Orientales* (Algiers), 10 (1952), p. 375.
25   Maqrizi, *Khitat*, p. 288.
26   Ibn al-Athir, *Kamil*, vol. 8, p. 128.
27   Ibid.
28   Ibid., p. 129.
29   Ibid.
30   Hanbali, *Shazarat* (see ch. 1 n. 31 above), vol. 3, p. 194.
31   Maqrizi, *Khitat*, vol. 2, p. 288.
32   For a discussion of the attitudes of hate and contempt toward the people, *al-'amma*, see the excellent summary in the article on it in the *Encyclopedia of Islam*. Also consult the books on proper behaviour for courtiers, like the essay attributed to al-Jahiz in *Le Livre de la couronne* (*Kitab al-taj*), which is an instructional manual on court etiquette, or how to please the prince. The basic idea is to humble oneself. Any show of dignity or self-respect annoys the leader. See al-Jahiz, *Le livre de la couronne*, tr. Charles Pellat (Paris: Les Belles Lettres, 1954), p. 49.
33   Ibn Battuta, *Travels of Ibn Battuta* (see ch. 1 n. 10 above), vol. 1, p. 41. However, it must be pointed out that the Cairo described by Ibn Battuta is the Cairo of the fourteenth century AD. Ibn Battuta, who was born in Tangier in 1304, made his first trip to Mecca in 1326. It was during this journey that he visited Egypt for the first time. I quote Ibn Battuta for the beauty of his description and its accuracy even for the Cairo of today. But for a description of the Cairo of al-Hakim, one should read Maqrizi, *Khitat*, where one finds a description of the city practically quarter by quarter, and especially a wealth of details about the public buildings.
34   Ibn Khallikan, *Wafayat*, vol. 5, p. 293; Maqrizi, *Khitat*, vol. 2, p. 285.
35   Maqrizi, *Khitat*, vol. 2, p. 286; Ibn Khallikan, *Wafayat*, vol. 5, p. 393.
36   Maqrizi, *Khitat*, vol. 2, p. 289.

37 Ibid., p. 285.
38 Ibid.
39 Ibid., p. 287.
40 Ibid.
41 *Encyclopedia of Islam*, article on 'Al-Hakim'.
42 Ibid.
43 Ibid.
44 Hanbali, *Shazarat*, vol. 2, p. 193.
45 Ibn al-Athir, *Kamil*, vol. 1, p. 129.
46 Ibid.
47 Ibid., vol. 8, pp. 129–30.
48 Hanbali, *Shazarat*, vol. 3, p. 173.
49 *Encyclopedia of Islam*, article on 'Al-Hakim'. 'A'isha and Mu'awiya were the enemies of Caliph 'Ali, who was considered by the Shi'ites as the only imam worthy of leading the Muslim community and the sole legitimate successor of the Prophet. 'A'isha launched and directed a civil war against 'Ali; and Mu'awiya succeeded in capturing power from 'Ali and having himself named caliph in his place through a mixture of military operations and trickery.
50 Maqrizi, *Khitat*, vol. 2, p. 287; Hanbali, *Shazarat*, vol. 3, p. 193.
51 Ibid.
52 Maqrizi, who clearly saw the link between the prohibitions on men's and women's moving about the city and the supply and inflation problems, constantly punctuates his text with insertions alongside each prohibition of the food supply problems experienced by the country (*Khitat*, vol. 2, pp. 285–9).
53 Hanbali, *Shazarat*, vol. 3, p. 194.
54 Ibid.
55 Al-Jahiz, *Le livre de la couronne*, p. 186.
56 Ibid., p. 184.
57 Ibid.
58 Ibid., pp. 184ff.
59 For all the details see: Maqrizi, *Khitat*, vol. 2, pp. 284–9; Ibn al-Athir, *Kamil*, vol. 8, pp. 128–31; Hanbali, *Shazarat*, vol. 2, pp. 192–5; Ibn Khallikan, *Wafayat*, vol. 5, pp. 292–8.
60 *Encyclopedia of Islam*, article on 'Al-Hakim'.
61 Hanbali, *Shazarat*, vol. 3, p. 194.
62 Ibid.
63 One can never emphasize too much the importance of mystery, that which is hidden, the non-apparent in the Shi'ite vision of the world and of its central axis, the imamate. The hidden imam is the pillar of that doctrine. See: Corbin, *Histoire de la philosophie islamique*, and *Encyclopedia of Islam*, article on 'Isma'iliyya'.
64 One of the best biographies of al-Hakim, which summarizes in a succinct but detailed fashion information that is otherwise scattered in

various volumes of certain sources like the *Wafayat* by Ibn Khallikan
and *Kamil* by Ibn al-Athir, is that of Zarkali in his *A'lam*, vol. 7, p.
304. The other excellent summary is that of the *Encyclopedia of Islam*.
65 How many of the admirers, like me, of the singers Farid al-Atrash
and his sister Asmahane know that they were Druze? They came from
a noted Druze family in al-Qarya, the Syrian part of the Druze
mountains. Farid was born in 1910, learned to play the lute from his
mother, and departed with Asmahane for Cairo at the time of the
Syrian revolt against the French in 1925. They continued their musical
training in Cairo. Asmahane was mysteriously killed when her automobile, travelling between Cairo and Suez in 1944, plunged into the
water. In 1960, when I had finished secondary school and left Fez for
the Mohammad V University in Rabat, we all obviously listened to
Elvis Presley and dreamed about Marilyn Monroe. But it was the
languorous manner of Asmahane, when she murmured 'Qahwa, asqini
ahwa' (Coffee, pour me a coffee), that I religiously tried to duplicate
in my apprenticeship in charm and seduction. Rumour had it that
Asmahane had been a spy during World War II and that was why she
had been killed. Some said that she was working for the Arabs, some
said for the English. The rumour that I hated was that she was in fact
connected to the Nazis, that to further the Arab cause against the
English she worked with the Germans. The men in her life? All the
princes and kings in the Middle East vied for her favour, and also
obviously workers and football players. What more could one dream
of? In any case, it was her air of mystery that released the dream that
was my ideal of femininity during the troubled years of adolescence;
and Farid, who lamented his loneliness in all the corners of the medina,
was my ideal of masculinity, real masculinity, who exuded gentleness
from every pore. Our obsession with Asmahane was so intense that
we almost bumped off the student from Marrakesh who told us that
she had died long before independence. We refused to believe it, just
as the followers of Hamza had refused to believe the death of al-
Hakim. As for me, when I got ready to undertake an operation of
seduction, whether romantic or professional, whether on a date or at
a conference, it was the languorous manner of Asmahane that I tried
to emulate. That is part of the reason that I always begin my lectures
in a soft little voice that is directed to the heart. After her death,
Farid al-Altrash had a meteoric career, becoming the famous singer
and actor that we know so well. He did the music for more than 500
films. He died in 1974. And some of us, like me, turn lamentably
romantic when his voice pours out of a transistor radio in all its
sweetness. *Allah yarhamu!*
66 Ibn al-Athir, *Kamil*, vol. 8, p. 128; Hanbali, *Shazarat*, vol. 3, p. 194;
Encyclopedia of Islam, article on 'Al-Hakim'.
67 Quoted by M. Canard in his article on al-Hakim in the *Encyclopedia*

of Islam, which is accompanied by one of the most complete bibliographies one can find.
68 Maqrizi, *Khitat*, p. 289.
69 Ibid.
70 Ibn Khallikan, *Wafayat*, vol. 5, p. 298; Ibn al-Athir, *Kamil*, vol. 8, p. 128.

CONCLUSION: THE MEDINA DEMOCRACY

1 Mas'udi, *Muruj al-dahab* (Beirut: Dar al-Ma'rifa, 1982), vol. 2, p. 329; *Les prairies d'or* (see ch. 2 n. 20 above), vol. 3, p. 607.
2 Ibid.
3 Ibn Khaldun, *Recueils de textes* (see ch. 1 n. 1 above), p. 89.
4 Ibid.
5 See Ibn Khaldun, *Al-Muqaddima* (Beirut: Dar al-Kitab al-'Arabi, n.d.), pp. 217ff.
6 Ibid.
7 Ibid.
8 Mas'udi, *Muruj*, vol. 3, p. 44; *Prairies d'or*, vol. 3, p. 729.
9 Ibid.
10 Tabari, *Tarikh al-umam wa al-muluk* (Beirut: Dar al-Fikr, 1979), vol. 10, p. 15.
11 Al-Mahdi is described here as dressed in white. Above it was said that the Abbasids dressed in black. There is, however, no contradiction. Black was the colour of their official garments, and white is for prayer robes for everyone, kings or humble people like you and me.
12 Tabari, *Tarikh*, vol. 10, p. 15.

Index

————————————————

Please remember that this is a library book, and that it belongs only temporarily to each person who uses it. Be considerate. Do not write in this, or any, library book.

Date Due

AP 1 '00			
SEP 2 2000			
12/11/01			
ILL			
13729243			
12/1/05			
5/4/09			